The Health of Britain's Ethnic Minorities

Policy Studies Institute (PSI) is one of Europe's leading independent research organisations undertaking studies of economic, industrial and social policy and the workings of political institutions.

PSI is a registered charity, run on a non-profit basis, and is not associated with any political party, pressure group or commercial interest.

PSI attaches great importance to covering a wide range of subject areas with its multi-disciplinary approach. The Institute's researchers are organised in groups which currently cover the following programmes:

Crime, Justice and Youth Studies – Employment – Ethnic Equality and Diversity – Family Finances – Information and Citizenship – Information and Cultural Studies – Social Care and Health Studies – Work, Benefits and Social Participation

This publication arises from the Ethnic Equality and Diversity Group and is one of over 30 publications made available by the Institute each year.

Information about the work of PSI and a catalogue of publications can be obtained from:

Publications Department
Policy Studies Institute
100 Park Village East
London NW1 3SR

The Fourth National Survey of Ethnic Minorities

The Health of Britain's Ethnic Minorities

Findings from a national survey

JAMES Y NAZROO

POLICY STUDIES INSTITUTE
LONDON

The publishing imprint of the independent
POLICY STUDIES INSTITUTE
100 Park Village East, London NW1 3SR
Tel. 0171 468 0468   Fax. 0171 388 0914

ISBN 0 85374 709 1
PSI Report 835

The Fourth National Survey of Ethnic Minorities was undertaken in partnership by
Policy Studies Institute
Social and Community Planning Research

It was supported by
Department of Health
Department of the Environment
The Joseph Rowntree Charitable Trust
Economic and Social Research Council
Department for Education and Employment/Employment Service

Cover design by Andrew Corbett
Laserset by Policy Studies Institute
Printed in Great Britain by Redwood Books, Trowbridge, Wilts.

level 5

Contents

Foreword

This is a significant text for two reasons. First, the PSI National Surveys have provided exceptional coverage of a variety of aspects of minority ethnic lives and thus, quite rightly, have been a major resource for policy makers and academics. Uniquely, the Fourth National Survey (Modood *et al.* 1997), as well as providing a wealth of contextual information on households, income, housing and identity, comes with a battery of well thought out and theoretically grounded questions on health and health care. This provides an unparalleled opportunity to exploit this data and explore the relationship between ethnicity and socioeconomic position in order to address ethnic inequalities in health and health care from within an empirically credible framework. Secondly, its significance lies in the quality and depth of analysis. Some of the extant epidemiological work on ethnicity and health in Britain epitomises mindless empiricism, bereft of an adequate understanding of minority ethnic people's lives; and reductionist in its explanations of ethnic inequalities in health and health care. On the other hand qualitative research on ethnicity and health remains limited. Nazroo's work is particularly welcome for its strong theoretical underpinnings, command of the relevant literature on ethnicity as well as health inequalities, and intimate knowledge of work on ethnicity and health. His use of the rich array of contextual information from the Fourth National Survey to examine the relationship between ethnicity and known determinants of health and health care provides his work a unique edge. The book provides an important benchmark in the field of ethnicity and health.

The text contains several important messages. The Fourth National Survey provides evidence of both disadvantage and diversity. This is reflected also in the current volume. Minority ethnic communities are disadvantaged in terms of health and access to health care but their experience is far from homogenous. The diversity witnessed in other aspects of life between the Indian and African Asians (relatively better off) and the Caribbeans, Pakistanis and Bangladeshis (relatively worse off) is reflected also in their experience of health and access to health services. The Chinese enjoy relatively good health but experience problems of access to health care. Such diversity has clear implications for health care agencies as well as other state and voluntary institutions.

A glaringly obvious gap in research on ethnicity and health relates to what can be termed 'the forgotten minorities'. This includes not only the relatively small groups (Somalis, Iraqis, etc.) but also the numerically large but widely dispersed communities such as the Chinese and Irish. The inclusion of the Chinese population in this survey is therefore particularly welcome.

Finally, the text demonstrates that a significant component of ethnic inequalities in health relates to the differentials in the socioeconomic position between different ethnic groups. Apprently clear differentials between ethnic groups substantially diminish when a relatively sophisticated composite measure of socioeconomic position is applied. This demonstrates the great importance of developing more meaningful measures of socioeconomic position which work across different ethnic communities within Britain; and the need to collect and use such data for policy and service delivery. Perhaps more importantly, it is a reminder that although health services have an important role to play in addressing inequalities in health and health care, substantial improvements in minority ethnic health will come from addressing socioeconomic inequalities between different ethnic groups.

Waqar Ahmad
Director, Ethnicity and Social Policy Research Unit
University of Bradford

Acknowledgements

This volume is one of a series based on the Fourth National Survey of Ethnic Minorities. The Fourth National Survey was supported and undertaken by several people and organisations. It was jointly sponsored by the Economic and Social Research Council, the Department of Health, the Department of the Environment, the Department for Education and Employment with the Employment Service, and the Joseph Rowntree Charitable Trust. The research team was advised throughout the study by an expert group chaired by *Professor Bhikhu Parekh* (University of Hull). Its members were:

Ameer Ali (Commission for Racial Equality)
Yasmin Alibhai-Brown (journalist and broadcaster)
Valerie Amos (Quality and Equality)
Muhammad Anwar (University of Warwick)
Paul Boateng (MP)
Godfrey Brandt (Joseph Rowntree Charitable Trust)
Dennis Brooks (Employment Department)
Ben Brown (Department for Education and Employment)
Bennie Bunsie (Anti-Racist Alliance)
Liza Catan (Department of Health)
Marian FitzGerald (Home Office)
Jenny Griffin (Department of Health)
Sanjay Gupta (Department of Health)
Colin Hann (Commission for Racial Equality)
Angelika Hibbett (Department of Employment)
Mike Hough (Home Office)
Kamaljeet Jandu (Transport and General Workers Union)
Keith Kirby (Department of the Environment)
Hans Kundnani (Commission for Racial Equality)
Juliet Mountford (Department of the Environment)
Kumar Murshid (London Borough of Tower Hamlets)
Ceri Peach (University of Oxford)
Usha Prashar, OBE (Chair, National Literacy Trust)
Bill Sheppard (Employment Service).

Apart from this formal group of advisers, the work on the survey benefitted from advice and commentary from a large number of friends and colleagues in universities and research institutes, in government, and elsewhere. I am particularly grateful to *Mel Bartley* and *George Davey Smith*, whose detailed comments on an initial draft of this volume led to significant improvements.

The research itself was undertaken in partnership by the Policy Studies Institute and Social and Community Planning Research. PSI had primary responsibility for the overall structure of the study, and for this book. SCPR was responsible primarily for the detailed design of the survey, and especially the sample; and for the massive tasks of data collection and preparation.

At Social and Community Planning Research, *Roger Jowell* held overall responsibility for the SCPR end of the partnership. *Patten Smith* undertook the primary role in designing and managing the survey, working during key periods with *Gillian Prior*.

A number of people at the Policy Studies Institute contributed to this volume. *David Smith* was originally responsible for getting the project off the ground, and led the team through the design phase before taking up a chair at the University of Edinburgh. *Richard Berthoud* then took over the overall responsibility for the study and made important contributions to the analysis presented in this volume before leaving PSI to take up a chair at the ESRC Research Centre on Micro-Social Change (University of Essex). *David Halpern* was responsible for the development and design of the health element of the questionnaire, before leaving PSI for Nuffield College Oxford and then the University of Cambridge. While working on other elements of the Fourth National Survey, *Sharon Beishon, Tariq Modood* and *Satnam Virdee* all contributed to this analysis and writing. Other PSI staff who made significant contributions to the study included *Karen Mackinnon, Lydia Maher* and *Chris Maynard* (data analysis), *Siân Putnam* (administrative support), *Karin Erskine* (typesetting) and *Jo O'Driscoll* (publications).

All of these people and organisations contributed to the research. Above all we are grateful to the 8000 people who took part in the survey and provided information about their experiences and opinions. Responsibility for this report, and its conclusions, lies with the author.

CHAPTER ONE

Introduction

The *Fourth National Survey of Ethnic Minorities* is the latest in a series of surveys undertaken by the Policy Studies Institute and it predecessor, Political and Economic Planning, which have charted the changing position of Britain's ethnic minorities from 1966 to the present day (Daniel 1968, Smith 1977, Brown 1984, Modood *et al.* 1997). This survey was undertaken jointly by the Policy Studies Institute and Social and Community Planning Research, and was funded by the Departments of Health, Employment and Environment, and the Economic and Social Research Council. It covers many of the traditional measures of social and economic disadvantage that have appeared in the previous studies, including sections on type and quality of housing, area of residence, employment and income, and education. In addition to this, several important new sections have been added, including a detailed exploration of ethnicity and how different ethnic groups view themselves and their lives in Britain, and the incidence and experience of racial violence and harassment. The other unique element to this survey was an extensive section on health and health related issues. These included perceptions of general health as well as specific illnesses, such as heart disease, diabetes, respiratory illness and accidents, and the use of health services. This provides the first detailed national morbidity survey that allows comparisons across ethnic groups for key dimensions of health to be made. Such a comparison is the focus of this volume, which presents the first comprehensive analysis of these data.

THE FOCUS OF EXISTING WORK

Since the early 1980s there has been considerable interest in the health of ethnic minority populations in Britain. There will be no attempt to provide an overview of existing research here, examples and summaries of current work can be found in: Balarajan and Soni Raleigh (1993 and 1995), who relate work on ethnic variations in health to the Health of the Nation targets; Smaje (1995a) who provides a comprehensive overview of the existing state of affairs in research on health and ethnicity; Ahmad (1993a), an edited volume that takes a critical perspective on several of the key issues in this area; Marmot *et al.* (1984), a classic epidemiological study of ethnicity and health that has provided the model followed by many others; and Donovan (1984), whose critical review of the state of research up to the early 1980s shows that despite the exponential growth in the number of publications, things have changed little since then.

Variations in health across ethnic groups appear to have been of interest for three, potentially conflicting, reasons. First, in an investigation, description and explanation of the position of ethnic minority groups in Britain, health is a crucial experience. How patterns of health and health care vary across and within ethnic groups is a reflection of both the social position of these groups and of the individual experiences of people who are members of these groups. Consequently, a description of ethnic variations in health and in the experience of health care, and an exploration of why these variations might occur, is an important part of under standing the disadvantages faced by ethnic minority groups. Second, how a disease is socially patterned provides important clues for an investigation of its aetiology. If a particular social group is at greater risk of a particular disease, then something about the attributes of that group must be elevating its risk. Consequently, in the investigation of the aetiology of specific diseases, key factors can be sought among the attributes of groups at greater risk. The third reason for the interest in the health of ethnic minority groups results from a concern with the planning and provision of appropriate health care services. However, the extent to which research has been carried out with this in mind, rather than satisfying this need as a by-product of the research process, is questionable. Indeed, Senior and Bhopal (1994) go so far as to argue that it is difficult to simultaneously meet the needs of both an aetiological approach and one directed at the planning of health care.

The tensions between the first two motives for carrying out work on ethnicity and health can be clearly seen from a comparison of existing work – for example, comparing that produced by Pilgrim *et al.* (1993) and found in the volume edited by Ahmad (1993a) with the work of Marmot *et al.* (1984) and McKeigue and colleagues (e.g. McKeigue *et al.* 1988, 1989 and 1991). The latter work clearly follows the tradition of classic epidemiological studies, with a focus on particular diseases, rather than health *per se*, and where the variation in disease patterns across ethnic groups is used to provide an understanding of aetiology. This is typically done with a focus on the biological or cultural characteristics of individuals within the ethnic/race group at greater risk and without an interest in the origins of the differential distribution of either the identified cultural attributes or their associated social factors. (Krieger (1994) provides a useful critique of this traditional epidemiological approach.) This can lead to a form of victim blaming, where the inherent characteristics of the ethnic (minority) group are seen to be at fault and in need of rectifying (Sheldon and Parker 1992). However, this need not be the case, particularly if factors beyond biology and culture are also considered and the complex and dynamic inter-relationships between relevant aetiological factors and their origins are acknowledged. In contrast, the former work is clearly in the tradition of work on race relations, it raises questions about the motives for, and methods used in, work on ethnicity and health and the implications that this has for the potentially discriminatory conclusions drawn. It also focuses on the health disadvantage faced by ethnic minority groups and how the health service, and social services more generally, may be failing to find appropriate ways to meet needs and, indeed, may be acting to promote disadvantage.

In many ways the work presented in this volume can, as a result of the advantages provided by the quality of the data set used, attempt to begin a synthesis between work based on a race relations perspective and that with a more epidemiological orientation. The concern here is to describe the extent of ill-health in different ethnic groups (both in terms of a general perception of health and for particular illnesses), to see how far ill-health for individuals within particular ethnic groups may be related to factors associated with the disadvantage faced by those groups, and how far any of the overall ethnic variations in health uncovered might be related to ethnic variations in other forms of social disadvantage. Unfortunately, the nature of a survey such as this means that the aetiological focus cannot be taken any further than this. Reliance on cross-sectional data means that causal direction can, at best, only be assumed. In addition, biological and cultural factors possibly associated with a health risk – apart from smoking and alcohol use – cannot be assessed, even though there is a need to explore the potentially complex inter-relationships between the social, cultural and biological factors involved in the aetiology of particular diseases.

Supplementing this focus, this volume is also concerned with explicitly addressing the needs of health care providers and policy makers. To this end, the volume contains direct estimates of the levels of ill-health in different ethnic groups, rather than only containing figures that have been adjusted to allow for comparisons across groups. It also contains a detailed exploration of the use made of available services and the ways in which health and social services may be failing to address certain needs.

THE DATA USED TO EXPLORE ETHNIC VARIATIONS IN HEALTH

The epidemiological approach to work on ethnic health variations must be understood in the light of the type of data that has, to date, been available to researchers to explore the relevant issues. The most influential work has been based on immigrant mortality statistics derived from national data sets. Country of birth is recorded on death certificates and has also been recorded in the decennial Census, allowing a thorough investigation of differences in mortality rates by both cause of death and country of birth (Marmot *et al.* 1984, Balarajan and Bulusu 1990, Balarajan 1996). However, despite the influence of these studies, there are several problems with data of this sort. Problems with the consistency of the recording of country of birth on death certificates and at the Census means that fairly diverse groups are included in the same category, the most obvious of these being a category that includes all of those born in the Indian sub-continent (Marmot *et al.* 1984) – although recent work attempts to improve on this situation (Balarajan 1996). In addition to this, assessing ethnicity using country of birth is far from adequate, misclassifying both ethnic minority people born in Britain and white people born overseas. Problems with assigning ethnicity during the research process will be discussed more fully later in this chapter. In addition, it seems that there is a degree of inaccuracy in the recording of cause of death on death certificates (Joint Committee of the Royal Colleges of Physicians and Pathologists 1982). The uncertainty in assigning cause of death has been shown to vary by occupational class (Bloor *et al.* 1989), so may also vary by other characteristics of the deceased, such as ethnic background. This leads to the possibility that the recording of cause of death might be systematically biased by the ethnic background of the deceased.

Also, if our concern is with the health of the population, mortality rates are a very crude indication of this complex multi-dimensional concept, an issue that is discussed more fully in the section in this chapter on measuring health. An equally important problem is that relying on Census figures to determine the size of the 'at-risk' population can exaggerate the estimated risk for any group that is undercounted in the Census and there is some evidence to suggest that such undercounting does vary by ethnicity (OPCS 1994). Finally, in terms of an epidemiological investigation that is concerned with exploring the aetiology of diseases that show variation, such data include no assessment of potential explanatory factors beyond occupational class as recorded at the Census and on death certificates (potential problems with the use of these data for exploring ethnic variations in health are discussed in Chapter 5). Certainly there is no assessment of the often favoured biological and cultural explanations that are consequently assumed, based on stereotypes and crudely used (see Bhopal (1995) for a critique of this 'Black Box' approach to epidemiology).

In terms of other nationally representative data, national surveys of the general population have not had sufficiently large samples of ethnic minority people for more than provisional conclusions to be drawn (see, for example, Benzeval *et al.* 1992), although this may change as the Health Survey for England is expanded (Markowe 1993). However, immigrant mortality data have been supplemented by smaller regional studies of the health of ethnic minority groups. Much of this work has had a more general perspective (Pilgrim 1993, Williams *et al.* 1993), but some has maintained an exclusive focus on aetiology, where data from immigrant mortality studies are used to identify an ethnic group at greater risk from a particular disease and then this greater risk is confirmed and aetiological factors explored in an in-depth local study. The work investigating whether the high rates of heart disease among South Asians are the result of an 'insulin resistance syndrome' is a good example of how this approach can be developed into a comprehensive research programme (Cruickshank *et al.* 1991, McKeigue *et al.* 1988 and 1991, Knight *et al.* 1992).

Despite the quality of much of this work, it still remains dependent on data that are far from adequate. Proportional mortality ratios are generally used for comparisons between ethnic groups by both local studies and national mortality studies that attempt to overcome crude ethnic classifications (Balarajan *et al.* 1984, McKeigue and Marmot 1988). This is because the size of the population of different ethnic groups is unknown, and if the size of the population in which deaths are occurring is unknown, then the death rate for that population and a comparison with the general population (usually expressed as a standardised mortality rate) cannot be calculated. To overcome this the proportion of *all* deaths in the group due to a *particular* disease can be calculated and that proportion can then be compared to that for the general population, giving a proportional mortality ratio. However, the limitations of proportional mortality ratios are well known (Roman *et al.* 1984). Particularly important is that they may not give a reliable estimate of comparative prevalence, because a high proportional mortality ratio for a particular disease can result from either a high relative prevalence of that disease or a low relative prevalence of other diseases. This means that such data require careful interpretation, particularly with regard to data on ethnicity as immigrant mortality statistics suggest that death rates for some diseases in ethnic minority groups are relatively low (Marmot *et al.* 1984).

In addition, because of the highly concentrated geographical locations of particular ethnic groups in Britain (Owen 1994), regional studies often cover only one specific ethnic group – such as Knight *et al.*'s (1992) study of insulin resistance and coronary heart disease among 'South Asian' men in Bradford who were, presumably, predominantly Pakistani, and McKeigue *et al.*'s (1988) study of coronary heart disease among Bangladeshis in East London – but then have their results generalised to the wider population within which this group is included. Both the potential impact of factors associated with the specific ethnic group considered, and the locality within which that group is resident, are often ignored.

In terms of improving the data available for the study of ethnic variations in health, progress has been made in three ways. For the first time the 1991 Census included a question on self-assigned ethnic group and another on the presence of a long-standing limiting illness. So far there has been little analysis of these data, although some is presented in Dunnell (1993) and in Chapter 3 of this volume. Nevertheless, the Sample of Anonymised Records, which contains full Census data for 2 per cent of the population, allows for a detailed investigation of responses to the question on long-standing limiting illness. The main limitation of these data is their restriction to only one assessment of health. This may be partly overcome by the routine and systematic collection of data on the ethnicity of patients admitted to hospital, introduced in April 1996, which can be related back to population data derived from the Census, although there may be some problems with this process (Aspinall 1995). Additional problems with such data are that they only reflect the small hospital-treated proportion of those that are ill, a proportion that may well vary according to ethnicity, and other factors of possible interest, such as socio-economic status, are not being collected alongside ethnicity.

Second, the Health Education Authority has carried out two surveys on the health and lifestyles of Black and Minority Ethnic Groups, the first of which has been published (Rudat 1994) and the second of which should appear shortly. These studies have provided useful and unique information on a range of health behaviours, health promotion issues and health care, together with some on health status, for several ethnic minority groups in Britain. The main disadvantage with these surveys is that they were undertaken in areas with relatively large ethnic minority populations – those areas that, according to the 1981 Census, had 10 per cent or more of households headed by someone born in the Caribbean, South Asia or Africa – and, consequently, they were not fully representative of the populations they covered. Indeed, the data presented by Smith (1996) suggest that such a strategy would only cover two-thirds of the ethnic minority population, and these two-thirds might differ from the remaining third in important respects. In addition, these surveys were unable to include a directly comparable general population group and could only contain a limited coverage of other factors relevant to the lives of ethnic minority people. Nevertheless, they provide an important addition to our relatively limited knowledge of these issues, as reflected in their use in this volume as a source of information on key issues.

The third step forward is the study reported here. The methods used in this survey will be described in full in the next section, however, the key points are: it is fully representative of the ethnic minority groups covered and includes a white comparison sample; health was assessed across a variety of dimensions, including both general health and specific illnesses; detailed information was collected on both ethnicity and features of the lives of ethnic minority people in Britain; and detailed information was also collected on demographic and socio-economic factors. This provides a rich and unique data source for examining the relationship between ethnicity and health. However, it does, inevitably, suffer from some disadvantages, two of which are worth mentioning here. First, its sample size was too small to explore the patterning of rare illnesses. In fact, the focus was exclusively on relatively common disorders that others have shown to vary by ethnic background. Second, it was based entirely on self-reported illness. No physical measurements were included and it is possible that the relationship between self-report of illness and actual disease varied across ethnic groups, as it appears to do by class (Blane *et al.* 1996). A more detailed discussion of this issue can be found later in this chapter in the section on measuring health.

METHODOLOGY[1]

Conduct of the survey

The survey was a national study covering England and Wales and carried out in 1993 and 1994. It was based on a structured questionnaire that, in addition to health and health service use, covered many traditional measures of social and economic disadvantage, including sections on type and quality of housing, area of residence, employment and income, and education. In addition to this, several important issues were covered for the first time, including those relating to ethnic identity and the incidence and experience of racial violence and harassment. Findings from these sections of the survey can be found in Modood *et al.* (1997) The survey was conducted in two phases: first, a screening phase for the identification of the sample of people of ethnic minority origin; second, the data collection phase, which covered both the identified ethnic minority sample and a white comparison sample. Interviewers were in most cases ethnically and language matched with respondents and interviews were carried out in the language(s) of the respondent's choice. The languages used included: Urdu; Punjabi; Gujarati; Bengali (Sylhethi); Hindi; and Chinese (Cantonese). Translations of questionnaires and other materials were carried out by a commercial translation agency and were checked by having the translation independently translated back into English. These were then tested in three small scale pilot studies and subsequently modified.

---

1   Full details of the survey methods, including copies of the materials used, can be found in the methodological report on this survey (Smith and Prior 1997).

Sampling

The sampling procedures were designed to select probability samples of both individuals and households. The areas used for sampling were selected on the basis of data from the 1991 Census on the ethnic minority population size in particular enumeration districts and electoral wards. For the ethnic minority sample they were designed to produce a sample that was fully representative of the groups covered, including respondents from areas with a low ethnic minority concentration, a population that has been ignored by other regional and national surveys of ethnic minority groups. This ensured that the wards and enumeration districts used represented those containing households of which less than 0.5 per cent were ethnic minority (low concentration), those containing between 0.5 and 10 per cent ethnic minority households (medium concentration), and those containing households of which more than 10 per cent were ethnic minority (high concentration). Once the sampling points were identified, the Postcode Address File was used as the sampling frame to identify households to be screened for inclusion in the study.

Screening for ethnic minority respondents was carried out in the field. In areas with a high ethnic minority concentration, suitable ethnic minority respondents were identified by asking at all of the selected addresses whether there was anyone living at the address who was of Caribbean, Asian or Chinese origin. In areas with medium and low ethnic minority concentrations, screening was based on the principle of focused enumeration, a method that has been shown to provide good coverage of the targeted populations (Brown and Ritchie 1981, Smith 1996). This involves interviewers visiting every nth (e.g. 6th) address in a defined area and asking about the ethnic origin of those living at both the visited address and at the n–1 (e.g. 5) addresses on each side of the visited address. Consequently, non-visited addresses are asked about at two visited addresses. If a positive or uncertain identification is made at either of the visited addresses for the non-visited addresses, the interviewer then goes on to visit them in person.

In practice the detail of this procedure varied according to the ethnic minority concentration in the area to be covered. In areas of medium ethnic minority density, on the whole every sixth address along the street was designated for an initial visit, but in some areas with more concentrated ethnic minority populations every fourth address was so designated. In these cases, when interviewers were told that there were no eligible ethnic minority people living at the non-visited addresses they were permitted to record them as having been covered with no further visit being made. However, if at either of the relevant visited addresses the interviewer was told that one or more ethnic minority people lived at *any* of the intervening non-visited addresses, they were asked to make personal calls at *all* of the intervening addresses to try to ascertain the ethnic origin of the people living at them. In contrast to this, in areas of low ethnic minority density every tenth address was used for the focused enumeration process and, if during this process the interviewer was told at exactly which address an ethnic minority person lived, the interviewer was instructed to visit that address directly rather than to visit *all* of the intervening addresses.

Any households identified in this way as containing one or more people with an ethnic minority origin were then used to obtain the ethnic minority sample. In order to maximise the efficiency of the sampling process, in households containing ethnic minority people two respondents were selected for interview whenever possible (if there were one or two eligible adults in the household all were selected, if there were three or more two were selected at random).

To draw the white sample a more straightforward three stage stratified design was used. First, a sample of wards was drawn. Second, from within each selected ward a sample of addresses were identified from the Postcode Address File. Finally, interviewers selected one random eligible adult (rather than a possible two, as in the case of ethnic minority households) from within each selected address. The sample of wards was drawn to include both those which, according to the 1991 Census, had a concentration of ethnic minority households above and below 0.5 per cent.

Six weighting factors were applied to the data in order to deal with the complex sample design and to ensure that the survey sample represented the populations under study as closely as possible. These accounted for differences in the probability of selection into the study, variations in the response rate by ethnicity, age and gender, and differences in the age profile of the sample compared to the 1991 Census figures.

Response rates were comparable to those for the third survey (Brown 1984). Among those who were approached for interview 71 per cent of white, 61 per cent of Caribbean, 74 per cent of Indian (including African Asian), 73 per cent of Pakistani, 83 per cent of Bangladeshi and 66 per cent of Chinese respondents agreed to take part. The final sample achieved consisted of 2867 white respondents (119 with Irish family origins and 94 with neither Irish nor British family origins) and 5196 respondents who were members of ethnic minority groups. If ethnicity is allocated according to family origins, of the 5196 ethnic minority respondents, 1205 were Caribbean, 1273 were Indian, 728 were African Asian, 1185 were Pakistani, 591 were Bangladeshi and 214 were Chinese. Other ethnic minority groups were not covered. The assignment of individuals into particular ethnic groups is, of course, a complex and controversial process. This is discussed in detail in the next section.

Measuring ethnicity

As Senior and Bhopal (1994) point out, the concept of ethnicity is by no means simple. It contains notions of shared origins, culture and tradition and, as such, its use allows us to move away from the biological/genetic determinism that is inherent in the concept of race. This move from a deterministic perspective becomes particularly likely if, in addition to recognising that ethnicity is a multi-dimensional concept, we also acknowledge that it is neither stable nor pure. This is illustrated in the exploration of ethnic identity in Modood *et al.* (1997). Indeed, ethnicity cannot be considered as fixed because culture is not an autonomous and static feature in an individual's life, it has a dynamic relationship to both the historical and contemporary experiences of social groups and is related to the living conditions of individuals. Central to the concept of ethnicity is that it is a reflection of the self-identification of individuals with particular cultural traditions. Certainly for members of ethnic minority groups there is an immediate and close link between self-identity and perceived ethnicity, although, as just suggested, perceived ethnicity and its link with identity is dependent on both immediate context and historical factors (Modood *et al.* 1994). In addition, there are competing claims on identity whose immediate relevance is also dependent on context, such as gender and class. The implication is that there are a range of (ethnic) identities that come into play at different times and even, possibly, at the same time, so that (ethnic) identity should be regarded as neither coherent nor secure (Hall 1992).

Despite the complexity of the concept of ethnicity, which has only been touched upon, most research on health and ethnicity has taken a crude approach to the allocation of individuals into ethnic groups. As a recent *British Medical Journal* editorial pointed out, the categories of ethnic group used in health related research are often undefined and inconsistently used (McKenzie and Crowcroft 1994). This allows the status of ethnicity as an explanatory variable to be assumed, treated as though objectively measured and, consequently, reified. The view of ethnicity as a natural division between social groups allows the *description* of ethnic variations in health to become their *explanation* (Sheldon and Parker 1992), leading to untested assumptions about the existence and importance of cultural and biological differences being asserted as fact without underlying explanations being explored.

This has partly been a consequence of the limitations of available data. For example, as already discussed, because country of birth is recorded on death certificates and in the Census, much of the published data in this area has allocated ethnicity according to country of birth, a strategy that is clearly inadequate. In addition, many studies use categories such as Black or South Asian to describe the ethnicity of those studied. Although some have suggested that this might be a useful starting point (Chaturvedi and McKeigue 1994), it is important to recognise that such categories are heterogeneous, containing ethnic groups with different cultures, religions, migration histories and geographical and socio-economic locations. In fact, rather than being a good starting point, combining ethnic groups leads to differences between them being ignored. For example, the differences between various South Asian groups' proportional mortality rates for myocardial infarction shown in Table III of Balarajan *et al.* (1984), which are potential highly important, have been repeatedly misconstrued (see, for example, McKeigue *et al.* 1989 and 1991, and Gupta *et al.* 1995, all of which cite this study as showing no differences), presumably because of assumptions that earlier studies that had combined South Asian groups had not been misleading. Also, as described earlier, local studies that contain representatives of only one component of such groups – such as Punjabis or Bangladeshis – but nevertheless have the population described in more global terms – such as South Asian – are potentially even more misleading, because the findings for one ethnic minority group in a particular location become generalised to others.

It seems that in order for work on ethnicity and health to progress further, assessments of ethnicity must be more adequate and the process used must be clearly defined (Senior and Bhopal 1994). One way forward is to allow individuals to assign themselves into an ethnic group, an approach that acknowledges the role of ethnicity in self-perception. This is the strategy adopted by the 1991 Census, however it suffers from a lack of stability. Individuals often move themselves from one category to another when the question is repeated at a later date (Sheldon and Parker 1992), a situation that is no doubt a reflection of the contextual nature of, ethnic identity. Another and important way forward is to actually acknowledge the contextual nature of ethnicity and to research the relationship between ethnicity and health with this explicitly in mind (Ahmad 1995). However, such a task is difficult, if not impossible, to undertake in a 'static' cross-sectional quantitative survey of this kind.

An alternative, and the option used in the majority of the investigation presented in this volume, is to largely ignore the role of perceived ethnicity and to assign ethnicity according to country of family origin. In this survey this was done by asking the question: 'Do you have family origins which are: Black Caribbean; Indian Caribbean; Pakistani; Bangladeshi; Indian; Chinese; Irish; white British; or did your family come from somewhere else?'. Not surprisingly, perceived ethnicity and country of family origin are highly related, as Table 1.1 shows.

Table 1.1   Self perceived ethnicity by ethnic family origins

column percentages

	White	Caribbean	Indian	African Asian	Pakistani	Bangladeshi	Chinese
				Ethnic family origins			
To which group do you belong?							
White	99.8	0.3	0.5	0.1	0.4	0.3	3.3
Black Caribbean	0	83.7	0	0	0	0	0
Black African	0	1.1	0	0	0	0	0
Black Other	0	0.3	0	0	0	0	0
Black British	0	10	< 0.1	0	0	0	0
Asian British	0	< 0.1	0.8	0.8	0.6	0.3	0
Indian	0	< 0.1	96.9	88.2	0.3	0	0
Pakistani	0	0	0.6	6.0	98.3	0.2	0
Bangladeshi	0	0	0.2	1.0	0	98.8	0
Chinese	0	0	0	0	0	0	92.5
Mixed	< 0.1	3.6	0.8	1.7	0	0.3	2.8
Other	0.1	0.2	0.2	2.1	0	0	1.4
Not anwered	0.1	0.7	0	0.1	0.4	0	0
Base	*2867*	*1205*	*1273*	*728*	*1185*	*591*	*214*

The approach based on country of family origin has the advantage of being a relatively straightforward and stable approach, although individuals within particular groups cannot be considered homogeneous in respect of a number of factors that may be related to both self-perceived ethnicity, such as religion or country of birth, and health, such as socio-economic status. Issues relating to this are discussed at some length in Chapters 4 and 5 and the conclusion to this volume and are also examined in detail in Modood *et al.* (1997). However, here it is particularly important to recognise that in this investigation the white comparison group has been treated as though it reflects a homogeneous ethnic group, and one that has had its ethnicity largely left unquestioned. This is clearly an issue that needs to be tackled in future work (Sheldon and Parker 1992, Bradby 1995). Related to this, the most obvious *practical* problem with this approach is how to deal with respondents who identify themselves as having mixed family origins. Here, a crude approach of wherever possible allowing ethnic minority status to over-ride white status has been taken.

Again, as Table 1.2 shows, this has only affected a small number of respondents in the South Asian groups and less than 10 per cent of those in the Caribbean and Chinese groups.

Table 1.2   Mixed ethnicity by ethnic family origins

column percentages

	White	Caribbean	Indian	African Asian	Pakistani	Bangladeshi	Chinese
				Ethnic family origins			
Those whose responses to family origins and group membership questions suggest mixed ethnicity	1.2	8.2	2.5	2.5	0.6	0.7	7.5
Base	*2867*	*1205*	*1273*	*728*	*1185*	*591*	*214*

Although the use of country of family origin to allocate ethnicity in this relatively crude and one-dimensional way is limited, it does enable a level of clarity to be maintained when making initial explorations of ethnic variations in health. And, importantly, it allows the exploration of this topic to move beyond the even cruder assessments of ethnicity that are based on country/continent of birth, or over-arching categories such as Black or South Asian. The implications of using more sophisticated attempts to assign ethnicity in a survey such as this are explored in Chapter 4 of this volume.

Measuring health

Much of the work that has explored the social patterning of health has concentrated on mortality rates (e.g. Townsend and Davidson 1982, Marmot *et al.* 1984). These have the advantages of being clearly defined, reasonably easily available from a combination of death certificate and Census data, and reasonably disease specific. However, they are a narrow reflection of what is clearly a complex concept. For example, the *Health and Lifestyle Survey* (Blaxter 1990) showed the multi-dimensional nature of lay concepts of health, which included, among others, notions of: 'not being ill'; not having or overcoming disease; a reserve or a source of energy; physical fitness or functional ability; and a sense of well-being. Certainly mortality rates reflect only a small element of these concepts. In addition, mortality rates may well not reflect even the narrowly defined disease-based definitions of health. The relationship between disease and death depends on a number of factors, including whether the disease is fatal, the types of treatment offered and used, and the wider resources available to individuals that affect the prognosis of a disease. Of particular importance to investigations of the social patterning of health is that such resources will vary across social groups. Given their differences, mortality and morbidity rates need not necessarily show the same social patterning.

In terms of asking questions about health in a survey such as this, with a focus on morbidity rather than mortality, a variety of strategies could be adopted. First, health can be considered in a medical sense as the absence or presence of recognised disease. For this questions can ask directly about the presence of particular diseases and this is one of the strategies adopted here. Data presented later will include responses to questions asking about the diagnosis of heart disease, hypertension and diabetes. However, such a strategy does raise certain problems, which partly result from how opportunities for the diagnosis of particular diseases may vary by social group. Certainly, a study of ethnic variations in health that relies solely on the identification of already diagnosed disease is particularly vulnerable to the criticism that differences in treatment rates and quality of treatment between ethnic groups may have produced the pattern of results reported. In addition to this, such questions are also dependent on the accuracy of respondents' knowledge and recollections of diagnoses that have been made. This will be influenced by the quality of the consultation with the doctor, which may also vary by social group.

Second, questions on disease can be extended beyond those on diagnosis to include coverage of symptoms. This helps to get around problems relating to differences in the access to or the use of medical services. Questions on symptoms were included in this survey, and will be reported later in relation to both heart disease and respiratory disease. However, such an approach cannot overcome possible differences between social groups in how these questions are interpreted and responded to. It is possible that an assessment of whether a particular symptom is severe enough to be worth mentioning will vary across social groups, particularly if the questions have been translated into different languages for different groups. Answers to such questions, consequently, may also produce misleading conclusions about differences between these groups.

A third approach is to ask about the effects of ill-health on the functioning of the respondent. For this survey the strategy adopted was to ask respondents to estimate the extent to which their performance of specific functions, such as climbing stairs, were restricted as a result of their poor health. A fourth possibility, also included here, is to ask respondents to provide a global self-assessment of their health. It has been suggested that the subjective nature of health makes this the most valid approach to assessing health (Benzeval *et al.* 1992), and there is some evidence that such self-assessments predict mortality rates (Mossey and Shapiro 1982). However, like reports of symptoms, differences across social groups in both the reporting of functional limitation as a result of ill-health and the reporting of self-assessed health may be a result of differences in the way these groups interpreted the questions used.

This discussion of the four types of morbidity assessment used in this survey illustrates one fundamental difficulty with the interpretation of responses – in terms of making comparisons across ethnic groups, differences in responses may be a reflection of differences in the ways that particular groups interpret and respond to questions and differences in their access to health care and the type of treatment received. Indeed, the problems faced here are similar to those discussed in some detail by Blane *et al.* (1996) in relation to assessing class differentials in morbidity. Despite the difficulties with these assessments of health, some confidence in the responses to them in this survey can be taken from two pieces of evidence. First, *within* particular ethnic groups the social patterning of ill-health for all four modes of questioning was as would be expected, with the rate of ill-health being related to age, gender, smoking and socio-economic status. Second, where comparisons can be made between the four modes of questioning – for example, comparing responses to questions on diagnosis with those to questions on symptoms, or responses to questions on general health with those to questions on functional limitation as a result of ill-health – similar patterns of response across ethnic groups are shown for all but one question. (The discrepancy involves responses to a question asking about 'long-standing illness', which others have suggested is interpreted differently by different ethnic groups (Pilgrim *et al.* 1993, Rudat 1994), and is explored at length in Chapter 3.) This suggests that on the whole all four types of questions on morbidity had some validity for exploring patterns of ill-health both within and across ethnic groups. In addition, the use of a 'battery of standardized instruments' in this survey increases the confidence with which we can interpret the findings (Blane et al., 1996).

Content of the survey

Much of the questionning on health used in the survey was derived from the Health Survey for England (White *et al.* 1993), which itself generally uses well established and validated questions. As a result of the large amount of material that was covered in this survey, some of the questions on health were only asked of half of the sample. These are identified in the text describing the results of the survey. In terms of the coverage of the interview, the health section tackled six broad areas:[2]

1. General health status
   a. Self-assessed health, including general health, long-standing illness and disability
   b. Activities limited by the respondent's health, using the physical functioning questions contained in the Medical Outcomes Study Short-Form Health Survey (Ware and Sherbourne 1992)

2. Cardiovascular disease
   a. Diagnosis of coronary heart disease, hypertension and stroke
   b. Symptoms of coronary heart disease, using some of the Rose Angina questions (Rose and Blackburn 1986)

3. Other specific physical health problems
   a. Diagnosis of diabetes
   b. Respiratory symptoms, using questions derived from the Medical Research Council Respiratory questionnaire (MRC 1982)

4. Perceived weight and health related behaviours, such as smoking and drinking

5. Accidents requiring hospital treatment, using questions derived from the 1989 General Household Survey (OPCS 1991)

6. Use of health services including hospital services, general practice, dentists, home helps etc.

---

2 The actual questions used can be found in Appendix A.

7 Mental health
  a Tiredness and problems with sleep.
  b Affective disorders, using questions derived from the revised version of the Clinical Interview Schedule (Lewis *et al.* 1992)
  c Psychotic disorders, using questions derived from the Psychosis Screening Questionnaire (Bebbington and Nayani 1995).

Data on the mental health aspects of this survey, together with that from the associated validation survey (which was undertaken because of the controversial nature of using standardised assessments of psychiatric disorder for comparisons across ethnic groups), are reported elsewhere (Nazroo 1997).

OVERVIEW OF THE VOLUME

Chapter 2 of this volume begins the exploration of the data from this survey. It shows the actual levels of ill-health across the dimensions assessed for each of the ethnic groups covered. Although differences in the age structure of ethnic minority and white groups means that this information does not allow a comparison between them to be made, these data are a crucial resource in terms of understanding the level of ill-health faced by different ethnic groups and for informing the planning of health care. It also provides a benchmark against which other studies, both on ethnic minority groups and the general population, can be compared.

Chapter 3 of this volume presents data on differences in the prevalence of ill-health between the various ethnic minority groups and whites. In order to allow for these comparisons, data here have been age and gender standardised so are, consequently, not directly comparable to those shown in the previous chapter. Ethnicity here, as in Chapter 2, is based on country of family origin. The data shown illustrate that the cruder ethnic categorisations used elsewhere, such as those based on country of birth or more global categories like South Asian, have resulted in misleading conclusions being drawn for both specific diseases and for more general perceptions about the health disadvantage of ethnic minority groups.

Chapter 4 of this volume begins to unpack the notion of ethnicity further. It does this by looking at the differences between those ethnic minority people who migrated to Britain and those born in Britain, and by looking at the differences in levels of ill-health between the religious groups that are contained in the Indian and African Asian categories. The implications of using an unproblematised ethnic classification for an explanatory or aetiological approach to ethnic variations in health are then examined.

Having established the extent and nature of ethnic health variations in the previous two chapters, Chapter 5 sets out to explore likely explanatory factors for the differences between ethnic groups. Although other factors are discussed, here the emphasis is very much on the association of health disadvantage with socio-economic position. It is argued that traditional approaches to the measurement of socio-economic position fail to take into account the extent of disadvantage faced by ethnic minority groups and new ways forward are taken.

Chapter 6 begins by exploring differences in medical health service use and, for the first time, includes data on need when assessing differences in use. Both primary and secondary medical care are considered, and discrepancies between the two are highlighted and discussed. The chapter than goes on to discuss differences in the quality of care offered to ethnic minority and majority patients. Here the focus is on the language needs of different groups and the preferences they have for the ethnicity and gender of the doctor they consult. The chapter concludes with an overview of the use made by different ethnic minority groups of other health and social care services.

Finally, the conclusion provides a summary of the key findings from the volume. It then goes on to discuss the implications of these for understanding ethnic variations in health and for future work on ethnicity and health. Once again the notion of a direct relationship between ethnicity/race and health is problematised and it is argued that ethnicity should be considered in terms of its role in increasing risk of socio-economic disadvantage. The extent to which the cultural and biological attributes associated with ethnicity play a role in understanding health disadvantage is questioned, although their importance in explaining the aetiology of specific diseases (perhaps through interaction with socio-economic factors), rather than overall variations in health, is acknowledged.

CHAPTER TWO

Health Status of Ethnic Minorities

INTRODUCTION

The previous chapter described the limitations of existing data on the health of Britain's ethnic minorities. In addition to this, it is worth restating that the vast majority of these data have been collected to explore the extent of the difference between the health of the white and ethnic minority populations, rather than levels of ill-health *per se,* with the aim of exploring the aetiology of particular disorders. This is done by identifying those groups that are at greater risk, who, presumably, have had greater exposure to certain aetiological factors that future research can set about identifying (see, for example, the rationale presented by Marmot *et al.* (1984) for undertaking their work on immigrant mortality rates). While there is a clear importance in describing and attempting to explain variations in health across social groups (indeed that is the focus of much of this report), such an approach has the disadvantage of obscuring the actual health status of the groups concerned. Aetiological analysis does not need to illustrate *actual* disease frequency, it only needs to demonstrate the rate of ill-health for a population that has been sampled and standardised to provide a valid comparison with other groups, and even standardised rates are often left out, with reports only containing a reference to odds ratios or relative risk.

An exclusive use of such a focus has several disadvantages. First, health service planners need data that reflect absolute need rather than relative need if they are to accurately predict the services they should provide. Second, a focus on relative risk only allows assessment of changes over time in relation to the comparison group, assessment of changes within the group under study cannot be directly made. Third, an aetiological focus will of necessity concentrate on those illnesses with a high relative risk for the population under study, which need not be those that contribute most to their burden of ill-health (Bhopal 1996). Fourth, a comparison with a majority population often leads to the assumption that the majority population's experience is 'normal' and reasons for deviation from this should be found among the characteristics of the minority population(s). Finally, the use of gender and age standardised data obscures gender and age effects and the interactions between these and ethnicity. For these reasons, it is important to begin by describing the health status of the groups we are concerned with. Consequently, this chapter will focus on providing benchmark data on the health of Britain's ethnic minority populations. It is also worth pointing out that this survey also provides a comprehensive coverage of the health of the white population, a nationally representative sample of almost 3,000 whites were interviewed. So, the data presented here will also provide a benchmark of the health of the white population and one that can be compared with other general population surveys.

A second concern of this chapter is to provide a comparison between the ethnic minority groups surveyed. Table 2.1, showing the age and gender structures of the different ethnic groups in the survey, illustrates the need for age and gender standardisation in order to make a comparison between ethnic minority groups and whites. The white sample has a greater proportion of women than African Asians, Pakistanis and Bangladeshis. It also has a three times greater proportion of respondents aged between 65 and 74 and a seven times greater proportion of respondents aged 75 or over compared with other ethnic groups. This is reflected in the mean age of the populations, which, when compared to others, is six years greater for white men and ten years greater for white women.

Table 2.1   Age and gender profiles

column percentages

	White	All ethnic minorities	Carib- bean	All South Asians	Indian	African Asian	Pakistani	Bangla- deshi	Chinese
Gender									
Male	45	49	45	51	47	55	51	55	47
Female	55	51	55	49	53	44	49	45	53
Age									
16 to 34	34	52	53	51	48	48	56	55	54
35 to 64	47	43	41	45	45	49	41	42	42
65 to 74	12	4	5	4	5	3	2	2	3
75 plus	7	1	1	1	2	1	1	1	1
Mean age in years (SD)									
Men	44 (18)	38 (16)	40 (17)	38 (15)	40 (16)	37 (14)	35 (15)	37 (16)	36 (13)
Women	46 (18)	36 (14)	37 (15)	36 (14)	37 (16)	36 (12)	34 (13)	33 (12)	35 (15)
Total	45 (18)	37 (15)	38 (16)	37 (15)	39 (16)	37 (13)	35 (14)	35 (15)	34 (14)
Weighted base	*2867*	*5196*	*1567*	*3238*	*1292*	*799*	*862*	*285*	*391*
Unweighted base	*2867*	*5196*	*1205*	*3777*	*1273*	*728*	*1185*	*591*	*214*

However, as explained in Chapter 3, this standardisation process requires some of the ethnic minority groups to be combined, a process which obscures differences across such groups. A closer look at Table 2.1 shows that the age profiles of the different ethnic minority groups are similar enough for differences between them to be commented on without standardisation – just as long as the reader remains aware of the differences that do exist. In this context two differences between these groups are worth highlighting. First, insofar as there are age differences, the Caribbean and the Indian populations have a slightly older age profile than the Pakistani, Bangladeshi and Chinese groups, with African Asians being somewhere in between. Second, for tables that do not include a gender dimension, it should be noted that the Caribbean, Indian and Chinese populations have a higher proportion of women than the others. In addition, in order to remind the reader that in the tables presented in this chapter the figures for whites should not be directly compared with those for ethnic minority groups, they are presented at the end of the table and separated from others by a dividing line.

SELF-ASSESSED GENERAL HEALTH

As described in Chapter 1, a number of questions were asked of respondents regarding their general health. Table 2.2 shows the responses to the question asking the respondent to assess his or her health in relation to other people of his or her age on a five point scale ranging from excellent to very poor.

Table 2.2   Report of health compared to others of same age

cell percentages

	All ethnic minorities	Carib-bean	All South Asians	Indian	African Asian	Pakistani	Bangla-deshi	Chinese	White
Men with fair/ poor health	29	33	29	26	26	34	35	20	26
Women with fair/ poor health	35	39	33	32	27	38	41	28	32
Total									
Excellent/good	68	64	69	71	74	64	62	76	71
Fair	20	24	19	17	18	22	21	16	19
Poor/very poor	12	12	12	12	8	14	17	9	10
Weighted base	*5180*	*1563*	*3226*	*1284*	*799*	*859*	*284*	*391*	*2863*
Unweighted base	*5182*	*1201*	*3767*	*1268*	*728*	*1181*	*590*	*214*	*2860*

It shows that overall a third of ethnic minority people described their health as fair or poor, and that the rate for this was highest for Caribbeans, Pakistanis and Bangladeshis. Chinese and African Asians reported the lowest rate, only a quarter of them said that their health was fair or poor, while Indians were somewhere between these groups. Focusing on just those who report their health as poor shows that over 10 per cent of people in ethnic minority groups described their health in this way, and that the figures were particularly high for Bangladeshis and Pakistanis – almost a fifth of Bangladeshis described their health as poor. Caribbeans and Indians have the next highest rate and African Asians and Chinese have the lowest rates. Interestingly, all of the ethnic minority groups showed the expected gender difference, women reported higher rates of fair or poor health than men. This is despite the slightly younger age profile of ethnic minority women (see Table 2.1). Of particular concern here is that two-fifths of Caribbean, Pakistani and Bangladeshi women described their health as less than good.

Table 2.3 shows responses to questions asking respondents whether they have a long-standing illness and, if so, whether it limits their ability to carry out paid work. It shows that a fifth of the people in ethnic minority groups reported that they had a long-standing illness, and over 10 per cent of them reported that they had a long-standing illness that effected their ability to work. There are some interesting variations between groups, with almost a third of Caribbeans having reported that they had a long-standing illness, while the African Asian and Chinese groups had half of the Caribbean rate. The other South Asian groups were somewhere in between these two extremes. There were also interesting gender variations, Caribbeans and African Asians had a similar pattern to whites – with women having slightly greater rates than men, while Indians and Pakistanis had no gender difference, and, surprisingly, Bangladeshi and Chinese men had higher rates than their female counterparts. This may be partly a reflection of variations in the interpretation of the question by different ethnic groups, as Pilgrim *et al.* (1993) and Rudat (1994) have suggested. This issue is explored further in Chapter 3.

Table 2.3   Rates of reported long-standing illness

cell percentages

	All ethnic minorities	Carib-bean	All South Asians	Indian	African Asian	Pakistani	Bangla-deshi	Chinese	White
Any long-standing illness									
Men	20	27	18	18	14	20	22	17	32
Women	21	30	18	18	16	20	15	13	34
Total	21	29	18	18	15	20	19	15	33
Long-standing illness that limits work									
Men	11	12	12	11	10	14	14	6	15
Women	12	16	11	12	9	10	9	6	16
Total	12	14	11	12	9	12	12	6	16
Weighted base	*5161*	*1556*	*3214*	*1283*	*797*	*850*	*284*	*391*	*2843*
Unweighted base	*5156*	*1194*	*3748*	*1267*	*725*	*1168*	*588*	*214*	*2839*

There was also a variable pattern of response by gender to the question asking about long-standing illness that limits work. This has implications for the interpretation of the overall differences between ethnic minority groups. While overall the pattern was similar to that for any long-standing illness – Caribbeans had the highest rate, African Asians and Chinese had the lowest rates, and the other ethnic minority groups were somewhere in between – this was, in fact, only approximately true for women and very misleading for men. Pakistani and Bangladeshi men had the highest rates of long-standing illness that limits work, almost one in six of them said that they had such an illness. Chinese men again had the lowest rate, with the other ethnic minority groups being between the Chinese and Pakistanis and Bangladeshis.

Table 2.4 allows for the possibility that respondents may have reported ill-health in response to one general question, but not another. It includes anyone who said they had fair or poor health, or a long-standing illness, or were registered disabled. (About 3 per cent of respondents reported themselves as registered disabled, with little variation across ethnic minority groups – the only notable ones being low rates for Bangladeshi, about 1 per cent, and Chinese, less than 1 per cent.)

The table shows that a third of all ethnic minority respondents reported that they had some form of ill-health. Comparing ethnic minority groups shows that the rates were highest for Caribbeans, Pakistanis and Bangladeshis, among whom almost two-fifths of respondents reported that they had ill-health. The Chinese had the lowest rates, only a quarter of them reported that they had ill-health. Looking at gender differences shows the expected result for all ethnic minority groups, women reported higher rates than men. It also shows that the low rate for Chinese people overall was a consequence of the very low rate among Chinese men, only one-fifth of them reported that they had ill-health. Chinese women had very similar rates to African Asian and Indian women.

Table 2.4   Rates of reported fair/poor health or long-standing illness or registered disability

cell percentages

	All ethnic minorities	Carib-bean	All South Asians	Indian	African Asian	Pakistani	Bangla-deshi	Chinese	White
Men	31	34	30	27	27	36	36	22	31
Women	36	41	34	32	29	39	42	30	36
Total	33	38	32	30	28	37	39	26	34
Weighted base	*5196*	*1567*	*3238*	*1292*	*799*	*862*	*285*	*391*	*2867*
Unweighted base	*5196*	*1205*	*3777*	*1273*	*728*	*1185*	*591*	*214*	*2867*

In order to get a more contextualised assessment of health, half of the respondents were asked if their abilities to perform a range of activities were limited by their health. Table 2.5 shows responses to these questions. Responses to the 'vigorous activities' question need to be interpreted with some caution as a large number of respondents reported that they would not ever do them – 13 per cent of all of the ethnic minority groups, and as many as 23 per cent of Bangladeshis and 22 per cent of whites said this. It is impossible to determine whether in some cases respondents had said that they would never perform vigorous activities because their ill-health meant they could not undertake them. This response was not used with any great frequency for any of the other categories. In order to provide an indication of moderately exerting activities limited by health, the final three rows of the table combine responses to four of the specific activities, namely: moderate activities; climbing one flight of stairs; walking half a mile or more; and carrying groceries.

The table shows that as many as one in five women and one in eight men in ethnic minority groups had their performance of moderately exerting activities limited by their health. The gender difference is consistent across ethnic minority groups except for the Bangladeshi group. Of the ethnic minority groups, Pakistanis and Bangladeshis had the highest rate, one in five of them reported that their health limited their performance of moderately exerting activities, compared to about one in six Caribbeans and Indians, one in eight African Asians and less than one in ten Chinese. Among the women, the highest rates were for Caribbeans, Pakistanis and Bangladeshis, with lower and similar rates for Indian, African Asian and Chinese women. The highest rates among the men were found for Bangladeshis, with particularly low rates among Chinese men (as seen in other tables presented so far) and, surprisingly given the pattern for other general health questions, Caribbean men.

Table 2.5   Activities limited by health

cell percentages

	All ethnic minorities	Carib-bean	All South Asians	Indian	African Asian	Pakistani	Bangla-deshi	Chinese	White
a. vigorous activities	18	17	18	17	14	23	19	19	22
b. moderate activities	9	8	10	9	7	13	18	6	10
c. several flights of stairs	14	15	16	15	11	20	19	5	17
d. one flight of stairs	7	6	7	6	4	11	11	1	7
e. walking >one mile	13	10	15	13	10	21	19	7	12
f. walking half a mile	8	6	10	8	6	15	12	6	7
g. walking 100 yards	4	3	5	5	2	7	6	1	4
h. carrying groceries	11	11	11	9	10	13	18	6	13
i. bending or kneeling	10	14	10	9	8	12	11	3	15
j. bathing or dressing	4	3	4	5	2	6	5	2	5
Any of b, d, f, h.									
Men	12	8	14	14	10	16	22	7	12
Women	19	22	18	15	15	24	21	12	22
Total	15	16	16	15	13	20	21	9	18
Weighted base	*2570*	*783*	*1592*	*645*	*390*	*420*	*138*	*195*	*2866*
Unweighted base	*2573*	*613*	*1856*	*637*	*348*	*582*	*289*	*104*	*2866*

Looking at responses to individual activities shows that Pakistanis and Bangladeshis were consistently more likely than other ethnic minority groups to report that their activities were limited by their health, followed by Caribbeans and Indians, then African Asians and finally Chinese, who consistently had the least limitation of all of the ethnic minority groups.

Summary

These results for a variety of indicators of general health illustrate the great burden of ill-health among Britain's ethnic minorities. As many as a third reported that they had fair or poor health, one-fifth that they had a long-standing illness and almost one in six that their performance of moderately exerting activities were limited by health. However, the pattern of responses was not uniform among the different ethnic minority groups. Caribbeans, Pakistanis and Bangladeshis reported the worst health across these three dimensions, while Indians and African Asians reported lower rates and Chinese had the lowest rates. Responses also varied across gender, women on the whole reported worse health than men for all of the ethnic minority groups. It is, at this stage, worth reconsidering the different gender and age profiles of the ethnic minority groups, shown in Table 2.1. Taking these into account suggests that Pakistanis and Bangladeshis had the worst health among the ethnic minority groups, followed by Caribbeans, then Indians and African Asians, and the Chinese group had the best health.

Psycho-social health

In addition to a detailed questioning on mental health, which is reported on elsewhere (Nazroo 1997), half of the ethnic minority and all of the white respondents were asked about tiredness and problems with sleep. This provides some indication of their overall sense of well-being. Table 2.6 shows responses to these questions and that a third of the ethnic minority respondents reported that they were tired or lacking in energy. In addition, a fifth reported that they had problems with sleep and two-fifths reported that they had either of these problems.

Table 2.6   Psycho-social health

cell percentages

	All ethnic minorities	Carib-bean	All South Asians	Indian	African Asian	Pakistani	Bangla-deshi	Chinese	White
Tired or lacking energy									
Men	28	30	26	26	25	30	23	35	37
Women	39	52	33	31	38	34	24	33	50
Total	34	42	30	29	31	32	23	34	44
Problems with sleep									
Men	18	19	16	15	17	14	16	29	28
Women	25	33	21	17	30	24	10	21	40
Total	21	26	19	16	24	19	13	25	35
Either of above									
Men	33	36	30	28	32	31	28	47	48
Women	45	60	38	35	44	41	25	40	62
Total	39	49	34	32	38	36	26	44	56
Weighted base	*2574*	*783*	*1595*	*646*	*392*	*420*	*138*	*195*	*2867*
Unweighted base	*2579*	*614*	*1861*	*638*	*350*	*584*	*289*	*104*	*2867*

However, Caribbeans were far more likely than other ethnic minority groups to have reported tiredness or that they were lacking in energy, and Bangladeshis were far less likely. The other groups had similar rates to each other. A similar pattern was found for sleep problems, although both the Chinese and African Asian groups had results that were similar to those for the Caribbean group. On the whole the results follow the gender pattern expected, women were more likely to report these symptoms than men. It is worth highlighting that over half of the Caribbean women reported that they suffered from tiredness or lack of energy, a third reported that they suffered from problems with sleep, and three out of five of them reported that they suffered with either of these. This almost entirely accounts for the higher rate among Caribbeans, differences between the men were not as great as those between the women. An unexpected exception to this gender pattern was present in the Bangladeshi and Chinese groups, for whom rates were highest among men. In fact, almost one in two Chinese men reported that they had tiredness, lacked energy or had problems with their sleep, making them the second highest group, after Caribbean women, with these problems. This is an interesting contrast to the results presented for general health indicators cited earlier, which suggested Chinese men were the healthiest of the groups studied here.

CARDIOVASCULAR DISEASE

Coronary heart disease

Respondents were asked several questions about coronary heart disease. Table 2.7 shows responses to the two questions that were asked of all respondents – whether they had ever had angina and whether they had ever had a heart attack 'including a heart murmur or a rapid heart'. The two questions overlap to some extent, someone with a heart attack may also have been diagnosed as having angina. Consequently, the final three rows of the table include respondents who said that they had had either of these.

Table 2.7   Prevalence of diagnosed heart disease

cell percentages

	All ethnic minorities	Carib-bean	All South Asians	Indian	African Asian	Pakistani	Bangla-deshi	Chinese	White
Angina	2.5	1.7	2.9	2.6	1.8	3.8	4.5	1.7	4.2
Heart attack	2.8	3.4	2.5	2.3	2.0	3.0	3.3	2.4	4.8
Either angina or heart attack									
Men	4.7	4.3	5.0	4.8	3.1	6.0	7.6	4.1	8.0
Women	3.3	4.3	2.9	2.7	2.2	3.8	3.7	1.7	6.2
Total	4.0	4.3	4.0	3.7	2.7	4.9	5.8	2.8	7.0
Weighted base	*5183*	*1563*	*3229*	*1287*	*799*	*860*	*283*	*391*	*2864*
Unweighted base	*5187*	*1202*	*3771*	*1270*	*728*	*1183*	*590*	*214*	*2864*

The table shows that as many as 4 per cent of ethnic minority people reported some form of heart disease. However, it also shows great variation between ethnic groups. First, the Chinese group had a low rate, under 3 per cent, followed by the combined South Asian groups, with the Caribbeans having the highest rate of these three groups. This is somewhat in contradiction to immigrant mortality data, which suggest that South Asians have higher rates than Caribbeans (Marmot *et al.* 1984, Balarajan 1991 and 1996). Second, within the South Asian group there was also considerable variation, African Asians reported low rates (again under 3 per cent) and Pakistanis and Bangladeshis reported high rates. In fact, Bangladeshis had the highest rate, almost 6 per cent reported that they had heart disease. Balarajan (1996) showed similar variations across the South Asian groups were present in the most recent immigrant mortality data. Third, women overall reported lower rates of heart disease than men, although this was not the case for Caribbeans. The pattern across ethnic groups within gender groups followed that just described, except that South Asian men reported slightly higher rates than Caribbean men. Of all of the groups, Pakistani and Bangladeshi men reported particularly high rates of heart disease – as many as one in 13 Bangladeshi men reported that they had diagnosed heart disease. Given the age profiles of the Pakistani and Bangladeshi populations, this is not only a current serious health problem, but, as this population gets older, one that is likely to have very important consequences for these communities and health care provision.

The questions on diagnosis may have under-counted prevalence, because they depend on respondents having consulted a doctor about cardiac symptoms and being aware of, understanding and remembering the diagnosis given. All of these factors could be related to ethnicity. In order to address this, those who had not reported heart disease and who were aged 40 or over were asked additional questions on the experience of chest pain. An introductory question simply asked whether the respondent had experienced any chest pain. This was followed by a question that asked about 'severe chest pain lasting more than half an hour', which is likely to be more useful in terms of reflecting actual coronary heart disease. Responses to these questions are shown in the first two rows of Table 2.8. They follow a similar pattern to those for the diagnosed heart disease questions, which are shown for those aged 40 or older in the third row of the table, and for all respondents in the previous table.

Table 2.8   Prevalence of chest pain and diagnosed heart disease for respondents aged 40 or older

cell percentages

	All ethnic minorities	Carib-bean	All South Asians	Indian	African Asian	Pakistani	Bangla-deshi	Chinese	White
Any chest pain	18	24	16	13	14	21	25	6	19
Severe chest pain	5	6	6	4	4	10	9	1	5
Diagnosed heart disease	10	9	10	8	7	14	14	7	12
Severe chest pain or diagnosed heart disease									
Men	16	16	16	13	12	23	28	12	19
Women	14	14	15	12	11	25	17	5	14
Total	15	15	16	13	12	24	24	8	16
Weighted base	*1525*	*586*	*1175*	*531*	*282*	*260*	*102*	*126*	*1525*
Unweighted base	*1592*	*494*	*1412*	*543*	*279*	*392*	*198*	*83*	*1592*

The final three rows of the table combine the question asking about severe chest pain with those asking about diagnosed heart disease. They again follow a similar pattern to the results shown in Table 2.7, Pakistanis and Bangladeshis reported the highest rates among the ethnic minority groups, followed by Caribbeans, then Indians and African Asians – both with half the Pakistani and Bangladeshi rates – and Chinese with the lowest rate – a third of the Pakistani and Bangladeshi rates. The result remains the same within gender groups, men on the whole had slightly higher rates than women, although they were much higher for Chinese and Bangladeshi men.

In terms of the prevalence of possible coronary heart disease among ethnic minority groups, the results are a cause of great concern. Among those aged 40 or over almost one in six people in ethnic minority groups reported heart disease or severe chest pain, while among the Pakistani and Bangladeshi groups this figure was one in four. Even if we ignore the reports of severe chest pain, one in ten people in ethnic minority groups aged 40 or over reported that they had heart disease, and this rose to one in seven among Pakistanis and Bangladeshis. This clearly has very serious implications for both the ethnic minority communities concerned and the health service. Again it is worth pointing out that even though this is a group aged 40 or more, it still has a relatively young age profile. For example, the median age for Pakistanis and Bangladeshis in the 40 or older age group is 50, while that for whites is 57.

Hypertension

Respondents were asked if they had ever suffered from hypertension. Table 2.9 shows that this is a common problem for people in ethnic minority groups, about one in ten reported they had hypertension. The figures show the variation across ethnic minority groups that would be expected from immigrant mortality data (Marmot *et al.* 1984, Balarajan 1991), Caribbeans reported the highest rates, followed by the South Asian groups – who had little variation between them – and the Chinese group with a low rate. The Caribbean rate is very high, one in five reported that they had hypertension. However, there is an important gender difference in the Caribbean group, one in four women reported hypertension compared to just under one in six men. This gender difference may be a consequence of the greater opportunities for women to be diagnosed as having hypertension, as this is a routine check prior to the prescription of oral contraception and is part of antenatal care, but it is not repeated consistently across other ethnic minority groups.

A question was also asked about strokes, but, not surprisingly, very few people reported such an event and rates were similar across the ethnic minority groups.

Table 2.9   Prevalence of hypertension

cell percentages

	All ethnic minorities	Carib-bean	All South Asians	Indian	African Asian	Pakistani	Bangla-deshi	Chinese	White
Men	10	15	9	10	11	6	10	4	15
Women	12	23	8	6	5	12	11	5	17
Total	11	19	8	8	8	9	11	4	16
Weighted base	*5171*	*1555*	*3225*	*1283*	*798*	*859*	*284*	*391*	*2862*
Unweighted base	*5173*	*1195*	*3764*	*1267*	*727*	*1181*	*589*	*214*	*2862*

OBESITY

Weight was not actually assessed in the interview. Instead half of the ethnic minority and all of the white respondents were asked if they considered themselves to be overweight and whether they had ever tried to lose weight. The highly subjective nature of these questions suggests that responses to them need to be interpreted with caution. However, as Table 2.10 shows, both questions gave a similar pattern of responses across ethnic minority groups. Caribbeans were far more likely to have said yes to either of the questions, followed by Indians, African Asians and Pakistanis, who all had similar rates, while the Bangladeshi and Chinese groups both had the lowest rates.

Table 2.10   Perceived obesity

cell percentages

	All ethnic minorities	Carib-bean	All South Asians	Indian	African Asian	Pakistani	Bangla-deshi	Chinese	White
Too heavy for height									
Men	18	19	19	21	21	18	7	11	40
Women	32	50	25	23	26	33	14	12	47
Total	25	36	22	22	23	25	10	12	43
Ever seriously tried to lose weight									
Men	4	15	14	15	14	16	10	5	24
Women	29	46	23	22	27	24	11	11	44
Total	22	32	19	19	20	20	11	8	35
Weighted base	*2524*	*774*	*1555*	*633*	*386*	*402*	*134*	*195*	*2845*
Unweighted base	*2524*	*608*	*1812*	*624*	*344*	*564*	*280*	*104*	*2846*

For all of the ethnic minority groups, women were more likely to have said that they considered themselves overweight and to have tried to lose weight. Interestingly, the ethnic variations just outlined were largely due to variations within the female group. Among the men there was much less variation, the only notable one being the relatively few positive responses to these questions among Bangladeshi and Chinese men.

DIABETES

Table 2.11 shows the number of people who reported that they had diabetes. The high rates for ethnic minority groups as a whole were the result of high rates among Caribbeans and South Asians, the Chinese group had a low rate compared to the others. Within the South Asian group there was an interesting variation, Pakistanis and Bangladeshis reported higher rates of diabetes than Indians and African Asians.

Table 2.11   Prevalence of diabetes

cell percentages

	All ethnic minorities	Carib-bean	All South Asians	Indian	African Asian	Pakistani	Bangla-deshi	Chinese	White
All respondents	5.6	5.9	5.9	5.5	4.0	7.6	7.4	2.2	2.2
Weighted base	*5196*	*1567*	*3238*	*1292*	*799*	*862*	*285*	*391*	*2867*
Unweighted base	*5196*	*1205*	*3777*	*1273*	*728*	*1185*	*591*	*214*	*2867*

Additional questions on type of diabetes were not asked, so it was not possible to distinguish between insulin dependent and non-insulin dependent diabetes (although the former is relatively rare), nor was it possible to identify those respondents who only had diabetes during pregnancy. In terms of the hypothesis relating insulin resistance to coronary heart disease (McKeigue *et al.* 1989), it is, of course, impossible to identify whether reported diabetes is a result of insulin resistance or not with survey research of this kind. Again, it is also worth pointing out that responses to the diabetes question were dependant on the respondent having consulted a doctor about possible symptoms and being aware of the diagnosis made.

RESPIRATORY DISEASE

Half of the ethnic minority and all of the white respondents were asked several questions in an attempt to identify possible respiratory illness. However, all of this questioning was around symptoms rather than diagnosis (which would have been very difficult to collect given both the number of sub-categories of diagnosis that could be given and the complexity of accurate diagnostic procedures). This means that the relationship between the data shown in Table 2.12 and actual respiratory disease should be treated with even more caution than in other cases. In fact, many of the questions used could have been answered positively by those with breathlessness as a result of heart failure. This is particularly the case for the first row of the table, which shows respondents who had been woken by shortness of breath. The small variations in response to this question suggested that this was a more common problem for Caribbeans, Pakistanis and Bangladeshis.

Table 2.12   Prevalence of respiratory symptoms

cell percentages

	All ethnic minorities	Carib-bean	All South Asians	Indian	African Asian	Pakistani	Bangla-deshi	Chinese	White
Woken by shortness of breath	4	5	4	3	2	5	6	3	6
Wheezing	14	21	11	11	9	12	12	10	26
Coughing up phlegm most days for three or more months a year	7	7	7	7	7	9	7	7	8
Wheezing or coughing up phlegm									
Men	18	21	16	14	15	19	17	18	27
Women	18	26	14	15	14	15	12	7	29
Total	18	24	15	15	14	17	15	13	28
Weighted base	2574	783	1595	646	392	420	138	195	2867
Unweighted base	2579	614	1861	638	350	584	289	104	2867

Responses to the wheezing question showed that this was a fairly common problem, about one in ten of the South Asian and Chinese groups and as many as one in five Caribbeans reported that they had this. Responses to the coughing up phlegm question showed little variation between ethnic groups.

The final three rows of Table 2.12 use an index of positive responses to the questions about symptoms that are most likely to be related to respiratory disease (wheezing or coughing up phlegm on most days for at least three months a year). They show that almost one in five people in ethnic minority groups reported such symptoms, and that this rose to one in four among the Caribbean group. The other ethnic minority groups reported similar rates. For most of the ethnic minority groups men had higher rates then women. Chinese women had rates that were clearly lower than other groups. However Caribbean women had higher rates than Caribbean men, and Indian and African Asian men and women had similar rates.

SMOKING, DRINKING ALCOHOL AND USE OF PAAN

Half of the ethnic minority and all of the white respondents were asked questions on these behaviours.

Smoking

Respondents were asked about their past and current smoking habits. Table 2.13 includes any past or current smoker, no matter how little they actually smoked. The patterns for ever and current smoking were very similar, Caribbeans had the highest rates, followed by Bangladeshis, then Chinese and Pakistanis, while Indians and African Asians reported the lowest rates. Although men were more likely than women to have reported smoking for all of the ethnic minority groups, this was particularly marked for the Asian groups among whom very few women reported that they smoked. Although one in three Caribbean women currently smoked, only very few women in the other ethnic minority groups smoked. In contrast, the rates of current smoking were one in two for Bangladeshi men, four out of ten for Caribbean men, one in three for Pakistani and Chinese men, and one in five for Indian and African Asian men. These rates are similar to, although slightly higher than, the findings reported by Rudat (1994).

Table 2.13   Smoking

cell percentages

	All ethnic minorities	Carib-bean	All South Asians	Indian	African Asian	Pakistani	Bangla-deshi	Chinese	White
Ever smoked									
Men	37	51	31	22	29	39	53	39	67
Women	15	36	4	5	4	4	< 1	6	56
Total	26	42	17	13	16	22	26	24	61
Current smoker									
Men	31	42	26	19	22	33	49	31	34
Women	12	31	4	5	3	4	< 1	3	37
Total	21	36	15	11	12	19	24	18	36
Smokers who have given up	16	16	15	13	24	13	8	24	42
Weighted base	*2574*	*783*	*1595*	*646*	*392*	*420*	*138*	*195*	*2867*
Unweighted base	*2579*	*614*	*1861*	*638*	*350*	*584*	*289*	*104*	*2867*

Also of concern is the small number of ever smokers who had successfully given up. While one in four African Asian and Chinese smokers had given up, only about one in seven Caribbean, Indian and Pakistani smokers, and only one in twelve Bangladeshi smokers had given up. Although these figures are not age and sex standardised, the rate of almost one in two white smokers successfully giving up is a stark contrast, which clearly has important implications for health promotion.

Table 2.14 shows the average number of cigarettes smoked per day by current smokers. Caribbeans, Indians, African Asians and Chinese reported relatively light smoking, 50 per cent of them said that they smoked ten or less cigarettes a day. In contrast, Pakistani and particularly Bangladeshi smokers were relatively heavy smokers, as many as one in three Bangladeshi smokers reporting that they smoked over 20 cigarettes a day.

Table 2.14   Average number of cigarettes smoked per day by current smokers

column percentages

	All ethnic minorities	Carib-bean	All South Asians	Indian	African Asian	Pakistani	Bangla-deshi	Chinese	White
1 to 5	22	25	18	19	22	13	21	21	17
6 to 10	32	33	30	35	29	31	18	34	19
11 to 20	27	27	24	14	23	32	27	39	47
Over 20	10	7	15	9	17	10	32	2	14
Not answered	10	7	14	23	9	13	2	4	4
Weighted base	*454*	*231*	*193*	*60*	*39*	*64*	*29*	*29*	*769*
Unweighted base	*456*	*182*	*255*	*56*	*40*	*95*	*64*	*19*	*786*

Alcohol use

Table 2.15 shows frequency of drinking alcohol. Very few of the almost entirely Muslim Pakistani and Bangladeshi respondents reported that they ever drank alcohol. Those among them who were most likely to drink alcohol were Pakistani men, of whom only 8 per cent ever drank and only 4 per cent drank regularly.

Of the other ethnic minority groups, one in three Caribbeans and about one in five Indians, African Asians and Chinese reported regularly drinking alcohol. If any alcohol drinking is considered, four out of five Caribbeans, three out of five Chinese and two out of five Indians and African Asians reported drinking. Of course a significant proportion of the Indian and African Asian groups were Muslim. Variations in alcohol use among these groups by religion are explored in Chapter 4, which confirms that few Muslims drank alcohol. For the Indian and African Asian groups, men were far more likely than women to report drinking alcohol. In contrast, this was only the case for regular drinking for Caribbean and Chinese respondents.

Table 2.15   Frequency of alcohol use

column percentages

	All ethnic minorities	Carib-bean	All South Asians	Indian	African Asian	Pakistani	Bangla-deshi	Chinese	White
Once a week or more									
Men	32	50	25	40	32	4	2	32	69
Women	11	23	4	6	8	0	0	11	46
Total	21	35	14	22	20	2	1	22	56
Less than once a week									
Men	25	37	17	26	24	4	1	37	23
Women	25	51	10	12	19	< 1	2	40	37
Total	25	45	13	19	21	2	2	38	31
Never									
Men	43	13	58	34	45	92	96	32	8
Women	64	26	86	82	74	100	98	49	17
Total	54	20	72	60	59	95	97	40	13
Weighted base	*2567*	*782*	*1591*	*643*	*391*	*419*	*138*	*195*	*2866*
Unweighted base	*2574*	*613*	*1857*	*637*	*349*	*582*	*289*	*104*	*2866*

Use of paan

Respondents were asked if they had 'ever had paan (betel)' and if so how frequently they currently used it. Table 2.16 shows surprising responses for the South Asian groups. While one in two of the African Asians and Bangladeshi respondents reported that they had used paan, this was only the case for one in five Indians and just over one in ten Pakistanis. Not shown in the table is that there were also differences between the Bangladeshi and African Asian use of paan. Almost half of the Bangladeshi users reported that they used paan regularly, while almost all of the African Asian users said that they only used paan occasionally.

Table 2.16   Use of paan by South Asian groups

cell percentages

	All South Asians	Indian	African Asian	Pakistani	Bangladeshi
Ever used paan					
Men	33	24	61	15	51
Women	27	22	42	10	55
Total	30	23	52	13	53
Currently use paan					
Men	22	14	43	7	45
Women	20	14	32	6	54
Total	21	14	38	7	50
Weighted base	*1588*	*641*	*391*	*419*	*138*
Unweighted base	*1856*	*636*	*349*	*582*	*289*

The contradiction between the African Asian and Indian result is at first sight hard to reconcile, as the former group largely have their roots in India. It may be possible that this is a result of regional influences within India. Very few African Asians had family origins in the Punjab, while over half the Indians did. Pakistanis, of course, were also originally from the Punjab. It may well be that the relatively low rate of paan use among Indians and Pakistanis is because its use in the Punjab is not as popular as in other parts of South Asia. This is explored in more detail in Chapter 4. There were few gender differences in the reported use of paan, apart from the lower rate for women among African Asians.

ACCIDENTS

Table 2.17 shows reports of accidents occurring in the previous 12 months that required some form of medical attention. These questions were only asked of half of the ethnic minority respondents so, because among the 104 Chinese respondents who were asked this question only eight such accidents were reported – too few for meaningful conclusions to be drawn – there is no separate column for the Chinese in this table. However, they are included in the 'all ethnic minorities' column. A similar argument holds for the African Asian and Bangladeshi samples. In order to keep them in the table, these groups have been combined with the Indian and Pakistani samples respectively.

Table 2.17   Accidents resulting in hospital treatment over the past 12 months

rate per 1000 people

	All ethnic minorities	Caribbeans	All South Asians	Indians and African Asians	Pakistanis and Bangladeshis	White
Sports accidents	15	19	9	10	9	22
Work/school/ college accidents	9	11	8	10	3	28
Home accidents	19	38	12	8	19	43
Road/pavement/ car accidents	14	20	12	10	18	25
All accidents						
Men	85	116	63	51	82	152
Women	33	63	21	26	11	90
Total	58	87	41	38	48	117
Weighted base	*2574*	*783*	*1595*	*1037*	*558*	*2867*
Unweighted base	*2579*	*614*	*1861*	*988*	*873*	*2967*

The final row of the table shows that Caribbeans were the most likely to have experienced such an accident, with a rate of almost one accident per ten people per year. The South Asian groups had about half that rate, with no great variation between them. Looking at the rows showing the locations of reported accidents, it can be seen that accidents occurring in the home were most frequent when ethnic minority groups are considered together, followed by accidents on the road and accidents related to sports activities. Work or study related accidents were the least frequent. However, this pattern did not hold for Indians and African Asians who reported a even spread of accidents over the various locations. For all groups women were considerably less likely than men to be at risk of such an accident.

CONCLUSION

The *Fourth National Survey* is the first fully representative assessment of the health of ethnic minority groups in England and Wales. Consequently, the data presented in this chapter provide a benchmark against which health needs can be assessed, changes determined, and comparisons with other groups made.

Given the relatively young age profile of ethnic minority groups in Britain, the figures do suggest a large burden of ill-health:

- One in three reported less than good health, or a long-standing illness or that they were registered disabled.
- Almost one in six reported that their health limited their performance of moderate activities, or climbing one flight of stairs, or walking half a mile, or carrying groceries.
- One in 25 reported a diagnosis of heart disease. While, among those aged 40 or older, one in ten reported a diagnosis of heart disease and almost one in six reported a diagnosis or symptoms suggestive of heart disease.
- One in ten reported a diagnosis of hypertension.
- One in 20 reported a diagnosis of diabetes.
- Almost one in five reported symptoms suggestive of respiratory disease.

There were also variations in the level of ill-health between the different ethnic minority groups. On the whole Pakistanis and Bangladeshis reported the poorest health. Almost two in five reported less than good health, or a long-standing illness or that they were disabled; one in five reported that their performance of moderately exerting activities was limited by their health; one in 20 reported a diagnosis of heart disease; while for those aged 40 or over as many as one in four reported a diagnosis of or symptoms suggestive of heart disease; finally, about one in 13 reported a diagnosis of diabetes. For all of these measures of health, the rates were lower for all of the other ethnic minority groups except Caribbeans, who had a similar rate of having any of: less than good health, or a long-standing illness, or registered disability.

Caribbeans were the group who reported the next worst health, almost one in five Caribbeans reported hypertension and about one in four Caribbeans reported symptoms of respiratory disease. There were also important gender differences within the Caribbean group, with the relative rates of hypertension and symptoms of respiratory disease being higher for Caribbean women than Caribbean men when compared to women and men in other ethnic minority groups.

Indians and African Asians had better health than Caribbeans, with African Asians being slightly better than Indians. Of all of the ethnic minority groups, the Chinese, and particularly Chinese men, reported the best health.

Many of these results are consistent with findings from immigrant mortality data (Marmot *et al.* 1984, Balarajan and Bulusu 1990, Balarajan 1996). The most important difference between the findings reported here and those published elsewhere, is that they suggest important differences between the South Asian groups. There are some suggestions of these differences in the most recent immigrant mortality data (Balarajan 1996).

CHAPTER THREE

Comparing the Health of Ethnic Minority Groups with Whites

INTRODUCTION

The previous chapter documented the levels of ill-health across a variety of dimensions for the main ethnic groups that make up the British population. It illustrated the variations in health that exist among ethnic minority groups, with Pakistanis and Bangladeshis reporting the worst health across a variety of dimensions, followed by Caribbeans, then Indians and African Asians, and Chinese having the best health. However, the differences in the age structure of the ethnic minority compared to the white population meant that a comparison between them could not be made there. Such a comparison is the concern of this chapter, which will focus on those issues identified by previous reports as having important differences between one or more of the ethnic minority groups and whites. These issues will now be introduced.

General health

Preliminary analysis of the 1991 Census data, which for the first time included a question asking about long-standing illness which limits activities, suggests that the rate of such illness (once the different age profiles of different ethnic groups is considered) is greater among all of the ethnic minority groups compared to whites, apart from the Chinese (Dunnell 1993). Figure 3.1 presents an analysis of the Census question for the age group (16 and older) and areas (England and Wales) used to sample for the *Fourth National Survey*. The age-standardised relative risks with 95 per cent confidence limits (see the next section of this chapter for a discussion of this statistic) by ethnic group confirm that Dunnell's conclusions apply to the population from which the Fourth National Survey sample was drawn. Limiting long-standing illness was almost 50 per cent greater among Pakistani/Bangladeshis compared to whites, about a quarter greater for Caribbeans and Indian/African Asians, and almost a quarter lower for Chinese respondents.

Analysis of the *Health and Lifestyles* national survey also suggested that ethnic minority groups report poorer health than whites, with non-whites being almost 25 per cent more likely than whites to have said that their health was fair or poor, although ethnicity for this survey was only assessed through interviewers

Figure 3.1 Relative risk of having a limiting long-standing illness at the Census compared with whites: England and Wales and aged 16 plus

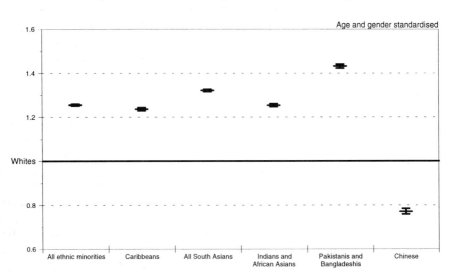

observations (Benzeval *et al.* 1992). Regional studies in Bristol and Glasgow confirm the reports of poorer health among ethnic minority groups (Pilgrim *et al.* 1993, Williams *et al.* 1993). For example, the Bristol study reported that 50 per cent of its respondents described their health as fair or poor, compared to a general population figure that ranged from 16 to 37 per cent, depending on household income (Pilgrim *et al.* 1993).

Cardiovascular disease

Cardiovascular disease is the area that has received the most attention from those interested in ethnic variations in health. It is also a major cause of ill-health, with around 40 per cent of deaths occurring in Britain being attributed to it. Both Marmot *et al.* (1984) and Balarajan (1991), using immigrant mortality data from 1970–1978 and 1979–1983 respectively, demonstrated ethnic variations in deaths attributed to cardiovascular disease. For example, Balarajan showed that both men and women born in South Asia had higher mortality rates from coronary heart disease than the national average (36 per cent and 46 per cent higher respectively). He was also able to demonstrate that this excess mortality was particularly significant for younger age groups, with those aged between 20 and 40 having more than twice the national average mortality rate. In addition, the comparison with Marmot *et al.*'s (1984) data that he presented suggested that this ethnic variation in coronary heart disease had not narrowed over time. This evidence is supported both by worldwide reports of higher rates of coronary heart disease among South Asians (McKeigue *et al.* 1989), and by the greater prevalence of indicators of coronary heart disease morbidity (rather than mortality) among South Asians in Britain. For example, McKeigue

(1993) demonstrated higher rates of abnormal Electro-cardiogram changes in South Asian men, and hospital admissions for coronary heart disease also appear to be higher for South Asians (Cruickshank *et al.* 1980, Fox and Shapiro 1988). In contrast to this, the data presented by Balarajan (1991) suggests that those born in the Caribbean had lower rates of mortality from coronary heart disease than the general population, with Caribbean men having less than half the national average rate and Caribbean women having three-quarters of the national average rate.

Balarajan (1991) also demonstrated that men and women born in the Caribbean were at much greater risk than others of dying from a stroke (76 per cent and 110 per cent higher respectively than that for those born in Britain), and the rates of mortality from stroke were also higher for those born in South Asia compared with those born in Britain (53 per cent higher for men and 25 per cent higher for women). One of the key risk factors for strokes is hypertension, and it also appears that those born in the Caribbean have much higher rates of hypertension than the general population. The rates of mortality from hypertensive disease are four times greater for men born in the Caribbean and seven times greater for women born in the Caribbean according to the data presented by Balarajan and Bulusu (1990), and Marmot *et al.* (1984) showed similarly high rates. Those born in South Asia also appear to have higher rates of hypertension than the general population, though relative mortality rates from hypertensive disease are not as great as they are for those born in the Caribbean (Cruickshank *et al.* 1980, Marmot *et al.* 1984, Balarajan and Bulusu 1990).

Non-insulin dependent diabetes

Non-insulin dependent diabetes is an important cause of both morbidity and mortality in its own right. In addition, it is also considered a risk factor for a variety of other diseases, such as cardiovascular disease and renal failure. In fact, it has been suggested that insulin resistance, a syndrome leading to non-insulin dependent diabetes, may be responsible for the higher reported rates of coronary heart disease among those born in South Asia (McKeigue *et al.* 1989). The prevalence of *diagnosed* non-insulin dependent diabetes among South Asians is reported to be over four times greater than that among the white population (Mather and Keen 1985, Mather *et al.* 1987, Simmons *et al.* 1989, McKeigue *et al.* 1991). If undiagnosed diabetes is also considered, this may well be an underestimation of the true differences in prevalence (Simmons *et al.* 1989). Also, mortality directly associated with diabetes among those born in South Asia is two to three times that in the general population (Marmot *et al.* 1984, Balarajan and Bulusu 1990). Those born in the Caribbean have a similar excess of mortality associated with diabetes (Marmot *et al.* 1984, Balarajan and Bulusu 1990) and the prevalence of diagnosed diabetes among Caribbeans is thought to be twice the rate in the general population (Odugbesan *et al.* 1989, McKeigue *et al.* 1991). However, the relatively high rate of non-insulin dependent diabetes among Caribbeans has not been linked to increased risk of coronary heart disease.

Respiratory disease

All ethnic minority groups appear to have lower rates of mortality from respiratory diseases (bronchitis, emphysema, asthma and pneumonias), apart from tuberculosis, than the general population (Marmot *et al.* 1984, Balarajan and Bulusu 1990). This appears to be particularly the case for chronic obstructive airways disease (bronchitis and emphysema). It has been suggested that this is a result of lower rates of smoking among the various ethnic minority groups (Marmot *et al.* 1984). However, mortality data are only available for South Asians as a combined group, and it has now been shown that some of the South Asian groups, particularly Bangladeshis, have high rates of smoking (Rudat 1994). This is confirmed by the data presented in Chapter 2, which showed that Bangladeshi men had particularly high rates of smoking, while Caribbean and Pakistani men and Caribbean women also had high rates (Table 2.13). However, rates among women for all of the South Asian groups were very low. Whether the high prevalence of smoking among particular South Asian groups translates into high rates of chronic obstructive airways disease for them is not known, although Table 2.12 does demonstrate higher rates of respiratory symptoms for Pakistani and Bangladeshi men compared to their Indian and African Asian counter-parts.

Accidents

One of the priority objectives of the Health of the Nation White Paper (1992) is a reduction of morbidity and mortality from accidents. However, very little is known about the rate of accidents among Britain's ethnic minority groups, nor where and how the accidents occurring to them happen, although immigrant mortality data suggest that they are at lower risk of motor vehicle accidents and at greater risk of fire-related accidents (Balarajan and Bulusu 1990).

AGE AND GENDER STANDARDISATION AND RELATIVE RISK

Given the large differences in the age profiles of ethnic minority compared to white groups (see Table 2.1), the data used for the figures and tables in this chapter have been age and gender standardised. This will allow a straightforward comparison to be made between the health of the white group and the various ethnic minority groups. The standardisation process involved using a weighting procedure to give each ethnic group the same age and gender structure. However, this procedure is dependent on having relatively large numbers in each age and gender group used for calculating the weights, to prevent any amplification of a chance response, and some ethnic groups had too small a sample size to be handled in this way. Consequently, Indians and African Asians have been combined, and Pakistanis and Bangladeshis have been combined. The small differences between the groups that have been combined can be seen by looking back to the relevant tables in Chapter 2. Even though the number of Chinese respondents was small and the standardisation procedure consequently more unreliable for them than any other group, given their very different health profile from all of the other ethnic minority groups (see Chapter

2) it was impossible to combine them with any another group. They have been included in figures and tables where possible in this chapter, however, results for them should be treated with caution. Finally, because of the small number of elderly people in the minority groups, the standardisation process was done to the age structure of the total ethnic minority population. This means that only relatively small weighting factors were applied to the few elderly ethnic minority respondents, reducing the chances of the weighting procedure biasing any result. Although standardisation means that this chapter can, on the whole, concentrate purely on ethnic variations without having to consider them separately for men and women or different age groups, in some cases there are important differences between gender and age groups and where this is the case the different groups are considered separately.[1]

Comparisons between ethnic minority groups and whites in this chapter were done using relative risk, with lower and upper 95 per cent confidence intervals calculated. Relative risk is simply the chance of a member of one group being in a particular illness category compared to a member of the other group, while the lower and upper limits give a range within which there is a 95 per cent probability that the true difference between the two populations compared lies. These comparisons are represented graphically in this chapter, and the tables that the figures are based on are presented in Appendix B. All comparisons in the following figures were made to the white group, who, consequently, are represented by a solid line at the value of '1'. The relative risk for each ethnic minority group compared to whites is represented as a range, with the top and bottom points of the 95 per cent probability range and the mid point indicated. Differences are only considered statistically significant if the full range of values does not cross the line indicating the white value.[2]

SELF-ASSESSED GENERAL HEALTH

Several questions about general health were asked of all respondents. The first question considered here asked the respondent to rate his or her health on a five point scale in relation to others of the same age. Most reports dichotomise responses to this question between those who report 'excellent' or 'good' health and those who report 'fair', 'poor' or 'very poor' health. Figure 3.2 is also based on this dichotomy, and shows that compared to whites Pakistani/Bangladeshis were 50 per cent more likely to have described their health as fair or poor and that Caribbeans were also more likely to have reported fair or poor health. In contrast, Indian/African

---

1 Gender and age differences in the reported ethnic variations in health were looked for routinely. This means that a large number of potential interactions between gender and ethnicity, and age and ethnicity were explored, which, of course, raises the possibility that some of those reported were present in these data purely by chance.

2 The graphical presentation of these data should, strictly speaking, be done using a logarithm scale rather than a linear scale. This was not done here because of the small relative risks reported. Logarithm scales would make a significant visual difference only if relative risks were below 0.5 or above 5, which occurs only in a few cases.

Figure 3.2   Relative risk of reporting fair or poor health compared with whites

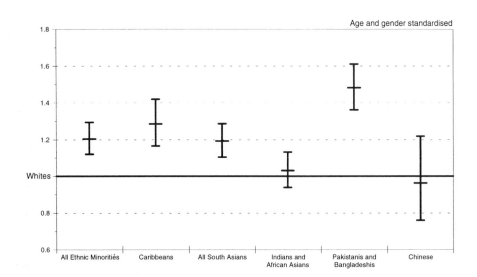

Asians and Chinese were very similar to whites. The difference between the overall South Asian grouping and whites was significant, but entirely due to the high rates among Pakistani/Bangladeshis.

This result was not confirmed by the second general health question asked of all respondents, which was whether they had a long-standing illness. This is similar to questions used in the General Household Survey and the 1991 Census, although it does not include the 'limiting' element of the equivalent Census question. The responses to this are shown in Figure 3.3, which demonstrates that members of all of the South Asian and the Chinese groups were less likely than whites to have reported such an illness. However, Caribbeans had the same rate as whites.

The two indicators of general health shown in Figures 3.2 and 3.3 lead to opposite conclusions on ethnic health variations. However, there has been a suggestion that ethnic minority groups interpret the long-standing illness question more restrictively than whites. A survey of ethnic minorities in Bristol (Pilgrim *et al.* 1993) reported that its ethnic minority sample was less likely than the pre-dominantly white sample in the *Health and Lifestyles* Survey (which it used for comparative purposes) to report a long-standing illness, a similar result to that shown in Figure 3.3. However, many of the Bristol respondents who *did not* report a long-standing illness *did* report having one of a fairly exhaustive list of specific illnesses used in that study. This implies that the long-standing illness question was not an accurate reflection of existing illness, at least as far as ethnic minority respondents were concerned. The authors suggested that ethnic minority groups may be less likely than whites to report an illness as long-standing because they have a more restrictive notion of what is serious enough to be included, saying:

Figure 3.3   Relative risk of long-standing illness compared with whites

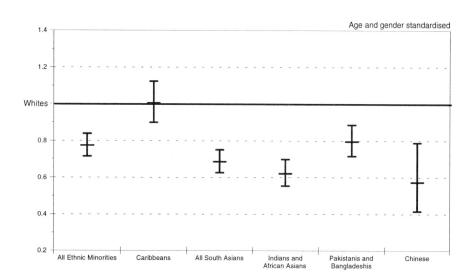

It is possible that, in the case of Black and minority ethnic group respondents, the difference in response to a check list and to a general question is greater than for others... It appears that people from Black and minority groups have a narrower interpretation of 'long-standing illness'. One explanation might be that 'long-standing illness' is interpreted as a condition which substantially and obviously affects daily living. Thus conditions such as asthma and diabetes are excluded. (Pilgrim *et al.* 1993:36)

This possibility is strengthened by Howlett *et al.*'s (1992) finding that Caribbean and white respondents to the Health and Lifestyles survey favoured describing their health in terms of strength and fitness, while Asians were more likely to favour describing their health in terms of being able to perform everyday activities. Interestingly, Rudat (1994) also reported difficulties with this question, and altered the wording in an attempt to overcome them.

In the *Fourth National Survey* it was not possible to make a direct comparison between a comprehensive list of illnesses and reports of long-standing illness, because no such list was used independently of the long-standing illness question. We did ask directly about diabetes, hypertension, cardiac disease and symptoms, and respiratory symptoms. For all of these except diabetes, ethnic minority respondents were no more likely than white respondents to say that they had the condition or symptoms while not reporting a long-standing illness. However, all of the South Asian groups were more likely than whites to say that they had diabetes while not reporting a long-standing illness. Of those South Asians reporting diabetes 26 per cent did not report that they had a long-standing illness compared to just 12 per cent for whites and 10 per cent for Caribbeans.

Figure 3.4   Relative risk of a long-standing illness that limits work compared with whites

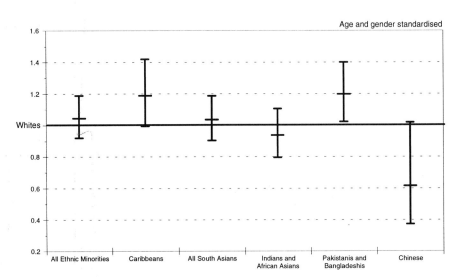

The *Fourth National Survey* did include a follow up question asking the respondent if a reported long-standing illness limited his or her ability to work. Figure 3.4 shows the relative risk compared to whites of having a long-standing illness that limited work.

This shows a pattern quite contradictory to the less restrictive notion of a 'long-standing illness', with Pakistani/Bangladeshis being statistically significantly more likely that whites to have a long-standing illness that limits the ability to work and the difference between Caribbeans and whites being close to statistical significance. Indian/African Asians had the same rate as whites and Chinese had lower rates, but not significantly so. This, in fact, is similar to the pattern shown in Figure 3.2 and, like the differences reported for diabetes, suggests that the conclusions drawn by Pilgrim *et al.* (1993) were correct.

A direct comparison between the two questions so far used to assess general health also provides useful information on their validity for exploring ethnic variations in health. Within both categories of response to the long-standing illness question (i.e. those reporting and those not reporting a long-standing illness) all ethnic minority respondents were more likely to report that they had fair or poor health, suggesting that for similar 'scores' on the long-standing illness question, ethnic minority respondents reported worse health than whites. Also, among those who reported good health, all South Asian and Chinese respondents were less likely than white respondents to report that they had a long-standing illness. Differences between whites and Caribbeans for this were small. These findings reinforce the belief that compared to the other ethnic groups South Asians and Chinese have to reach a higher threshold before they report a long-standing illness. Whether this is a

Figure 3.5   **Relative risk of a score of 3 or more on a general health index*
compared with whites**

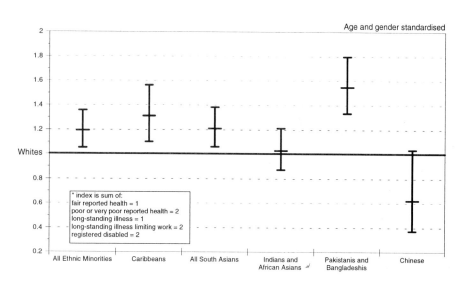

result of 'under-reporting' on the part of ethnic minority groups or 'over-reporting' on the part of whites is not clear from these data, which suggest a combination of both explanations. Among those with diabetes some ethnic minority groups seem to 'under-report' the presence of a long-standing illness. However, among those with good health whites appear to 'over-report' the presence of a long-standing illness.

A third question asked of all respondents about their general health was whether they were registered disabled. Too few respondents reported being registered disabled (less that 3 per cent in each group except Caribbeans who had 3.1 per cent) for a comparison of ethnic groups to be made. However, this question was combined with the reported health and long-standing illness questions to provide an index of general health. This index was then dichotomised at a level above which the respondent must have reported a minimum of one of the following

- poor or very poor health *and* a long-standing illness;
- a long-standing illness that limits work *and* fair, poor or very poor health;
- being registered disabled *and* either a long-standing illness or fair, poor or very poor health.

That is, the respondent must have had a high score on one of the three questions and also be positive on at least one of the other two. The relative risk of being positive on this general health index is shown in Figure 3.5.

Overall this shows almost identical results to the reported health question, except that differences between white and Chinese respondents were greater,

Figure 3.6   Relative risk of a score of 3 or more on a general health index* compared with whites – Caribbean men and women

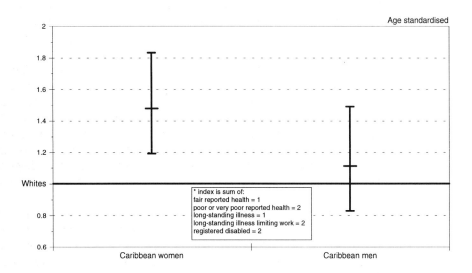

Figure 3.7   Per cent with a score of 3 or more on a general health index* by age

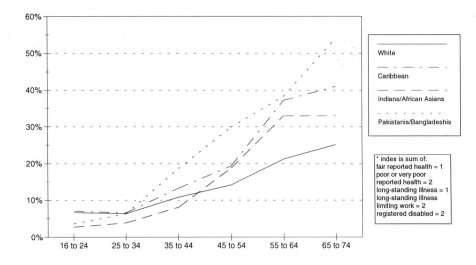

although still not statistically significant. However, this index does have a gender variation in response that was not present for the reported health question, with all of the difference between Caribbeans and whites being accounted for by the 50 per cent higher rate among Caribbean compared to white women. Caribbean and white men had similar rates – see Figure 3.6. There was no great gender variation in relative risk compared to whites for the other ethnic minority groups.

Ethnic variations in risk of being positive on the general health index also differed by age. Figure 3.7 shows that variations only emerged above the age of 35 and became greater with increasing age. Between the ages of 16 and 34 both Pakistani/Bangladeshis and Indian/African Asians had lower rates than whites, although the difference from whites at these ages was only statistically significant for Indian/African Asians. Interestingly, this pattern is also present in data relating to social class variations in health and it has been suggested that such findings are an 'artefact' resulting from the very low levels of poor health among the young (Blane *et al.* 1994).

For half of the ethnic minority sample, but all of the white sample, an additional series of questions were asked to assess the functional impact of any poor health, that is whether the respondent felt certain activities were limited because of his or her health. Table 3.1 shows responses to this series of questions and that Pakistani/Bangladeshis were consistently more likely to report limitation than other ethnic groups. The pattern for the other ethnic groups is a little inconsistent, but there appear to have been only small differences between the Indian/African Asians and Caribbeans and both seem to have had higher rates of limited activity than whites, while Chinese respondents appear to have had lower rates than whites.

Table 3.1   Activities limited by health

cell percentages: age and gender standardised

	White	All ethnic minorites	Caribbean	All South Asians	Indian or African Asian	Pakistani or Bangladeshi	Chinese
Vigorous activities	19	18	17	19	16	24	20
Moderate activities	6	9	7	11	8	15	6
Several flights of stairs	12	15	13	16	13	22	6
One flight of stairs	4	6	5	8	5	13	1
Walking more than one mile	7	13	9	16	11	23	8
Walking half a mile	4	9	5	10	7	17	6
Walking 100 yards	2	4	3	5	4	8	1
Carrying groceries	8	11	10	12	10	16	6
Bending, kneeling or stooping	9	10	12	10	8	13	4
Bathing or dressing	3	4	3	5	4	6	2
Weighted base	2866	2584	795	1590	1035	554	199
Unweighted base	2866	2573	613	1856	985	871	104

Figure 3.8 **Relative risk of health limiting moderately exerting activities* compared with whites**

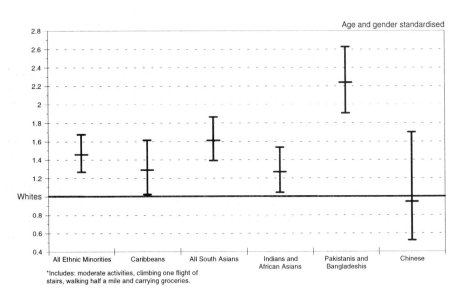

*Includes: moderate activities, climbing one flight of stairs, walking half a mile and carrying groceries.

Figure 3.9 **Relative risk of health limiting moderately exerting activities* compared with whites – Caribbean and Indian/African Asian men and women**

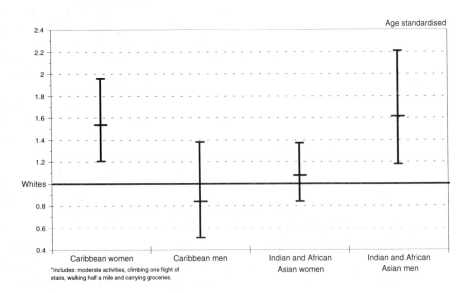

*Includes: moderate activities, climbing one flight of stairs, walking half a mile and carrying groceries.

Figure 3.8 shows the relative risks of health limiting one or more of the moderately exerting activities listed in Table 3.1, namely: moderate activities; climbing one flight of stairs; walking half a mile; and carrying groceries.

According to this overall assessment, all ethnic minority groups except the Chinese had poorer health than whites. Compared to whites, Caribbeans and Indian/African Asians were 30 per cent more likely to report one or more moderately exerting activity limited by health, while Pakistani/Bangladeshis were over twice as likely. This is consistent with the pattern of results for reported health (Figure 3.2), long-standing illness that limits work (Figure 3.4) and the general health index (Figure 3.5).

Like the general health index, responses to the questions on activities limited by health also showed important gender variations. Caribbean men had a very similar risk to white men of having one or more moderately exerting activities limited by health, while Caribbean women had a much greater risk than white women – see Figure 3.9. This figure also shows that the pattern is exactly the opposite for Indian/African Asians, where women had the same rate as white women and men had higher rates than white men. There was no great gender variation in relative risk for Pakistani/Bangladeshis and Chinese.

Summary

Most of the assessments of general health used here lead to the conclusion that Pakistani/Bangladeshis had considerably worse health than whites. Caribbeans also had significantly worse health than whites, although for two of the indicators used this was the result of particularly poor health among Caribbean women. Indian/African Asians had similar health to whites, although for one of the indicators male Indian/African Asians had a statistically significantly higher rate of ill health. Chinese respondents appeared to have had better health than whites, although, perhaps because of the small numbers of Chinese respondents in the survey, at no stage was the difference between them and whites statistically significant. Differences between ethnic minority groups and whites also appeared to only emerge above the age of 34. However, this could be a result of the very low rate of reported general ill-health among the young (Blane *et al.* 1994).

Responses to the question asking respondents if they have a long-standing illness did not follow the pattern of response for other general health questions, with all ethnic minority respondents being less likely than whites to have such an illness. However, as others have shown (Pilgrim *et al.* 1993), there is some evidence to suggest that the long-standing illness question is not valid for making comparisons across ethnic groups, with some indication that whites 'over-report' and Asians 'under-report' such illness (whites reporting good health are more likely to report a long-standing illness and Asians with diabetes are less likely to report a long-standing illness).

For these findings there is only one other national dataset with which comparisons can be made – the 1991 Census question asking about a limiting long-standing illness. During the development of the Census question considerable work was put into assessing its reliability and validity (Thomas and Purdon 1994).

Figure 3.10   Relative risk of tiredness, lack of energy or sleep problems compared with whites

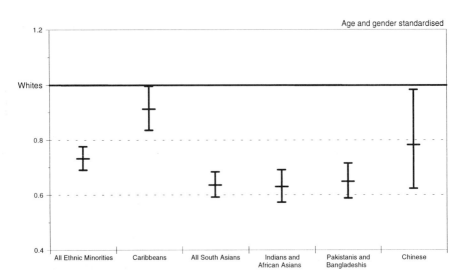

Although these assessments have not been reported by the ethnicity of respondents, responses to a follow-up interview during piloting do suggest that it is highly reliable. Of those reported as having a limiting long-standing illness on the Census form, 88 per cent had this confirmed at the follow-up interview, while for those not reported as having a limiting long-standing illness, only 4 per cent were reported to have such an illness at the follow-up interview. In terms of validity, it was concluded that the Census question 'functions empirically as a (rough and imperfect) measure of disability' (Thomas and Purdon 1994:10). In Figure 3.1 the relative risk of being positive on the Census question was presented for the population from which the *Fourth National Survey* was drawn. Comparing Figure 3.1 with Figures 3.2, 3.3, 3.4, 3.5 and 3.8 shows that responses to the Census question are consistent with responses to all of the *Fourth National Survey* questions except that on long-standing illness, which follows a very different pattern. If the Census question is a valid indicator of health among whites, as the Census reliability and validity assessment suggests, this would imply that here it is the long-standing illness question that is most misleading and that the other indicators, which follow a similar pattern to both the Census question and each other, should be regarded as the most valid indicators of ethnic differences. This supports the conclusions drawn in the previous paragraph.

PSYCHO-SOCIAL HEALTH

Half of the ethnic minority respondents and all of the white respondents were asked questions on tiredness/lack of energy and problems with sleep, giving an indication

Figure 3.11 Relative risk of diagnosed heart disease compared with whites

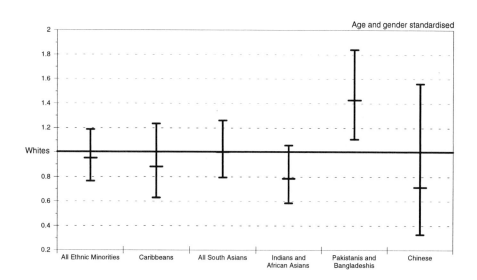

of psycho-social health. (There was also a great deal of information collected on mental health that is reported in Nazroo (1997).) Figure 3.10 shows the relative risk for ethnic minorities of having one or more of these problems compared with whites. All of the Asian groups had a much lower risk than whites. Caribbeans also had a statistically significant lower risk than whites, although the difference between these two groups was not large. Not shown in the figure is that this difference was entirely due to low rates among Caribbean men, Caribbean women had the same rate as white women. There was also a gender variation in risk for the Chinese group that went in the opposite direction to that for Caribbeans, Chinese men had the same rate as white men while Chinese women had lower rates than white women. However, the number of Chinese respondents asked this question was very small, making it difficult to draw conclusions about the importance of this.

CORONARY HEART DISEASE

All respondents were asked whether they had ever been diagnosed as suffering from angina and whether they had ever been diagnosed as suffering from a heart attack 'including a heart murmur, a damaged heart or a rapid heart'. Figure 3.11 shows the relative risk for ethnic minority groups to have either of these compared to whites.

There were only small and statistically non-significant differences between whites and Caribbeans and Chinese. Somewhat surprisingly given the mortality data already discussed, Figure 3.11 also shows that the overall South Asian group had similar rates of diagnosed heart disease to whites and the rate for Indian/African

**Figure 3.12 Relative risk of diagnosed heart disease or severe chest pain
compared with whites**

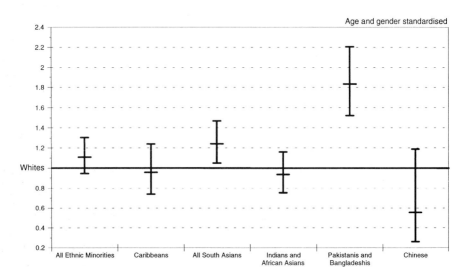

Asians was close to being statistically significantly lower than that for whites.
Pakistani/Bangladeshis, however, had much higher rates than the other groups,
close to 50 per cent greater than that for whites. This suggests the possibility that all
of the reported difference in coronary heart disease between South Asians and
whites can be attributed to greater rates among the Pakistani and Bangladeshi
communities. There were no great variations in relative risk when comparing
genders, nor when comparing responses to the two questions on diagnosis that were
used.

The questions on diagnosis may have been misleading because they depend on
respondents having consulted a doctor about cardiac symptoms and being aware of
and remembering the diagnosis given. Both of these factors could be related to
ethnicity. Consequently, those who had not reported diagnosed heart disease and
who were aged 40 or over, were asked whether they had experienced any chest pain,
followed by an additional question asking if any pain reported was severe and lasted
more than half an hour. For those aged 40 or over, Figure 3.12 shows the relative
risk for ethnic minority groups compared to whites to have either diagnosed heart
disease or severe chest pain.

Chinese respondents had lower rates than whites, although the difference was
not statistically significant. Caribbeans had a rate very similar to that for whites,
while the combined South Asian group had a rate that was 25 per cent higher,
consistent with the mortality data. However, splitting this group into its constituent
parts shows that Indian/African Asians had the same rate as whites, while Pakistani/
Bangladeshis had a rate that was much higher, over 80 per cent greater than that for
any of the other ethnic groups. Others have reported that the differences between
South Asians and whites in mortality from heart disease are particularly large for the

young (Balarajan 1991). If the relative risk of having diagnosed heart disease or severe chest pain is explored across three age groups (40–44, 45–59 and 60 or older), the overall pattern remains stable. Caribbeans and Indian/African Asians had the same rate as whites across the age groups (although there is a suggestion that the rate for Indian/African Asians may have been lower than the white rate for the youngest age group, although not statistically significantly so) and Pakistani/Bangladeshis had a higher rate than whites. (There were too few Chinese respondents for their responses to be analysed by age.) However, the relative risk for Pakistani/Bangladeshis was particularly large for those aged 40–44, being three times the white rate. For those aged 45–59 and 60 or older, the Pakistani/Bangladeshi rate was 70 per cent greater than the white rate (full details are shown in Table B.8 in Appendix B).

The figures presented in this section confirm previous findings that suggest that South Asians as a whole have higher rates of coronary heart disease than whites (Marmot *et al.* 1984, Balarajan 1991 and 1996), but they also suggest that all of this difference can be attributed to higher rates among Pakistani/Bangladeshis. In fact, whites and Indian/African Asians seemed to have almost identical rates of coronary heart disease. The result seems robust in that it is repeated at each stage in the questioning, from questions addressing experience of symptoms to those asking about diagnosed heart disease, and across age and gender groups. The figures also suggest that Caribbeans have similar rates of heart disease to whites, rather than the lower rates suggested by mortality data. Chinese respondents appear to have had lower rates than whites, although the difference was not statistically significant. Compatible with immigrant mortality data, which shows that differences between those born in South Asia and those born in Britain are greater for the young, is that much, but not all, of the greater heart disease morbidity among Pakistani/Bangladeshis also appeared to occur among younger age groups here.

HYPERTENSION

Figure 3.13 shows responses to the question asked of all respondents about whether they had been diagnosed as having hypertension. It broadly confirms other studies on hypertension, whites and Pakistani/Bangladeshis reported similar rates, Indian/African Asians and Chinese had lower rates than whites and Caribbeans had rates almost 50 per cent higher than whites.

However, the relatively high rate for Caribbeans showed an interesting gender variation. Figure 3.14 shows that for men the Caribbean rate was only slightly and not significantly higher than the white rate, while for women the Caribbean rate was almost 80 per cent higher than the white rate. Mortality data also suggest that the difference between Caribbean and white women is greater than that between Caribbean and white men (Marmot *et al.* 1984, Balarajan and Bulusu 1990), but, unlike the data presented here, does still have a difference between men.

The data presented on hypertension clearly need to be treated with some caution. Hypertension is an asymptomatic condition and we have no knowledge of undiagnosed hypertension in this sample, nor how the process of diagnosis may be

Figure 3.13 Relative risk of diagnosed hypertension compared with whites

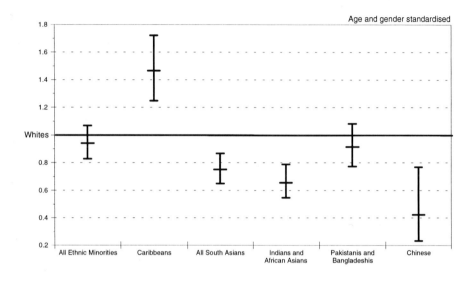

**Figure 3.14 Relative risk of diagnosed hypertension compared with whites –
Caribbean men and women**

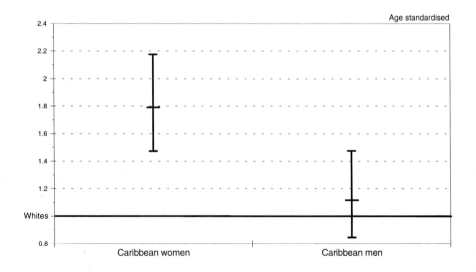

Figure 3.15 Relative risk of perceived obesity compared with whites

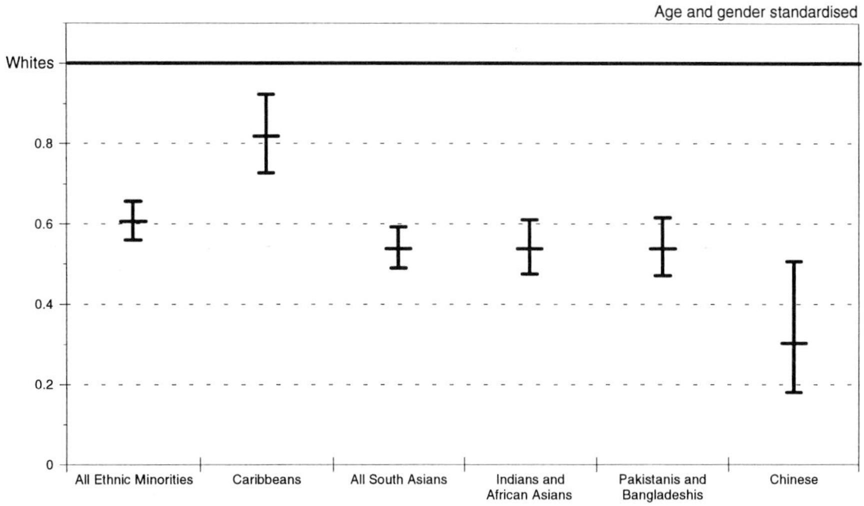

associated with both gender and ethnicity. It certainly seems possible that the routine checks carried out on women in family planning and ante-natal clinics will increase detection rates of hypertension for them compared to men, and this may partly explain the differences in relative risks shown for Caribbean men and women.

OBESITY

As for hypertension, there was no direct assessment of obesity in this survey. Half of the ethnic minority and all of the white respondents were asked if they considered themselves overweight and if they had ever tried to lose weight, but data resulting from such questions clearly needs to be treated with some caution. Responses to both questions showed very similar variations by ethnicity, so only those to the perceived obesity question are shown in Figure 3.15.

This shows that all ethnic minority groups were less likely than whites to consider themselves overweight. Not shown in the figure is that for Caribbeans there was a difference according to gender, with Caribbean men having lower rates than white men and Caribbean women having the same rate as white women.

DIABETES

All respondents were asked whether they had ever had diabetes. Figure 3.16 shows that all ethnic minority groups had higher rates than whites, although the size of the

Figure 3.16   Relative risk of diabetes compared with whites

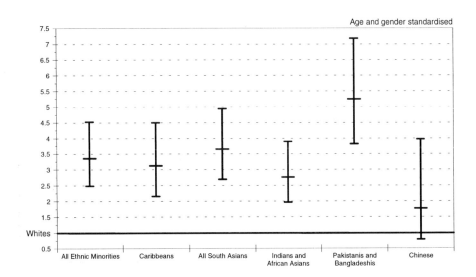

difference was smaller and not statistically significant for Chinese respondents. Indian/African Asians and Caribbeans had similar rates, about three times the white rate. Pakistani/Bangladeshis had much higher rates than any other group, over five times the white rate.

Additional questions on type of diabetes were not asked, so distinctions cannot be made between insulin dependant and non-insulin dependant diabetes (although the former is relatively rare), nor can those who only had diabetes during pregnancy be identified. Like other reports of specific illness, it is again worth pointing out that responses to the diabetes question were dependant on the respondent consulting a doctor about possible symptoms and being aware of the diagnosis made.

RESPIRATORY DISEASE

Half of the ethnic minority and all of the white respondents were asked several questions about symptoms suggestive of respiratory illness, which covered wheezing, coughing up phlegm and being woken by shortness of breath. Figure 3.17 shows the relative risk for ethnic minorities compared to whites to either have a wheeze or to cough up phlegm on most days for at least three months a year (respiratory symptoms). All of the Asian groups had a statistically significant and markedly lower risk of this than whites. Caribbeans, however, had a similar risk to whites.

This difference was entirely due to responses to the wheezing question, Caribbeans, Indian/African Asians and Chinese were just as likely as whites to cough

Figure 3.17 Relative risk of respiratory symptoms compared with whites

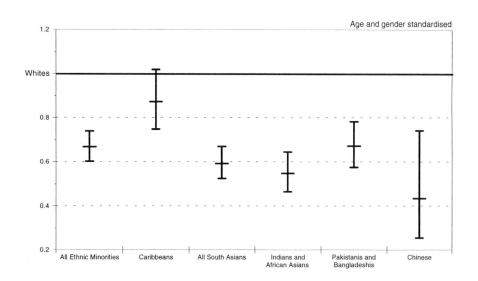

up phlegm and Pakistani/Bangladeshis were more likely (see the total row of the 'coughing up phlegm' section in Table B.12, Appendix B). The previous chapter illustrated ethnic variations in rates of smoking (see Table 2.13) and it is possible that the low risk of respiratory symptoms among Asians shown in Figure 3.17 is the result of their relatively low rates of smoking. Figures 3.18 and 3.19 show the relative risk of ethnic minorities to have respiratory symptoms for both those who had ever regularly smoked and those who had never smoked.

For smokers South Asians were just as likely as whites to have respiratory symptoms, the lower risk among South Asians only applied to non-smokers. (Numbers were too few for the Chinese respondents to be analysed in this way.) In this context it is again worth looking back at Table 2.13, which shows that smoking among South Asians was almost entirely restricted to men. Despite this, there was only a gender difference in relative risk of respiratory symptoms compared to whites for the Pakistani/Bangladeshi group, with Pakistani/Bangladeshi men having a greater relative risk than Pakistani/Bangladeshi women (compare their percentages with the equivalent white group in Table B.12, Appendix B). Also of significance is that ethnic minority smokers were less likely than whites to have given up smoking (Table 2.13).

Respondents were also asked whether they had ever been woken by shortness of breath. Responses to this question, shown in Figure 3.20, show that Caribbeans and Pakistani/Bangladeshis had similar rates of this symptom to whites, while Chinese and Indian/African Asians had lower rates than whites (although the result was not statistically significant for the Chinese group). It is by no means clear whether this symptom represents respiratory illness or coronary heart disease, or both of these. Consequently, the significance of this pattern cannot be fully assessed.

Figure 3.18 Relative risk of respiratory symptoms for smokers compared with whites

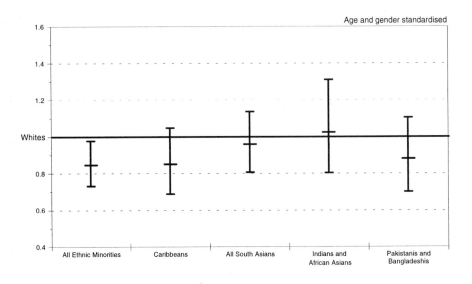

Figure 3.19 Relative risk of respiratory symptoms for non-smokers compared with whites

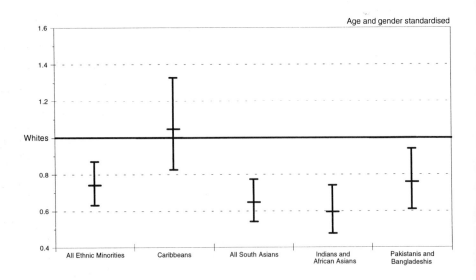

Figure 3.20 Relative risk of being woken by shortness of breath compared with whites

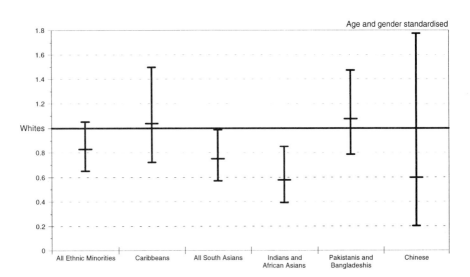

ACCIDENTS

Half of the ethnic minority and all of the white respondents were asked the number of accidents they had had in the last 12 months that had resulted in hospital treatment, and where the accidents had occurred. Figure 3.21 shows the overall relative risk of having such an accident and that it was much lower for all ethnic minority groups than whites, although for Chinese respondents this difference was not statistically significant. All of the South Asian groups had well under half the risk of whites, while the differences was not so great for Caribbeans.

Table 3.2 details the rate of reported accidents by where the accident took place, and shows that the ethnic variation illustrated by Figure 3.21 was generally consistent across location. However, it is worth noting that for home accidents Caribbeans reported a similar rate to whites and for road/pavement accidents both Caribbeans and Pakistani/Bangladeshis reported rates that were not much below the white rate.

These results are unexpected, particularly considering that accidents are known to be associated with poverty and poor housing and ethnic minority groups have lower incomes and poorer housing than whites (see Chapter 5 of this volume and Modood *et al.* 1997). The low rate of accidents reported by ethnic minorities should be considered in relation to two factors. First, the question asked about accidents requiring hospital treatment. It may be the case that attendance at a hospital following an accident varies across ethnic groups. Second, this survey does not

Figure 3.21 Relative risk of having an accident resulting in hospital treatment compared with whites

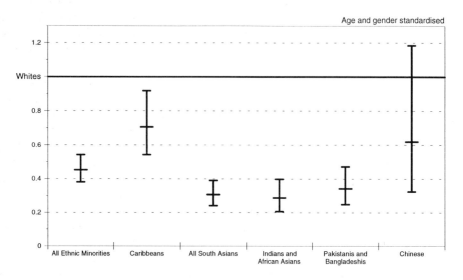

include anyone below the age of 16. It may well be that high rates of accidents among those in poor socio-economic situations are largely a result of accidents occurring to children (Balarajan and Soni Raleigh, 1995). Certainly, one study that explored the relationship between ethnicity, socio-economic status and accidents among children found that socio-economic status was a crucial factor (Alwash and McCarthy 1988).

Table 3.2   Accidents resulting in hospital treatment by location of accident

rate per 1000: age and gender standardised

	White	All ethnic minorites	Caribbean	All South Asians	Indian or African Asian	Pakistani or Bangladeshi	Chinese
Sports accidents	29	16	19	9	10	7	52
Workplace accidents[1]	50	17	24	14	16	5	9
School/college accidents[2]	15	16	*	9	12	0	*
Home accidents	44	20	40	13	8	21	0
Road/pavement/ car accidents	24	14	21	11	9	16	8
Weighted base (full sample)	*2867*	*2587*	*795*	*1593*	*1038*	*555*	*199*
Unweighted base (full sample)	*2867*	*2579*	*614*	*1861*	*988*	*873*	*104*

1 Base = only those who work.
2 Base = only those in full-time education.
*   Too few respondents for a reliable estimate.

Conclusion

The data presented in this chapter illustrate important variations between ethnic minority groups and whites in reported health. They broadly confirm differences suggested by other studies based on morbidity and mortality data. However, there are also some important discrepancies between the data presented here and conclusions reached elsewhere. As far as general health is concerned, the data indicate that Pakistani/Bangladeshis were particularly disadvantaged compared to whites, having a 50 per cent greater risk of reported fair or poor health (see Figure 3.2), and over twice the risk of having their performance of moderately exerting activities limited by their health (see Figure 3.8). Caribbeans were also disadvantaged compared to whites, being about 30 per cent more likely to have reported fair or poor health or that their performance of moderately exerting activities was limited by their health. Although previous research has indicated that all ethnic minority groups have poorer general health than whites (Benzeval *et al.* 1992, Pilgrim *et al.* 1993, Williams *et al.* 1993, Rudat 1994), differences between the Indian/African Asian and Chinese groups and the white group reported here were small and not statistically significant. This discrepancy may be a result of more effective sampling in this survey – the sample used here is nationally representative rather than either reflecting a local situation, or only being drawn from areas with a relatively large ethnic minority population – and careful allocation of individuals into specific ethnic groups. The Census also meets both of these criteria, and the question on general health used in it showed a very similar pattern of response to all but one of the indicators of general health used here.

The indicator of general health used here which did not follow the pattern of the others, or that of the Census, was whether the respondent reported a long-standing illness. All ethnic minority groups did better on this indicator than whites, except Caribbeans who had the same rate as whites (see Figure 3.3). Evidence presented here and elsewhere (Pilgrim *et al.* 1993) suggests that this may be due to problems with the use of such a question for making comparisons across ethnic groups, unless its phrasing includes some notion of the illness limiting the respondent in some way.

Interestingly, the ethnic variations in response to general health questions did not emerge until the age of 35 and above, for those aged 16 to 34 there were no or minimal differences between ethnic groups. This may be a result of the very low rates of ill-health in this age group (Blane *et al.* 1994), or because ethnic variations in the key forms of material, cultural or biological disadvantage that are related to poor health do not emerge until early middle age.

Immigrant mortality data suggest that those born in South Asia have higher rates of coronary heart disease than those born in Britain, and that those born in the Caribbean have lower rates (Marmot *et al.* 1984, Balarajan 1991 and 1996). The morbidity data presented here indicate that Caribbeans had lower rates of coronary heart disease than whites, but not statistically significantly so, as did the Chinese. Of the South Asian ethnic minority groups, somewhat unexpectedly Indian/African Asians also appeared to have similar rates of coronary heart disease to whites. However, Pakistani/Bangladeshis had considerably higher rates of coronary heart disease than whites according to the measures used in this survey. Examining differences between Pakistani/Bangladeshis and whites by age showed a pattern that was consistent with the differences in age-related mortality that are reported for those born in the Indian sub-continent and those born in Britain. When considering the differences between the morbidity data presented here and the mortality data presented elsewhere, it is important to keep in mind three factors. First, as described in Chapter 1, ethnicity for mortality data is not adequately collected, being based on country of birth, so real differences in mortality rates between the various South Asian groups may not have been identified by previous studies. Indeed, the data presented by Balarajan *et al.* (1984) suggests that Muslims may have higher mortality rates from ischaemic heart disease than other South Asians, and the recent immigrant mortality data presented by Balarajan (1996) suggests that those born in Bangladesh and Pakistan have higher rates of mortality from heart disease than those born in India. Second, mortality rates and reported morbidity rates do not necessarily co-vary. As a result of differences in access to treatment, or in the natural progression of the disease, or in exposure to environmental or social factors which may influence the progression of the disease, coronary heart morbidity may well lead to different rates of mortality among different social groups. Indeed, rates of survival following myocardial infarction have been shown to vary for both socio-economic group (Morrison *et al.* 1997) and for ethnic group, with South Asians appearing to have lower survival rates than white comparisons (Shaukat *et al.* 1997, Wilkinson *et al.* 1996).[3] Third, there may be important cohort differences between the populations included in the immigrant mortality data collected over the past two decades and those included in this morbidity survey carried out in 1993 and 1994. Indeed, there is some suggestion of a possible cohort effect in a recently published comparison of immigrant mortality statistics from 1989–92 with those from 1970–72 (Wild and McKeigue 1997).

The data presented on rates of hypertension show higher rates among Caribbeans, confirming previous findings of higher rates of mortality related to hypertension among those born in the Caribbean compared with those born in Britain (Marmot *et al.* 1984, Balarajan and Bulusu 1990), although the higher rates here applied only to female Caribbeans. Chinese respondents reported lower rates of hypertension than white respondents. Among the South Asians in this sample, the rate of hypertension for Indian/African Asians was lower than that for whites, while it was about the same as whites for Pakistani/Bangladeshis. This is again in contrast to data on immigrant mortality from hypertensive disease and mortality from strokes. These suggest that South Asians should have higher rates of hypertension than whites (Balarajan and Bulusu 1990). Some of the explanations presented above may apply to this discrepancy. However, it is also worth noting that in a survey such as this the recognition of hypertension is totally dependent on diagnosis by a doctor. Different ethnic groups may well have had different opportunities for such a diagnosis to be made.

---

3   Interestingly, the two papers showing higher mortality rates for South Asians compared to whites following a myocardial infarct favoured different explanations. Shaukar *et al.* (1997) based their explanation on the presence of more extensive arterial disease, while Wilkinson *et al.* (1996) suggested that differences were a consequence of greater co-morbidity with diabetes.

In this sample rates of diabetes showed the expected ethnic variation, with all of the ethnic minority groups having higher rates than whites. Interestingly, the difference between the South Asian groups and whites was much greater for Pakistani/Bangladeshis than for Indian/African Asians. Also Indian/African Asians and Caribbeans had similar rates of diabetes. In contrast to this, as far as perceived obesity is concerned all of the ethnic minority groups had lower rates than whites.

According to the other indicators of morbidity presented in this chapter, the South Asian and Chinese groups were on the whole advantaged compared to whites and Caribbeans. The indicators of psycho-social health used here – tiredness, lack of energy and problems with sleep – had a higher rate among whites than all of the other ethnic groups. These indicators are closely related to mental health, issues relating to ethnic variations in mental health are explored in more detail elsewhere (Nazroo 1997).

Table 2.13 shows that whites were far more likely than the other groups to have reported ever smoking, although differences for current smoking among men were smaller. One of the consequences of smoking is respiratory disease. Across almost all of the indicators of respiratory disease whites did worse than the other ethnic groups. This is consistent with immigrant mortality data (Marmot *et al. 1984,* Balarajan and Bulusu 1990). However, if patterns of smoking are considered, the size of the ethnic differences was much reduced and not significant among those who had ever regularly smoked, suggesting that the differences reported overall were largely a result of different patterns of smoking. (As a result of the small number of Chinese respondents asked this question, it was not possible to test whether this also held for the Chinese group.) This possibility is slightly weakened by the fact that there was a greater rate of respiratory symptoms among white non-smokers compared with South Asian non-smokers, although other factors, such as passive smoking, might be important here.

All of the ethnic minority groups had lower rates than whites for all types of accident (although, perhaps because of its small sample size, this difference was not statistically significant for the Chinese group). This is somewhat puzzling as accidents are known to be associated with poverty and poor housing (e.g. Kelly and Miles-Doan 1997), and that people from certain ethnic minority groups are more likely to be in such situations (see Chapter 5 of this volume and Modood *et al.* 1997). Three factors may be important in explaining this: the question asked about accidents requiring hospital treatment and there may be ethnic variations in attendance at hospital following an accident; the sample did not include any children and it may be that socio-economic factors have their strongest influence for accidents with children; and ethnic minorities are less likely to use alcohol (see Table 2.15), which is related to all forms of accident.

One important issue concerning gender also emerged in the data presented. For many of the indicators of health, Caribbean men did better than Caribbean women when compared to their white counterparts. The higher rate of ill-health among Caribbeans compared to whites according to most indicators of general health was the result differences between Caribbean and white women. This also applied to differences in the rate of diagnosed hypertension, with Caribbean men having the same rate as white men and Caribbean women having much higher rates than white

Exploring Ethnicity Further: the Effect of Migration and Differences Between Ethnic Sub-Groups

INTRODUCTION

The previous chapters have used country of family origin to explore ethnic variations in health. This has considerable advantages over the use of country of birth as a proxy for ethnicity, which most other national studies have been forced to rely on (e.g. Marmot *et al.* 1984, Balarajan 1991 and 1996), but it is not without its own disadvantages. These issues and their implications have been discussed in the introduction to this volume. However, in the light of the findings presented in Chapters 2 and 3, two are worth returning to and exploring further. First, as suggested earlier, one of the problems with the majority of epidemiological work on ethnic variations in health is that it has only focused on migrants to Britain. However, a significant number of ethnic minority respondents to the *Fourth National Survey* were born in Britain, which gives us the opportunity to provide a comparison between those born in Britain and those born abroad. This would be useful in a number of ways. In particular, it will allow an exploration of the implications of using country of birth as a surrogate ethnic classification, and how far this may have resulted in the discrepancies between the findings reported here and published data on immigrant mortality rates. Such a comparison will also aid us in understanding the processes that might lead to ethnic variations in health.

Second, the use of overarching and misleading ethnic categories, such as South Asian, in research on ethnic variations in health has been widely criticised, because they combine distinct ethnic groups with different cultural traditions, migration experiences and socio-economic positions. In fact, tables presented in Chapter 2 showed that the South Asian ethnic category contained groups with very diverse health experiences, and figures in Chapter 3 showed that its use led to misleading comparisons with the white population. However, it is possible that an ethnic classification based on country of family origin is itself too crude. For example, the Indian category includes populations from distinct regions and, again, with different cultural traditions, migration histories and socio-economic positions. In this context, it is worth recognising that a number of local studies of South Asians have, in fact, been studies of particular sub-groups within this Indian category (e.g. Williams *et al.*'s (1993) study of the Punjabi population in Glasgow, Cruikshank *et al.*'s (1991) study of glucose resistance in the predominantly Gujarati population of north-west London and Mather and Keen's (1985) study of diabetes in the Punjabi population of Southall, London). In order to explore the implications of this further, and to allow comparisons to be made with regional studies that have focused on particular sub-groups of Indians, in this chapter the ethnic category of Indian/African Asian will be sub-divided according to religion to see whether important differences between groups emerge.

Much of the data for this chapter are presented in the form of figures. The tables on which these figures are based can be found in Appendix C.

THE RELATIONSHIP BETWEEN MIGRATION AND HEALTH

There have been a number of discussions of how the process of migration could be directly related to health. These clearly have direct implications for the interpretation of data that uses country of birth to allocate ethnic group. However, the large number of migrants among the ethnic minority populations of Britain means that they also have implications for the interpretation of ethnic variations in health in studies that have used more appropriate assessments of ethnicity.

The first issue of relevance here is a consideration of how health may be related to the selection of individuals into a migrant group. Migrants may well differ from non-migrants in their country of origin in a number of ways, including age, gender and socio-economic status. Many of these factors will be related to health and if, as seems possible, migrants are younger and better educated than those who remain, they will have better health. The Nuffield Social Mobility Survey found that nearly a quarter of non-white migrants to Britain had professional class origins (Heath and Ridge 1983). In addition, health itself may be one of the factors that differs between the migrant and non-migrant populations of a country. On the one hand, those who are in poor health may, because of the difficulties they will face, be less likely to migrate than those who are healthy – a 'healthy migrant effect'. In support of this possibility, Marmot *et al.* (1984) presented data that suggested that migrants to England and Wales from all countries where comparisons could be made (which, unfortunately, did not include the Indian sub-continent) had a lower mortality rate than those in their country of birth, with the exception of Ireland – although there are a number of competing explanations for this finding. Alternatively, migration may be inversely related to health. Marmot *et al.* (1984) suggested that migrants to England and Wales from Ireland did not follow the pattern described above for two reasons. Geographical and political differences in the process of migration for the Irish meant that they did not face a health barrier when migrating, so, rather than migrants being selected from the more advantaged groups in Ireland, they may have been selected from the more disadvantaged groups (presumably also because of different socio-economic pressures to migrate in the country of origin) who had poorer health. Indeed, it seems quite possible that those who are more marginal in society and, consequently, more disadvantaged will be more likely to migrate if an opportunity arises. In addition, poor health itself may directly lead to migration –

perhaps as a result of exclusion from the society of birth because of the presence of a stigmatising illness, or possibly in search of better health care. There is, however, little empirical evidence beyond Heath and Ridge's (1983) work to support any of these possibilities. It is also the case that where whole communities have been forced to migrate, as happened to African Asians in the late 1960s and early 1970s, neither negative nor positive health selection would have played a role in the process of migration (although it may have influenced which country the migrant moved to).

The second issue that needs consideration is the direct effect of the process of migration on health. Migration involves a great deal of social disruption and stress. Social networks break down and are often reformed in new and unexpected ways (Khan 1979). This will have implications for the extent and nature of the social support that exists in migrant communities. There will also be changes in economic position and economic opportunity once migration has occurred and the movement into an unfamiliar and probably hostile environment will undoubtably cause considerable stress. All of these factors may have an adverse impact on the health of migrant ethnic minority populations.

A third issue that is of relevance here is the importance of environmental experiences on health. The impact of environmental factors during childhood on adult health is a topic that has raised considerable interest (Barker 1991, Vågerö and Illsley 1995) and this may be of particular relevance to ethnic variations in health. It certainly seems possible that greater environmental deprivation in the country of birth for migrants compared to others is one of the explanatory factors for the ethnic variations in health that have been reported in immigrant mortality studies. In support of this, Williams *et al.* (1993) concluded that differences in the physical development of members of the Punjabi population in Glasgow compared to the white population were the result of childhood environmental deprivation in the Punjab. If this is the case, we would expect ethnic variations in health to diminish as new generations are born in Britain. In fact, there is some evidence from the USA to suggest that within one or two generations the health of ethnic minority populations becomes similar to that of others in the country to which they migrated (e.g. Syme *et al.* 1975, Gordon 1982), supporting the possibility that ethnic variations in health are a consequence of differences in environmental risk in different countries of birth.

USING THE FOURTH NATIONAL SURVEY TO COMPARE THE HEALTH OF MIGRANTS AND NON-MIGRANTS

A more direct test of the health consequences of possible disadvantage associated with migration is to compare the health of migrants with that of members of ethnic minority groups who were born in Britain. These data will be presented next, however a number of technical problems occur when a comparison of this sort is made. First, a decision has to be made between what is and what is not a migrant population. Should respondents who migrated in childhood be regarded as migrants, or, because of their exposure to British schooling and a British childhood environment, should they be considered as non-migrants? If we agree with the latter decision, at what age should the cut-off between migrants and non-migrants be made? For the purposes of the comparisons made here, a distinction has been drawn between those who were born in Britain or who migrated below the age of eleven (called non-migrants in the rest of the chapter) and those who migrated aged eleven or older (called migrants in the rest of the chapter). This is somewhat arbitrary and chosen to provide as numerically balanced a sample as possible. However, perhaps because of the small number of respondents affected by such a decision, the results presented are similar to those that are produced if the cut-off is made at the age of five or based on country of birth.

The second and perhaps most obvious problem is that the ages of migrant and non-migrant ethnic minority populations in Britain are very different, with little overlap in age groups. For example, in this sample the mean age of Caribbeans born in Britain was 26 (standard deviation = 6) while that of Caribbeans born elsewhere was 50 (standard deviation = 13); the mean age of Indians and African Asians born in Britain was 22 (standard deviation = 5) while that of Indians and African Asians born elsewhere was 43 (standard deviation = 14); and the mean age of Pakistanis and Bangladeshis born in Britain was 21 (standard deviation = 4) while that of Pakistanis and Bangladeshis born elsewhere was 39 (standard deviation = 14). This means that only respondents within specific age bands can be used to make the comparison between migrants and non-migrants and even within these fairly narrow age bands the data need to be age and gender standardised. As before, small sample sizes mean that for the process of standardisation certain ethnic groups have had to be combined and the Chinese group has been dropped (see Chapter 3 for a description of the rational behind this). Because of similarities in their health profiles (shown in Chapter 2), African Asians are combined with Indians, and Pakistanis are combined with Bangladeshis.

Third, because of differences in when different ethnic groups migrated to Britain, the age bands that are focused on vary from ethnic group to ethnic group. For Caribbeans the age group is 30 to 44, for Indian/African Asians it is 25 to 39 and for Pakistani/Bangladeshis it is 20 to 34. This also means that these groups cannot be combined to provide summary figures.

Fourth, the need to focus on these relatively young age groups means that the prevalence of ill-health was low among the respondents included for this comparison. Together with the small sample sizes used, this means that comparisons cannot be made for certain illnesses, such as heart disease and diabetes, and for other health assessments differences found will inevitably be small. We consequently need to be sensitive to the risk of type II statistical errors, where relevant differences between groups are ignored because they do not meet the criteria for statistical significance (see Blalock (1985) for a full discussion of this issue).

Self-assessed general health

Global assessments of health will be covered first. Figure 4.1 is based on responses to the question asking respondents to assess their health on a five point scale ranging from excellent to very poor, compared to others of the same age. It shows the percentage of respondents who rated their health as fair or worse and that those

Figure 4.1   Reported fair or poor health by age on migration to Britain

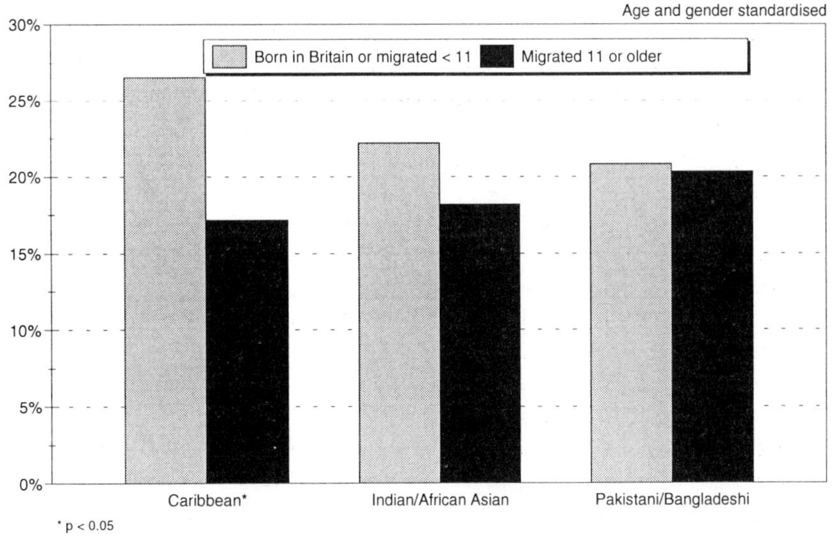

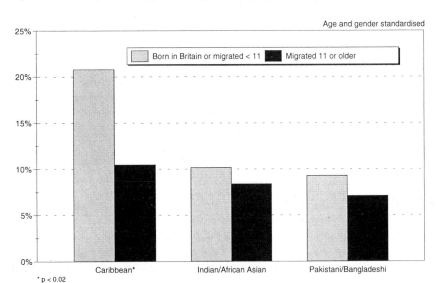

who migrated aged eleven or older were less likely to have bad health for all ethnic groups. However, differences were only statistically significant for the Caribbean group and were small for the Pakistani/Bangladeshi group.

Figure 4.2 charts the number of respondents who reported that they had a long-standing illness. The pattern of response is very similar to that for Figure 4.1. Those

Figure 4.2   Reported long-standing illness by age on migration to Britain

Figure 4.3   Hypertension by age on migration to Britain

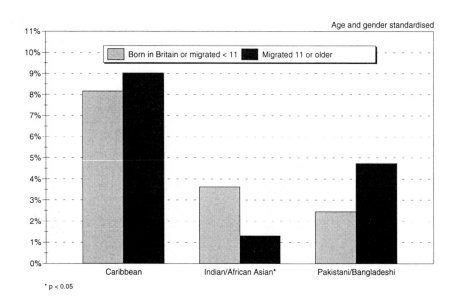

* p < 0.05

aged 11 or older at the time of migration were less likely than others to have reported such an illness for all three ethnic groups. Once again, these differences were only statistically significant for Caribbeans.

Specific illnesses

Of the five categories of ill-health explored in detail in earlier chapters (heart disease, hypertension, diabetes, respiratory symptoms and accidents) only hypertension and respiratory symptoms occurred frequently enough in the age groups considered here for any meaningful comparisons to be made. Figure 4.3 shows responses to the question asking respondents if they had ever had hypertension. Differences for Indian/African Asians followed the pattern reported above for self-assessed health, non-migrants were more likely than migrants to report hypertension and this difference was statistically significant. Differences for the other two groups go in the opposite direction, but were not statistically significant.

Half of the ethnic minority sample were asked a series of questions about respiratory symptoms. Figure 4.4 shows the rate of positive response to having either a wheeze or coughing up phlegm for at least three months of the year. Two of the three groups showed marked differences, with those who migrated to Britain aged 11 or older having lower rates than others. However, despite the fact that the size of the difference was two-fold for Caribbeans, once again these differences were not statistically significant. The Pakistani/Bangladeshi group showed only small differences between the migrant and non-migrant groups.

Figure 4.4   Respiratory symptoms by age on migration to Britain

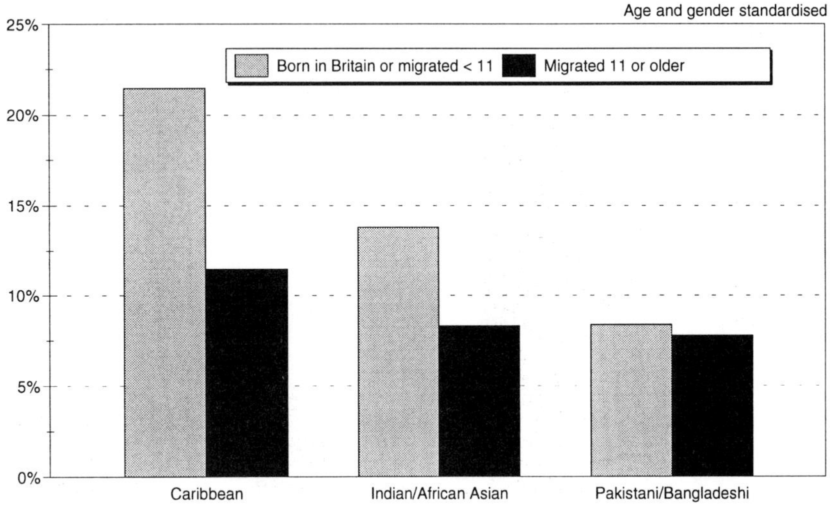

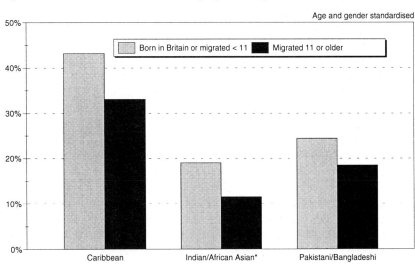

Health-related behaviour

Questions on smoking behaviour and alcohol consumption were asked of half of the ethnic minority respondents. Consistent with responses to questions on health, Figure 4.5 shows that migrants were less likely than non-migrants to have ever smoked for all of the ethnic groups included here. However, these differences were

Figure 4.5   Whether ever smoked by age on migration to Britain

* p < 0.05

Figure 4.6   Alcohol consumption by age on migration to Britain

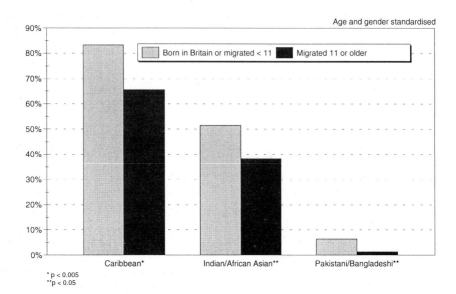

* p < 0.005
**p < 0.05

only statistically significant for the Indian/African Asian group, for whom non-migrants were almost twice as likely as migrants to have reported smoking.

Figure 4.6 considers whether the respondent reported ever drinking alcohol. Once again migrants were less likely than non-migrants to be alcohol drinkers for all ethnic groups. Here differences were also statistically significant for all of the groups, including Pakistani/Bangladeshis among whom very few respondents reported drinking.

Summary and implications of differences between migrants and non-migrants

The assessments of health presented in Figures 4.1 to 4.6 followed the same overall pattern. Although many of the differences between the migrant and non-migrant populations were not statistically significant, in virtually all cases migrants reported better health than non-migrants. In addition, in all cases where the differences *were* statistically significant, migrants reported better health than non-migrants. Taking into account the small size and relatively young age, with consequent low rates of ill-health, of the samples considered (which, as described above, leads to an increased risk of statistical tests missing important differences between groups), the consistency of this evidence across several indicators strongly suggests that for ethnic minority populations in Britain, the health of migrants is as good as that of non-migrants and is probably better.

Although this conclusion is clear, its implications for the issues discussed earlier are not so straightforward. This is largely a result of a dependence on cross-sectional survey data. However, data presented by Marmot *et al.* (1984) suggested that the health of migrants was better than that of those who remained in the country migrated from. This, together with the data presented here, does raise the possibility that selection into migrant groups was at least partly dependent on good health or factors associated with good health, as such an effect would be expected to be diminished for those born in Britain. The data also indicate that the ethnic variations in health, suggested by the findings reported in Chapters 2 and 3 of this volume and immigrant mortality data published elsewhere (e.g. Marmot *et al.* 1984), are not the result of environmental factors operating prior to entry to Britain. Such an hypothesis would suggest that those born in Britain, or who migrated at an early age, should be advantaged compared to the migrant population, which is clearly not the case. Finally, the data also suggest that ethnic variations in health cannot be attributed to the stresses and disruptions produced by the process of migration itself. Again, the fact that migrants did not report worse health than non-migrants and, in fact, possibly had better health, is inconsistent with that perspective.

Taken together with the data on health-related behaviours, the suggestion that migrants had better health than non-migrants raises an interesting set of further possibilities. Figures 4.5 and 4.6 show migrants were less likely than non-migrants to have reported that they smoked or drank alcohol. Consequently, differences in health-related behaviour may have contributed to differences in the health of migrants and non-migrants. Differences in health-related behaviour presumably occur because childhood environment is an important influence on the degree to which such practices become culturally acceptable. In addition, an adverse childhood environment in Britain for non-migrants, compared to the childhood environment of migrants, may also have damaged their adult health more directly (Barker 1991). Indeed, there is the possibility that differences in the health of migrants and non-migrants are the result of the latter's greater ongoing exposure to an adverse environment in Britain, rather than a healthy migrant effect. This is supported by evidence suggesting that for migrants health deteriorates with increasing time spent in Britain (Williams 1993), although such findings could also be a consequence of positive health selection effects wearing off with time.

THE CONSISTENCY OF HEALTH STATUS ACROSS ETHNIC SUB-GROUPS

As mentioned in the introduction to this chapter, the use of overarching and internally heterogeneous ethnic categories when exploring ethnic variations in health can be misleading. In fact, the extent to which analyses based on such categories have in the past led to erroneous conclusions can be seen by comparing the responses shown in Chapters 2 and 3 of this volume for the ethnic groups included in the category South Asian. Also of concern is that regional studies in Britain that have focused on particular ethnic minority populations, such as Knight *et al.*'s (1992) study of insulin resistance and coronary heart disease among 'South Asian' men in Bradford, who were presumably predominantly Pakistani, and McKeigue *et al.*'s (1988) study of coronary heart disease among Bangladeshis in East London, have had their results described using the term 'South Asian' and their findings consequently interpreted as if they apply to all components of this group. Similar criticisms could, however, be levelled at the use of ethnic categories based on country of family origin in Chapters 2 and 3. This is particularly the case for the Indian and African Asian categories, which cover respondents who have family origins in a geographically, economically and culturally diverse region. In fact, a unique study by Balarajan *et al.* (1984), which used an analysis of names to sub-divide those born in India into regional and religious groups, demonstrates that such groups may well show different patterns of disease.

The intention of this section of the chapter is to explore how useful it is to use geographical, cultural or religious markers to deconstruct ethnic categories that are based on country of family origin into ethnic sub-groupings. This is most easily done for those with Indian family origins, who can be conveniently divided into three cultural/geographical groups: Hindus from the Gujarati region of India; Sikhs from the Punjabi region of India; and Muslims from a number of areas. For the purposes of the analysis carried out here, religion has been used as a marker of ethnic sub-group. This involves focusing on three main groups: Hindus; Sikhs; and Muslims. Where possible, a fourth group has also been considered, Indian Christians (for some of the analyses here this group was too small in size to be reliably used for comparisons). Other studies, which have used an analysis of names to determine ethnic (sub-) group, have tended to include Indian Christians in a white group on the basis that: 'Anglo-Indians and Indians with English names (mostly Christians)... probably have a lifestyle similar to that of people of English descent' (Balarajan *et al.* 1984:1185) and: 'Counting "Anglo-Indian" as British is justified by their way of life and easy entry to the UK, governed as it is by having a British parent or grandparent' (Marmot *et al.* 1984:9). This perspective clearly prejudges the explanatory focus of the analysis that is to be undertaken (i.e. that it will be based on cultural factors) and when exploring the diversity of health experience among Indians in Britain it seems useful to include, rather than exclude, a group whose family origins are Indian and who are Christians.

USING THE FOURTH NATIONAL SURVEY TO COMPARE THE HEALTH OF ETHNIC SUB-GROUPS

As explained earlier, religion is used as the marker for determining ethnic sub-group. Indians and African Asians are considered jointly as both groups describe their family origins as Indian and combing these groups gives a large enough sample size for such an analysis to be carried out. Also, as shown in Chapter 2, these two groups have similar levels of ill health across a variety of dimensions. However, it should be noted that the categories of Indian and African Asian are related to religion. As shown in Table 4.1, Indians were more likely to be Sikhs than African Asians who, in turn, were more likely to be Hindus or Muslims. The table also shows that a small percentage of respondents in these ethnic groups said that they had no religion or a religion other than Hindu, Sikh, Muslim or Christian. This group is almost certainly heterogeneous in make-up and, consequently, is not considered separately in this section, although these respondents are included in the totals in the following figures.

Table 4.1   Religion for Indians and African Asians

column percentages

	Indian	African Asian	Total
Religion			
Hindu	33	58	42
Sikh	50	19	38
Muslim	6	15	9
Christian	5	3	4
Other or none	6	5	6
Weighted base	*1292*	*799*	*2091*
Unweighted base	*1273*	*728*	*2001*

The comparisons between the religious groups have not been standardised for age and gender, since differences between the groups were only minor. However, it is worth bearing in mind that the Hindu group had slightly more men than the other groups (52 per cent compared to 50 per cent for all Indian/African Asians) and that the Sikh group was slightly younger than the other groups (median age for Sikhs was 34 compared to 36 for all Indian/African Asians).

Self-assessed general health

All respondents were asked two questions about their general health. The first asked the respondent to rate his or her health on a five point scale ranging from very poor to excellent. Figure 4.7 shows that Muslims were more likely to report that their health was fair or poor than other groups. This is confirmed in Figure 4.8, which

Figure 4.7   Reported fair or poor health by religious group for Indians/African Asians

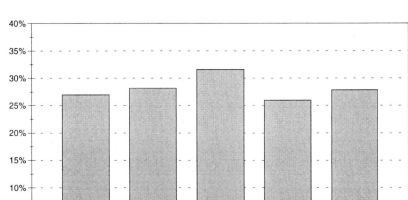

*Includes those with another or no religion

Figure 4.8   Reported long-standing illness by religious group for Indians/African Asians

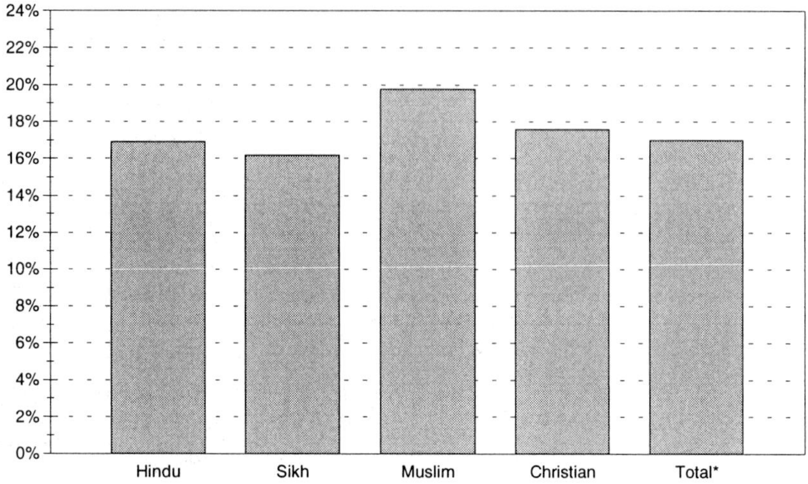

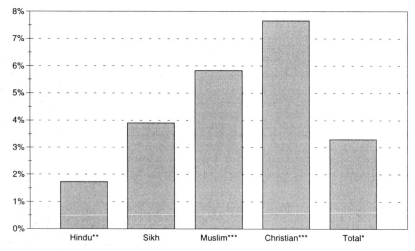

*Includes those with another or no religion

shows that Muslims were more likely than others to report that they had a long-standing illness. However, the differences in both of these figures were not statistically significant.

Figure 4.9   Diagnosed heart disease by religious group for Indians/African Asians

*Includes those with another or no religion
**P < 0.001 compared to other religious groups
***P < 0.05 compared to other religious groups

Figure 4.10   **Diagnosed heart disease or severe chest pain by religious group for Indians/African Asians**

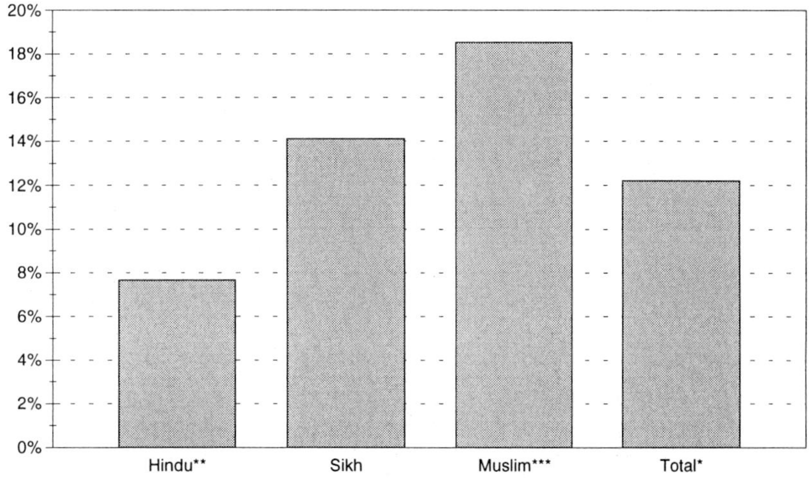

*Includes those with another or no religion
**p < 0.01 compared to other religious groups
***p < 0.05 compared to other religious groups

Heart disease

All respondents were asked whether they had had angina or 'a heart attack – including a heart murmur, a damaged heart or a rapid heart'. Figure 4.9 includes respondents who said that they had had either of these. It shows that Muslims and Christians were more likely than others to have had diagnosed heart disease, and that Hindus were less likely. The differences shown in this figure were all statistically significant.

In addition to questions on the diagnosis of heart disease, respondents aged 40 or more were asked questions about the experience of severe chest pain. Figure 4.10 shows respondents who had had either diagnosed heart disease or severe chest pain (it does not include Christians because there were too few in this age group). As in Figure 4.9, Muslims were more likely than others and Hindus were less likely than others to meet these criteria. The differences shown in response to these questions were statistically significant.

Other specific illness

Figure 4.11 shows the percentage of respondents who reported that they had had hypertension. Although the differences shown were not significant, there is a suggestion that Hindus were less likely and Christians were more likely than others to have had hypertension.

Figure 4.11 Hypertension by religious group for Indians/African Asians

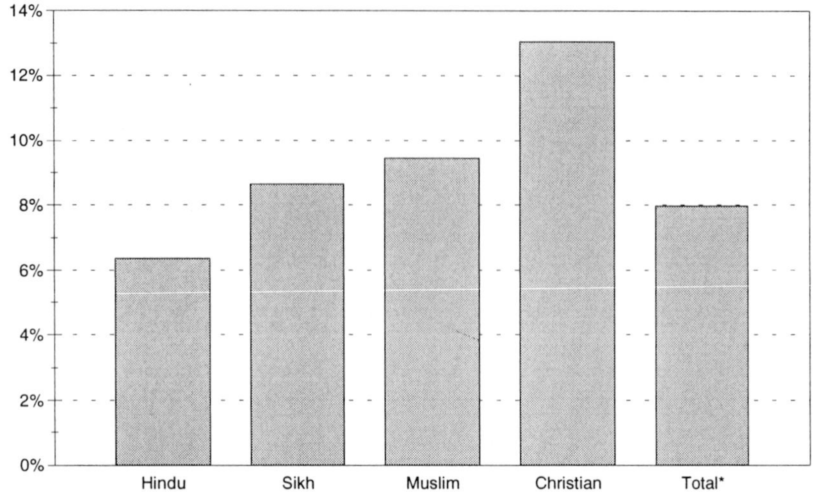

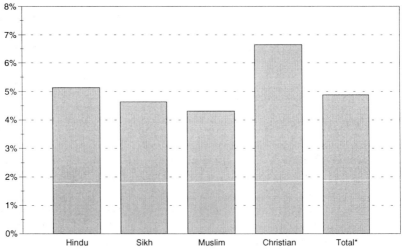

*Includes those with another or no religion

Figure 4.12 shows that Christians were also more likely to have reported that they had diabetes and, unlike the situation for all of the other assessments of health reported in this section, Muslims were the least likely to have reported that they had had diabetes. Again the differences shown in Figure 4.12 were not statistically significant.

Figure 4.12 Diabetes by religious group for Indians/African Asians

*Includes those with another or no religion

Figure 4.13 Respiratory symptoms by religious group for Indians/African Asians

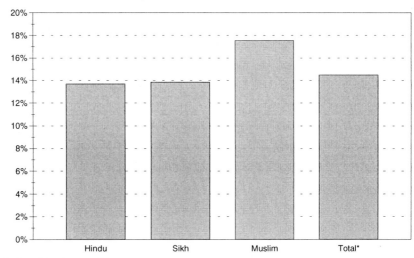

*Includes those with another or no religion

Half of the respondents were asked whether they had had a variety of respiratory symptoms. Figure 4.13 shows the percentage of respondents who reported that they either had a wheeze or had coughed up phlegm for at least three months of the year. Muslims were more likely than others to have reported these symptoms, although again the differences were not statistically significant. (Christians were not included because there were too few in the half of the sample who were asked this question for results for them to be considered reliable.)

Health-related behaviour

Half of the ethnic minority sample were asked questions on smoking, drinking alcohol and use of paan (as these questions were only asked of half of the sample, there are too few Christians for them to be included as a separate group). Figure 4.14 shows the percentage of respondents who reported that they had ever smoked. Muslims were more likely than the other groups to have smoked and Sikhs, whose religion is anti-smoking, were the least likely. Both of these differences were statistically significant.

Figure 4.15 shows whether the respondent reported drinking alcohol. Not surprisingly Muslims were much (and statistically significantly) less likely than others to have reported drinking alcohol, although they were slightly more likely than the predominantely Muslim populations from Pakistan and Bangladesh to have said that they were drinkers (see Table 2.15).

Figure 4.16 shows responses to the question asking respondents if they had ever used paan. Sikhs were much less likely than the others to say that they had used paan and this difference was statistically significant.

Figure 4.14 Whether ever smoked by religious group for Indians/African Asians

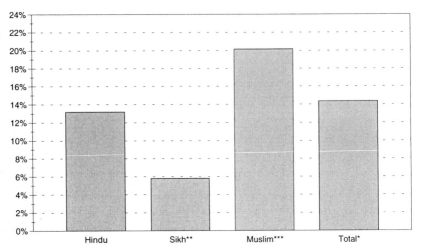

*Includes those with another or no religion
**p < 0.001 compared to other religious groups
***p < 0.01 compared to other religious groups

Figure 4.15 Alcohol consumption by religious group for Indians/African Asians

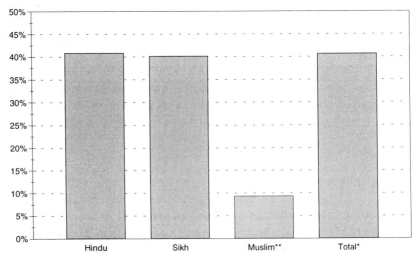

*Includes those with another or no religion
**p < 0.001 compared to other religious groups

Figure 4.16 Use of paan by religious group for Indians/African Asians

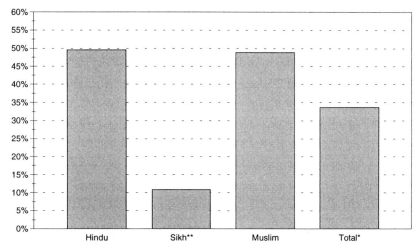

*Includes those with another or no religion
**p < 0.001 compared to other religious groups

Summary and implications of differences between religious groups

Figures 4.7 to 4.13 show the extent of variations in health by religious group for those with Indian family origins. The most striking differences were found for heart disease. Both Muslims and Christians reported higher rates of diagnosed heart disease than Hindus and Sikhs, and this finding was repeated for Muslims when, for those age 40 or older, either diagnosed heart disease or severe chest pain was considered. (There were too few Christians in this age group for them to be considered separately here.) Other assessments of health did not show statistically significant differences between groups. However, all but one – whether the respondent reported having diabetes – suggested that Muslims had worse health than Hindus and Sikhs. The consistency of this result across a variety of health indicators, together with the relatively small sample size of Muslims (285 respondents when the full sample is considered and 139 when half the sample is considered), suggests that there were genuine differences in the health of these groups. Indeed, as for the differences between migrants and non-migrants reported earlier, an inflexible interpretation of the lack of statistical significance for these health indicators (except those assessing heart disease) could lead to type II errors being made (where genuine differences are ignored (Blalock 1985)).

Differences in health-related behaviour showed even more striking differences between the religious groups. Muslims were the most likely to have ever smoked – one in five Muslims said that they had smoked, compared to about one in eight Hindus and only one in seventeen Sikhs. In contrast to this, two in five Hindus and Sikhs said that they drank alcohol compared to less than one in ten Muslims. The use of paan also showed differences, with just over one in ten Sikhs saying that they had ever used it compared to almost one in two Hindus and Muslims. This pattern of response has parallels with findings presented in Table 2.16, which shows Pakistanis, who are from a geographically related area to Sikhs, although members of a different religious group, had a similar rate of paan use to Sikhs, that African Asians had a similar rate of paan use to that reported by Hindus and Indian/African Asian Muslims, and that Indians had a rate somewhere between the Pakistani and African Asian rates. This suggests that variations in paan use in the Indian/African Asian group (and South Asians as whole) may be a regional rather than religious effect, despite the fact that it has been uncovered using a religious ethnic classification. This possibility highlights the difficulties that exist when interpreting the findings for variations in health by ethnic (sub-)group, problems exist in identifying what the associated risk factors are unless they have been clearly identified in the research process. These difficulties will be discussed further next, but what is clear from these data is that considering ethnic groupings as internally homogeneous, whether they are based on continent of birth, country of birth or country of family origin, is potentially misleading. Evidence presented here confirms the conclusions drawn in Chapters 2 and 3, that there are important differences in both health and health behaviour *within* these ethnic groupings.

DISCUSSION

Chapters 2 and 3 clearly illustrated that the use of overarching ethnic categories, such as South Asian, are misleading when considering ethnic variations in health. Classifying those within the South Asian group by their country of family origin showed a diversity of health experiences within this group, with those with Indian and African Asian family origins having much better health across a variety of dimensions than those with Pakistani and Bangladeshi family origins. The data presented here show that this process can be taken at least one step further. By classifying Indians and African Asians according to their religion – which for Hindus and Sikhs is closely related to geographical origin within India – differences in health and health-related behaviour emerged. These differences were particularly striking for heart disease, where they were statistically significant, but were also consistent across virtually all of the health outcomes covered. The apparent usefulness of this approach raises the question of how much further the process of refining a classification scheme for ethnicity should be taken and whether such refining really is as useful as it appears.

As described in the introduction to this volume, one of the purposes of exploring ethnic variations in health and health-related behaviour is to inform those who are responsible for providing health care. Such care should be acceptable and accessible to groups with very different cultural backgrounds and should be targeted to meet their diverse needs. Consequently, an understanding of the differences in health and health-related behaviour between ethnic groups should be of great use to the process of health care provision, so attempts to identify the needs of ethnic sub-groups should also be beneficial. In fact, Chapter 6 of this volume is concerned with exploring differences in the use and experience of health services for different ethnic groups in Britain.

However, the two other reasons for exploring ethnic variations in health, also described in Chapter 1, need to be considered. The first of these was clearly laid out by Marmot *et al.* (1984), who saw work on the epidemiology of ill-health across different ethnic groups to have a direct bearing on an understanding of the aetiology of diseases that showed a variation:

> Comparisons of disease rates between immigrants and non-immigrants in the 'old' country, between immigrants and residents of the 'new' country, and between different immigrant groups in the new country have helped elucidate the relative importance of genetic and environmental factors in many diseases. (Marmot *et al.* 1984:4)

To this list of comparisons we can add that between migrant and non-migrant ethnic minority groups, while to the list of explanatory factors we can add factors related to cultural differences. Further refining the classification of ethnicity used in such epidemiological work would no doubt improve its power. However, in this work 'environmental factors' are rarely assessed and explanation is often based on genetic and cultural factors. This is because their existence, while often also not measured, can easily be assumed (see Sheldon and Parker (1992) and Bhopal (1995) for critiques of this 'Black Box' approach to epidemiology). In this context, it would not be helpful to refine an ethnic classification scheme in a way that allows further assumptions to be made about the importance of culture and genetics while neither are measured and environment continues to be ignored.

Similar issues arise when considering the third reason for exploring ethnic variations in health. In our desire to investigate, describe and explain the position of ethnic minority groups in Britain, health is a crucial experience. Ethnic minority groups' experiences across a number of dimensions – such as economic position, housing, and racial discrimination and harassment – are described in *Ethnic Minorities in Britain: Diversity and Disadvantage* (Modood *et al.* 1997). As the title implies, this report shows that, like ill-health, the extent of other forms of disadvantage varies between ethnic minority groups. However, while a description of health disadvantage is an important part of this overall investigation into the disadvantages faced by ethnic minority groups in Britain, a descriptive approach adds little to an understanding of the reasons for such disadvantages. In fact, if anything, such a process only aids in the racialisation of the issue of ethnic variations in health. As explained above, when describing how health varies across ethnic (sub-)groups it becomes easy to attribute disadvantages to inherent properties of the ethnic group itself, such as culture or race, without considering the context in which health disadvantage exists. And more sophisticated assessments of ethnicity potentially allow this racialisation to be taken further.

An example of this process can be seen in attempts to understand the high rate of coronary heart disease among South Asians. A *British Medical Journal* editorial (Gupta *et al.* 1995) used existing research to attribute this problem to a combination of genetic and cultural factors that are apparently associated with being South Asian. In terms of cultural factors, the use of ghee in cooking, a lack of physical exercise and a reluctance to use health services were all mentioned – despite the fact that the use of ghee is hardly universal across all of the ethnic groups that comprise South Asians, and evidence presented here and elsewhere suggests that South Asians do use medical services (Chapter 6 of this volume, Rudat 1994) and do understand the importance of exercise (Beishon and Nazroo 1997). The ease with which a de-contextualised description of ethnic variations in health can lead to the use of explanations based on (often unfounded) cultural stereotypes or suppositions about genetic differences is of crucial importance to attempts to further refine ethnic classifications. Data presented in Chapters 2 and 3 clearly show that Pakistanis and Bangladeshis had a high risk of heart disease compared to both whites and other South Asians (Tables 2.7 and 2.8, and Figures 3.11 and 3.12). Data presented in this chapter show that among Indians and African Asians, who generally have an average risk of heart disease (Figures 3.11 and 3.12) Hindus had a low rate, Sikhs had an average rate and Muslims had a high rate (Figure 4.10). On the one hand, such an approach is useful in uncovering the extent to which this issue has been racialised. However, on the other hand, rather than 'South Asian heart disease' we could now use the term 'Muslim heart disease', or 'Pakistani and Bangladeshi heart disease', to describe the situation, and explanations could be sought in assumptions about Muslim, Pakistani and Bangladeshi cultural practices or their shared evolutionary history.

It is important to recognise that this parody is not intended to imply that cultural or genetic factors are of no use in explaining ethnic variations in health. Indeed, Chapter 3 goes some way towards explaining ethnic variations in respiratory symptoms by exploring differences in the culturally related practice of smoking (see Figures 3.18 and 3.19). Rather, cultural practices and genetic differences need to be directly assessed, rather than assumed, and their association with health outcomes measured. In addition, other explanatory factors need to be considered. Given the pattern of socio-economic deprivation faced by ethnic minority groups in Britain (Modood *et al.* 1997) and the clearly established relationship between socio-economic factors and health (Townsend and Davidson 1982, Blaxter 1990, Davey-Smith *et al.* 1990a, Benzeval *et al.* 1995), it seems that the most important context that needs to be taken into account when explaining ethnic variations in health is socio-economic position, although other aspects of the environment, such as the impact of racism (Benzeval *et al.* 1992) and the geographical locations of ethnic minority groups in Britain (Robinson 1989, Owen 1994) are also worth considering.

In fact, the comparison between migrant and non-migrant ethnic minority groups presented in the first half of the chapter emphasised the need to consider environmental context when considering ethnic variations in health. Figures 4.1 to 4.4 show that ethnic minority people who migrated aged 11 or older were healthy than those who were born in Britain or who migrated younger than 11, while Figures 4.5 and 4.6 show that they were also less likely to smoke and drink alcohol. Differences in health-related behaviours are almost certainly related to differences in the cultural context of migrants' and non-migrants' childhoods. In addition, differences in the health of these two groups could be related to either, or both, of two other factors. First, they could be the result of more healthy individuals being selected into groups that migrate, an effect that wears off with subsequent generations. This possibility is consistent with both the data presented here and that presented by Marmot *et al.* (1984). Second, they could be the result of a negative impact of the British environment on the health of ethnic minority groups – perhaps particularly those who spent their early childhood in Britain. Again, this could be a result of greater poverty, living in disadvantaged inner-city environments or experiences of discrimination and harassment. This possibility is strengthened by evidence suggesting that the length of time spent in Britain is directly related to poorer health for migrants from South Asia living in Glasgow (Williams 1993), with the implication that something about the British environment is damaging their health.

CHAPTER FIVE

Explaining the Relationship Between Ethnicity and Health: the Importance of Socio-Economic Factors

INTRODUCTION

Chapters 2 to 4 demonstrate clear ethnic variations in health. If ethnic minorities in Britain as a whole are considered, on most indicators of general health they show poorer health than the white majority. However, this pattern is not uniform across the ethnic minority groups that are represented in the sample used for this survey. Across virtually all of the dimensions considered, the health of Chinese, Indian and African Asian respondents was similar to that of whites and better than that of other ethnic minority groups. In contrast, Caribbeans, Pakistanis and Bangladeshis reported poorer health than whites. These findings clearly indicate that members of ethnic minority groups cannot be considered to be uniformly disadvantaged in respect of their health and, consequently, investigations of the health of ethnic minority people need to carefully consider which groups they are studying. In addition, these findings suggest a need to consider the extent to which factors that may result in a health disadvantage might vary across ethnic minority groups.

A number of factors may play an important role in determining ethnic variations in health. These include the following possibilities: they are an artefact resulting from the way data have been collected; they are a result of cultural differences between ethnic groups; they are a consequence of biological/genetic differences in risk; health-related selection into a migrant group or the consequences of migration itself might be responsible; they are a direct consequence of racism; or they are the result of the relationship between socio-economic status and both health and ethnicity. (See Smaje (1995a) for a detailed discussion of most of these possibilities, but note that to date there has only been limited empirical exploration of these issues.)

Concerns that uncovered ethnic variations in health are a result of an artefact of the way in which data have been collected have largely centred around the possibility that members of ethnic minority groups are under-counted in the population from which statistics are calculated – producing a smaller denominator in the calculation of the percentage and consequently elevating the per cent of the population who are ill. An alternative possibility is that members of ethnic minority groups are over/under-counted in the ill group, perhaps as a result of being more or less likely to be treated than equivalent white people. Given the population-based, rather than treatment-based, nature of the sample used here, the first of these concerns does not apply to the data presented in this volume. The second of these concerns might have some bearing on the questions concerning the diagnosis of, rather than symptoms of, particular conditions, especially where the condition may be asymptomatic, as in the case of hypertension. A further concern regarding the quality of the data may, however, apply. This is that members of different ethnic groups may interpret differently and respond differently to the same questions about their health. This possibility was examined in some detail in Chapter 3 for the questions on general health, and it was concluded that one of the questions used, whether the respondent had a long-standing illness, did in fact have this problem. This clearly is an issue that merits consideration, although as far as it has been possible to explore the validity of the questions used here, the evidence suggests that they operate consistently across the ethnic groups under consideration (see Chapter 1).

The contribution that biological/genetic factors and cultural factors might have made to the ethnic variations in health reported here could not be directly considered. Biological indicators could not be estimated in a survey of this kind. Cultural factors relating to health, such as diet, are also difficult to estimate so, with the exception of smoking, no attempt was made. Although, factors relating to both culture and biology are commonly used as explanations for the health disadvantage of particular ethnic groups, just as in this survey, they are rarely assessed. This means that postulated cultural and biological differences are assumed rather than directly considered, and assumed on the basis of cultural/biological stereotypes (Ahmad (1993b) provides a useful critique of this approach). So, once other factors have been 'controlled' for,[1] culture and biology are used to explain 'residual' differences between ethnic groups in ethnocentric and simplistic ways, which rely on notions of culture and biology that are divorced from the contexts in which they might operate.

Of course there may be some merit in considering cultural or biological factors as important, particularly insofar as they might be related to, and interact with, other factors of importance, such as socio-economic status. However, it seems unlikely that they would play the key role in explaining the overall health disadvantage of Caribbean, Pakistani and Bangladeshi ethnic groups compared to the white, Indian, African Asian and Chinese groups This is because the cultural and biological variations between the different 'unhealthy' ethnic groups and between the different 'healthy' ethnic groups are likely to be just as great as the variations across the 'unhealthy' and 'healthy' divide.

The most researched example of a biological/genetic explanation is the 'insulin resistance syndrome', which has been the focus of a number of researchers (e.g. McKeigue 1992, Knight *et al.* 1992). Here it is postulated that the evolutionary development of a 'thrifty' gene in South Asian populations, to deal with inconsistent food supplies, has led to a greater likelihood for these ethnic groups to develop both non-insulin dependent diabetes and coronary heart disease. This appears to be an

---

1   Later in the chapter there is a discussion of the process of controlling out 'confounding' factors to expose an ethnicity/race effect.

attractive biological/genetic explanation for ethnic variations in coronary heart disease, which to date have been considered to be greater for all South Asian groups. However, given the data presented in Chapters 2 and 3, which demonstrate that the greater South Asian risk could be entirely attributed to the greater risk of Pakistanis and Bangladeshis, and that insulin resistance has been shown to be elevated in all South Asian groups, rather than being a specific risk for Pakistanis and Bangladeshis (McKeigue *et al.* 1991), this biological/genetic explanation might not be as important as anticipated. However, it is worth considering the ability of the insulin resistance hypothesis to survive evidence that showed that Caribbeans had high rates of non-insulin dependent diabetes and low rates of coronary heart disease. Its proponents (e.g. Shaukat and Cruickshank 1993) did this by suggesting that the high rates of diabetes might be a result of insulin deficiency rather than insulin resistance for Caribbeans, or that the component of insulin that caused coronary heart disease for South Asians was not to be found in Caribbean insulin.

Explanations around migration were considered in the previous chapter. Particularly important here is the possibility that ethnic minority groups have poorer health than the indigenous population either because of problems directly associated with the process of migration, such as the cultural dislocation that may result or the stresses that may occur, or because of greater environmental deprivation in migrants' country of birth. However, the previous chapter showed that ethnic minority people who were migrants had, if anything, better health than those who were born in Britain. This of course might be evidence for the hypothesis of positive health selection into migrant groups, or that the British environment was damaging to the health of ethnic minorities.

In addition to racism and discrimination possibly having an effect on health as a result of consequent socio-economic disadvantage, it is also possible that the experience of racial discrimination and harassment might have a direct detrimental effect on health. For example, Benzeval *et al.* (1992) demonstrated that experiencing racial harassment was significantly associated with reported acute illness (after controlling for other relevant variables) and that experiencing any form of discrimination at work was significantly associated with both acute and long-standing illness. However, in terms of explaining the pattern of results presented here, Chapter 7 in the main report of the *Fourth National Survey* (Modood *et al.* 1997) shows that variations across ethnic minority groups in the reported experiences of racial harassment did not match those for health. For example, Bangladeshi respondents were less likely than both African Asian and Chinese respondents to report that they had been racially harassed.

Poorer access to health care services might also help explain the poorer health of certain ethnic groups. However, Chapter 6 in this volume shows that ethnic minority respondents reported using primary health care services more often than white respondents, even after their reported level of health had been controlled for – although the quality of the care received may not have matched that for white respondents.

Although the review of the evidence for the possibilities so far discussed suggests that they are not crucial to explaining the described ethnic variations in health, it is by no means a robust rejection of their contribution. In fact, each does warrant a far more detailed exploration. However, given the clearly documented relationship between socio-economic status and health (see for example, Townsend and Davidson 1982, Blaxter 1987 and 1990, Davey-Smith *et al.* 1990a, Benzeval *et al.* 1995) and the relatively deprived position of many ethnic minority groups, it seems that any exploration of ethnic variations in health needs to seriously consider socio-economic effects. Table 5.1 looks at some indicators of socio-economic status for this sample, showing the class distributions of different ethnic minority groups, together with their unemployment rates and the number that live in poor housing.

Table 5.1   Socio-economic status

column percentages

	White	Caribbean	Indian	African Asian	Pakistani	Bangladeshi	Chinese
Registrar General's Class							
I/II	35	22	30	35	20	11	40
IIIn	15	18	19	23	15	18	26
IIIm	31	30	21	23	32	32	20
IV	20	30	30	19	33	40	13
Weighted base	*2364*	*1402*	*1133*	*723*	*618*	*190*	*334*
Unweighted base	*2239*	*1057*	*1122*	*650*	*856*	*406*	*187*
Per cent of economically active unemployed	11	24	16	13	38	42	7
Weighted base	*1727*	*1102*	*753*	*555*	*405*	*123*	*257*
Unweighted base	*1603*	*814*	*747*	*491*	*564*	*248*	*143*
Per cent lacking one or more basic housing amenities*	16	17	19	10	39	32	19
Weighted base	*2867*	*1567*	*1292*	*799*	*862*	*285*	*391*
Unweighted base	*2867*	*1205*	*1273*	*728*	*1185*	*591*	*214*

* i.e. excluse use of: bath or shower; bathroom; inside toilet; kitchen; hot water from a tap; and central heating.

Across all three of these dimensions of socio-economic status both the Chinese and African Asian groups compared favourably to whites, Indians were similar to, but slightly worse off than, whites, and Caribbeans, Pakistanis and Bangladeshis were clearly worse off, with Bangladeshis the most disadvantaged. The fact that variations in socio-economic status across ethnic groups follow the pattern for health, while the other explanatory factors do not, adds weight to the suggestion that this may, on prima facie grounds, be a fruitful avenue to explore.

However, attempts to explore the relationship between socio-economic status, ethnicity and health have generally not lent support to this perspective. For example, Marmot *et al.*'s (1984) classic study of immigrant mortality found that for both overall mortality rates and those for specific causes of death there was no, or an inconsistent, relationship with the Registrar General's class for most immigrant groups. Indeed, for one group, those born in the 'Caribbean Commonwealth', the relationship between class and overall mortality rates was the opposite of that for the general population. In addition to this, Marmot *et al.* (1984) found that once they had controlled for class, ethnic differences in mortality rates remained the same, leading them to conclude that: 'differences in social class distribution are not the explanation of the overall different mortality of migrants' (21). Other studies have also failed to find a relationship between socio-economic status and health within certain ethnic groups for specific illnesses (e.g. Clarke *et al.* 1988) and they have also found that standardising for socio-economic status across ethnic groups did not greatly diminish the relationship between ethnicity and health, even if within ethnic groups there was an association between socio-economic status and health (e.g. Fenton *et al.* 1995, Smaje 1995b). (However, Ahmad *et al.* (1989) were able to show that once unemployment had been controlled for, South Asian men living in Bradford had better, rather than worse, health than their white counterparts.)

It is possible, however, that both the within and between group negative findings for the relationship between socio-economic status and health are a result of an overly crude assessment of ethnicity (such as the use of country of birth in immigrant mortality data) and the use of socio-economic indicators that inadequately reflect the position of ethnic minority groups. In fact, there has been an increasing recognition of the limitations of traditional class groupings, which are far from internally homogeneous. A number of studies have drawn attention to variations in income levels and death rates among the occupations that comprise each occupational class (e.g. Davey Smith *et al.* 1990b). And within an occupational group, ethnic minorities may be more likely to be found in lower or less prestigious occupational grades, to have poorer job security, to endure more stressful working conditions and to be more likely to work unsocial hours. Bartley's (1994) work, which demonstrates that those who have insecure work or who have been obliged to take on low status jobs have a similar risk of poor health to the unemployed, illustrates the significance of this.

Alternative measures of material circumstances, which are easy to collect and apparently universally applicable, have also been used as socio-economic indicators in epidemiological work; typically housing tenure and car ownership. An increasing number of studies report large variations in health associated with these measures of socio-economic status (e.g. Townsend *et al.* 1988). However, advocates of the use of such measures have often failed to consider how ethnicity interacts with them. For example, the proportion of home owners is higher in most South Asian groups than among whites, but the quality of their accommodation tends to be poor (Brown 1984, Modood *et al.* 1997). In fact, the most disadvantaged, who undoubtedly include a large proportion of certain ethnic minority groups, probably suffer disproportionately from the cumulative impact of different forms of deprivation, an effect which cannot be identified by a one-dimensional indicator of socio-economic status.

Thought also needs to be given to the possibility that relative deprivation may play a role in producing the poorer health of ethnic minority groups, in addition to that played by absolute deprivation. Here it is suggested that inequality in social position in itself can damage health, perhaps as a result of psychological processes that operate when social comparisons are made (Wilkinson 1994). There is growing evidence to support this possibility, for example Ben-Shlomo *et al.* (1996) showed that the extent of *variation in income* in a location was related to increased mortality rates even after the relationship between average income in the location and mortality rates had been accounted for. It seems likely that the process of social comparison will be of more significance to the health of ethnic minority groups than the general population, as any social comparison made by ethnic minority people will clearly illustrate the obvious inequalities, discrimination, and racism, that they face in virtually every sphere of their lives (Modood *et al.* 1997).

It is also likely that much of the material, social and psychological disadvantage faced by ethnic minorities is structured by their geographical location, which differs markedly from that of the white population. Over 60 per cent of ethnic minorities live in the urban areas of Greater London, West Yorkshire and the West Midlands, where only 18 per cent of the total white population live (Owen 1994). There are even greater differences when smaller areas are considered, more than half of ethnic minority people live in areas where the total ethnic minority population exceeds 44 per cent (Owen 1994). There has been a great deal of research into the extent to which socio-economic variations in health are the result of the attributes of the areas where people live rather than the characteristics of individuals themselves (Townsend *et al.* 1988, Humphrey and Carr-Hill 1991, Macintyre *et al.* 1993, Sloggett and Joshi 1994). Aspects of the physical and social environment may influence both mental and physical health by influencing attitudes, structuring social interaction, limiting access to resources and increasing exposure to hazards (Robinson 1989). For example, Macintyre *et al.* (1993) found that middle-class compared to working-class areas in Glasgow had easier access to, and cheaper, healthy food, more sporting and recreational facilities within easy reach, more extensive primary health services and lower perceived crime risk.

The particular urban locations of the majority of ethnic minority people make them far more likely to have poor access to employment opportunities, good housing and other services, despite attempts to link resource allocation to patterns of deprivation (Robinson 1989). These areas may also be more likely to be subjected to pollution and other environmental toxins that will have a detrimental impact on health. On the other hand, there is evidence to suggest that the concentration of ethnic minority groups in particular locations may be protective of health, allowing the development of a community with a strong ethnic identity that enhances social support, reduces the sense of alienation, increases the group's access to political power and protects against the direct effects of racism (Halpern 1993, Smaje 1995b).

THE IMPACT OF CLASS AND TENURE WITHIN ETHNIC GROUPS

Clearly the issues discussed in the introduction to this chapter require detailed consideration and the data available from the Fourth National Survey provide a unique opportunity to do this. To begin with the relationship between two standard indicators of socio-economic status – class and tenure – and the health assessments for each of the ethnic groups is explored. For tenure a simple distinction between owner-occupiers and renters is made. For class a distinction is drawn between households that are manual and those that are non-manual, according to the

Registrar General's criteria,[2] and, in addition to this, a third group of respondents from households containing no full-time worker is included (for reasons described later, respondents aged 65 or older have not been included in this analysis). Once these issues have been explored the limitations of these standard indicators of socio-economic status for making comparisons across ethnic groups are examined, and a possible way forward is developed. This shows how controlling for socio-economic status in different ways alters the extent of ethnic variations in health.

The health indicators used here reflect the broad topics covered in earlier chapters and include: self assessed health compared to others of the same age; diagnosed heart disease; diagnosed heart disease or severe chest pain; hypertension; diabetes; and symptoms suggestive of respiratory disease. Some health related behaviours, smoking and alcohol use, have also been included as this allows some exploration of the inter-relationships between socio-economic status and culture.

Once again the data presented in this chapter have been age and gender standardised to allow for immediate comparisons across both socio-economic and ethnic groups. As explained in Chapter 3, this means that certain ethnic groups have had to be combined – Indians are combined with African Asians, and Pakistanis are combined with Bangladeshis. In addition, Chinese respondents cannot be considered separately, because of extremely small numbers of respondents in particular age/class/gender weighting cells, although they are included in the 'All Ethnic Minorities' group. Similarly, because of small numbers in particular weighting cells, the 65 and older age group have also not been included, which means that these data are not directly comparable with those shown in earlier chapters. Much of the data presented here is in the form of figures. Tables containing the raw data upon which these figures are derived can be found in Appendix D.

General health

Respondents were asked to rate their health in comparison with others of the same age on a five point scale ranging from very poor to very good. Figure 5.1 shows the percentage of respondents in each ethnic group who said that they had fair, poor or very poor health by whether they lived in a household that had no full-time worker, or was manual or non-manual. It shows a very clear relationship between this indicator of general health and socio-economic status for all ethnic groups. Interestingly, the difference between individuals in manual and non-manual households appears to be much more marked for ethnic minority respondents than white respondents.

Figure 5.2 looks at how responses to the same question varied between those who rented their accommodation and those who owned it. Those who owned their homes were less likely than those who rented to report fair or worse health for all of the ethnic groups.

---

2   Class was assigned using the head of the household's occupation. Where it was not clear which household member was the head of the household (e.g. where there was more than one working adult), class was allocated on the basis of gender (with men's occupations being used in preference to women's) and age (e.g. a father's occupations being used in preference to a son's if the father was below retirement age).

Figure 5.1   Reported fair or poor health by class

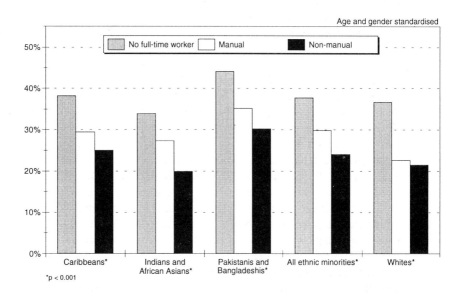

Age and gender standardised

No full-time worker   Manual   Non-manual

*p < 0.001

Figure 5.2   Reported fair or poor health by tenure

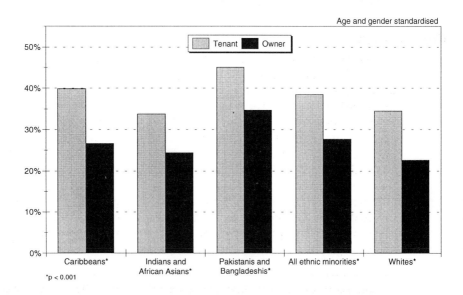

Age and gender standardised

Tenant   Owner

*p < 0.001

Figure 5.3   Diagnosed heart disease by class

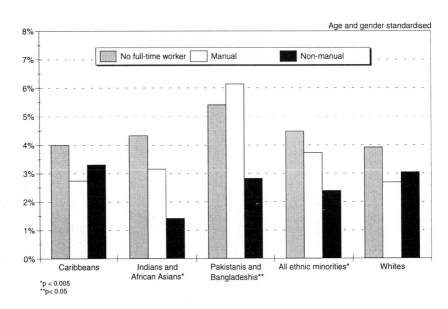

Heart disease

Figures 5.3 and 5.4 show the percentage of respondents who reported a diagnosis of angina or heart attack within each ethnic group by class and tenure respectively. They show a similar pattern to that for self-assessed general health, although not

Figure 5.4   Diagnosed heart disease by tenure

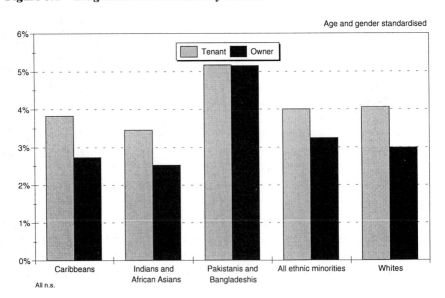

All n.s.

Figure 5.5　　**Diagnosed heart disease and severe chest pain by class**

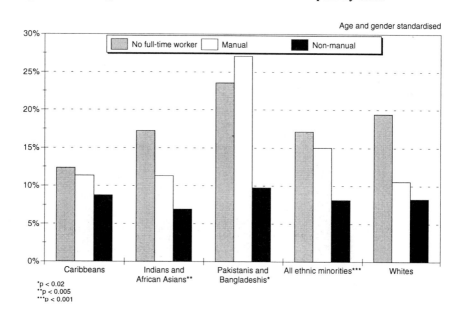

quite as clear. In Figure 5.3 the expected relationship between class and diagnosed heart disease is present for the Indian/African Asian, Pakistani/Bangladeshi and All Ethnic Minorities groups. However, for the Caribbean and white groups, individuals in non-manual households were more likely to report a diagnosis of heart disease than those in manual households.

Figure 5.4 shows that home owners were less likely to report diagnosed heart disease than renters for all of the ethnic groups except Pakistani/Bangladeshis, although none of the differences shown were statistically significant.

Respondents aged 40 or over were also asked questions about the experience of chest pain. Figure 5.5 shows that for all ethnic groups there was the expected relationship between class and either having a diagnosis of heart disease or experiencing severe chest pain, although for the Pakistani/Bangladeshi group those in households without a full-time worker were less likely than those in manual households to have reported one of these indicators of heart disease.

Figure 5.6 shows that home owners were less likely than those who rent to report either a diagnosis of heart disease or severe chest pain for all ethnic groups except Pakistani/Bangladeshis, although differences for Caribbeans were small.

Hypertension

Figure 5.7 shows the relationship between class and reporting a diagnosis of hypertension. Although for Indians/African Asians and whites those in households with no full-time worker were less likely than those in manual households to report such a diagnosis, and there was no difference between manual and non-manual

Figure 5.6   Diagnosed heart disease or severe chest pain by tenure

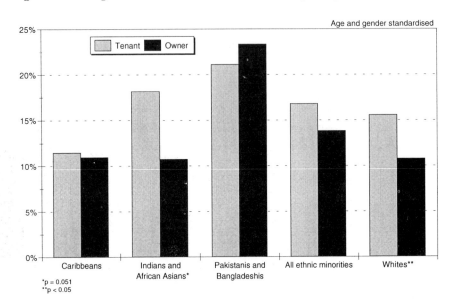

*p = 0.051
**p < 0.05

Caribbeans, overall the figure shows the expected inverse relationship between class and a diagnosis of hypertension.

Figure 5.8 confirms the relationship between socio-economic status and likelihood to have reported a diagnosis of hypertension for all ethnic groups, although the differences for the Caribbean group were again not statistically significant.

Figure 5.7   Hypertension by class

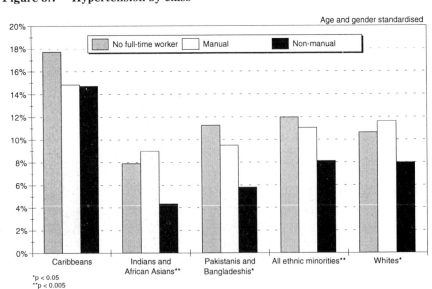

*p < 0.05
**p < 0.005

Figure 5.8   Hypertention by tenure

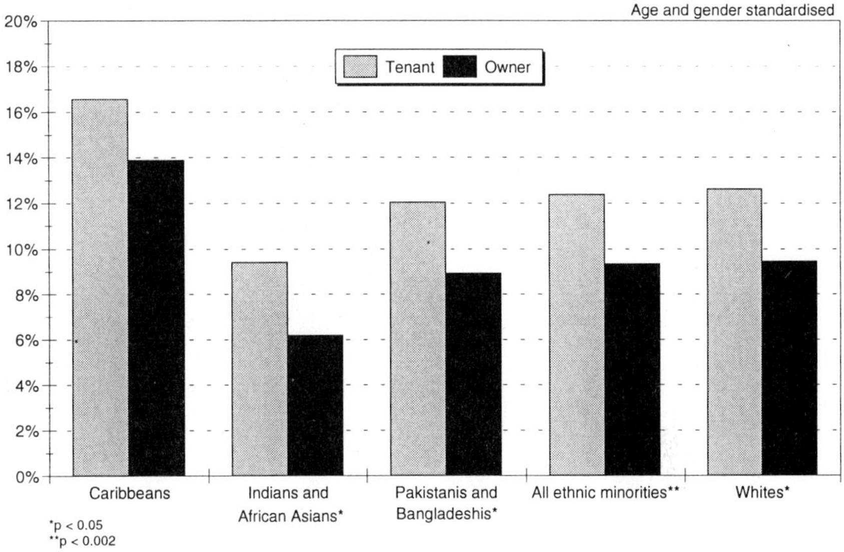

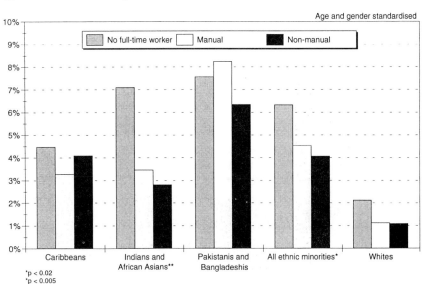

Age and gender standardised

Legend: Tenant ■ Owner

Categories: Caribbeans | Indians and African Asians* | Pakistanis and Bangladeshis* | All ethnic minorities** | Whites*

*p < 0.05
**p < 0.002

Diabetes

Figures 5.9 and 5.10 show the relationship between reporting a diagnosis of diabetes and class and tenure respectively. Although the relationship is not entirely consistent, Figure 5.9 does suggest that there was a relationship between class and such a diagnosis for all ethnic groups except, possibly, Caribbeans. This is confirmed

Figure 5.9   Diabetes by class

Age and gender standardised

Legend: No full-time worker | Manual | ■ Non-manual

Categories: Caribbeans | Indians and African Asians** | Pakistanis and Bangladeshis | All ethnic minorities* | Whites

*p < 0.02
*p < 0.005

Figure 5.10 Diabetes by tenure

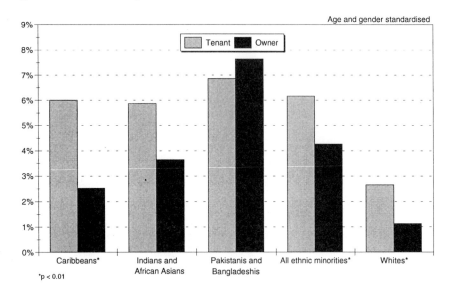

*p < 0.01

in Figure 5.10 which shows that for all groups except Pakistani/Bangladeshis, homeowners were less likely than renters to have reported a diagnosis of diabetes.

Respiratory disease

Half of the ethnic minority and all of the white respondents were asked a number of questions about symptoms relating to respiratory disease. Figures 5.11 and 5.12 show the percentage of respondents who reported that they either had a wheeze or had coughed up phlegm for at least three months of the year by class and tenure. Again, Figure 5.11 suggests a relationship between socio-economic status and respiratory symptoms, although it is not completely consistent. Figure 5.12 shows the relationship between socio-economic status and respiratory symptoms more clearly – for each ethnic group, those who owned their homes were less likely than renters to have reported respiratory symptoms.

Health-related behaviours

Figures 5.13 and 5.14 show the relationship between current regular smoking and class and tenure for each ethnic group. Figure 5.13 shows that those with no full-time worker in the home were more likely than those in manual homes to smoke and that those in non-manual homes were the least likely to smoke, although the relationship was not entirely consistent for the two South Asian groups.

This finding is confirmed in Figure 5.14, which shows that home owners were much less likely to be smokers than renters for all ethnic groups.

Figure 5.11 Respiratory symptoms by class

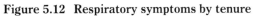

*p < 0.05
**p < 0.02
***p < 0.001

Figure 5.12 Respiratory symptoms by tenure

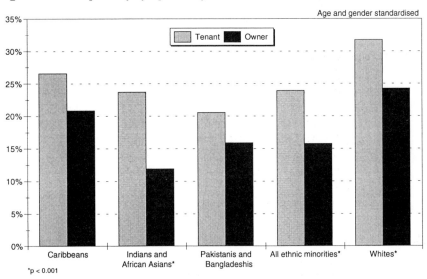

*p < 0.001

Findings for alcohol use show the opposite effect for all ethnic groups except Caribbeans. Figure 5.15 and 5.16 show that those in higher socio-economic groups were slightly less likely to drink alcohol for Caribbeans, while Figure 5.15 shows that for all of the other ethnic groups, those in non-manual households were slightly more likely to drink than others and Figure 5.16 shows that for Indian/African Asians and for whites, home owners were *more* likely to drink than renters.

Figure 5.13 Regular current smoking by class

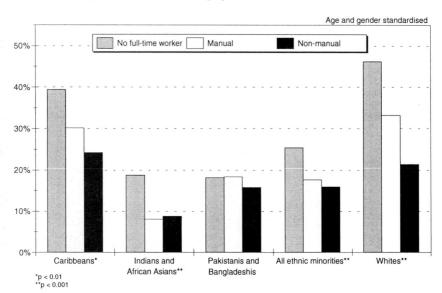

*p < 0.01
**p < 0.001

Figure 5.14 Regular current smoking by tenure

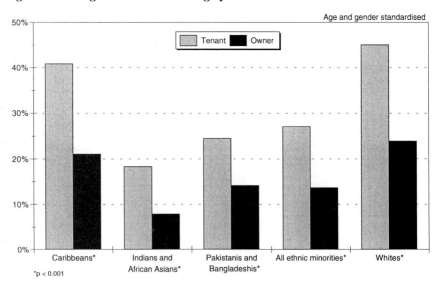

*p < 0.001

Summary

The data presented in Figures 5.1 to 5.12 show a reasonably clear and consistent relationship between socio-economic status and health for all of the main health indicators used in this survey and for each of the ethnic groups covered. This is much as might be expected from studies of the general population and, like such studies, tenure on the whole had a stronger and more consistent relationship with

Figure 5.15 Alcohol use by class

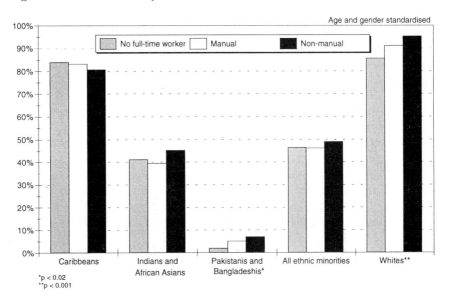

Figure 5.16 Alcohol use by tenure

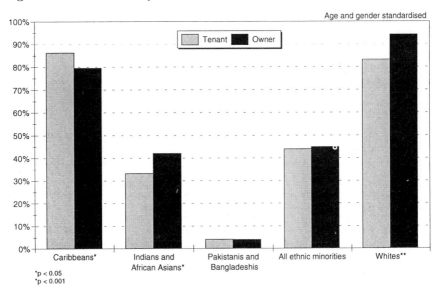

health outcomes than a combined indicator of Registrar General's class and unemployment (see, for example, Haynes 1991). Interestingly, however, the opposite was the case for the Pakistani/Bangladeshi group. Some thought needs to given to why such a clear relationship between socio-economic status and health emerges here, while it did not in the immigrant mortality data presented by Marmot *et al.* (1984). This is an issue which will be returned to in the conclusion to this chapter.

STANDARDISING FOR SOCIO-ECONOMIC EFFECTS FOR COMPARISONS ACROSS ETHNIC GROUPS

Given that there is such a strong relationship between socio-economic status and health within particular ethnic groups and there are important differences in the socio-economic positions of different ethnic groups (as illustrated in Table 5.1), it would seem to make sense to explore how far ethnic variations in health remain once socio-economic differences between ethnic groups had been controlled. This is the strategy adopted by Marmot *et al.* (1984), but, as previously described, they found that once they had standardised for class differences in the immigrant mortality data they used, ethnic variations in health remained more or less unchanged. A similar impression might be formed from the data presented in Figures 5.1 to 5.12. For example, in Figure 5.1, within each class group Pakistani/ Bangladeshis were more likely than the equivalent white group to report fair or poor health, and a similar pattern is found in Figure 5.2, which looks at the relationship between tenure and likelihood to report fair or poor health. Indeed, if all of the figures are looked at in this way, it seems that we should conclude that while there are important socio-economic effects within ethnic groups, differences between ethnic groups remain once these have been accounted for. That is, socio-economic factors do not explain ethnic variations in health.

However, some thought has to be given to how adequate variables such as class and tenure are for controlling out socio-economic effects when exploring ethnic variations in health. In effect, we have to ask ourselves whether individuals from different ethnic groups, but within the same broad socio-economic band – such as non-manual or owner-occupier – are really in an equivalent socio-economic position. As already discussed, it certainly seems likely that, as a result of the racialisation of disadvantage, within these broad bands ethnic minority groups will be worse off relative to the equivalent white group, suggesting that the use of such indicators of socio-economic status does not apply adequate controls when making comparisons across ethnic groups. This issue is explored empirically in Table 5.2.

The first part of Table 5.2 shows the mean equivalised household income for individuals within particular classes by ethnic group. This statistic needs to be treated with some caution for a number of reasons. First, a large number of individuals did not reply to the question asking about household income. Second, although the calculation is weighted to take into account the number of adults and children in the household, it is based on income bands rather than actual incomes. In order to perform the calculations the mid-point of each band has been taken, but this inevitably produces some inaccuracy, particularly if members of different ethnic groups are differentially located within the bands used. Nevertheless, the table does show that Caribbeans and Indian/African Asians appear to have similar locations within each class, while whites were better off and Pakistani/Bangladeshis were worse off. Despite the element of inaccuracy in the calculation of this figure, the consistency of the pattern in each class suggests that standardising for Registrar General's class is a far from adequate method of dealing with socio-economic effects for comparisons across ethnic groups.

Table 5.2   Ethnic variations within socio-economic bands

	Whites	Caribbeans	Indians and African Asians	Pakistanis and Bangladeshis
Mean income by Registrar General's class ($£$)[1]				
I/II	250	210	210	125
IIIn	185	145	135	95
IIIm	160	145	120	70
IV/V	130	120	110	65
Weighted base	*1937*	*1144*	*1173*	*600*
Unweighted base	*1894*	*869*	*1142*	*969*
Median duration of un-employment (months)	7	21	12	24
Weighted base	*134*	*126*	*92*	*100*
Unweighted base	*128*	*91*	*91*	*166*
Per cent lacking one or more basic housing amenities[2]				
Owner occupiers	11	12	14	38
Renters	27	23	28	37
Weighted base	*2867*	*1567*	*2091*	*1147*
Unweighted base	*2867*	*1205*	*2001*	*1776*

1 based on bands of equivalised household income: the mean point of each band is used to make this calculation, which is rounded to the nearest £5.
2 i.e exclusive use of: bath or shower; bathroom; inside toilet; kitchen; hot water from a tap; and central heating.

The second part of the table shows the median length of unemployment for those who were currently unemployed at interview. It again shows diverse patterns across ethnic groups, whites and Indian/African Asians were unemployed for a considerably shorter period than Caribbeans and Pakistani/Bangladeshis. Here it is worth noting that Bartley *et al.* (1996) clearly showed that length of unemployment, rather than unemployment *per se*, was an important determinant of health.

The third part of Table 5.2 gives an indication of the quality of housing occupied by owners and renters for different ethnic groups. It shows the percentage of respondents who reported that their household did not have sole access to certain amenities: a bath or shower; a bathroom; an inside toilet; a kitchen; hot water from a tap; and central heating. Again the table shows interesting variations across ethnic groups. For both owners and renters, whites, Caribbeans and Indian/African Asians showed a similar pattern, while Pakistani/Bangladeshis were far more likely to be lacking exclusive use of such an amenity than any other group in both the owner and the renter groups. In addition, while owners appeared to have better housing than renters for the white, Caribbean and Indian/African Asian groups, this was not the case for Pakistani/Bangladeshis. This, of course, suggests that tenure may not only be an inadequate means of controlling for socio-economic status when making comparisons across ethnic groups, but also that tenure is an inadequate reflection of socio-economic status within the Pakistani/Bangladeshi group. This might explain why tenure was less likely to be associated with health status for Pakistani/ Bangladeshis than for the other ethnic groups.

The overall conclusion to be drawn from Table 5.2 is that, while these indicators of socio-economic status might have some use for making comparisons within ethnic groups (for example the first part of the table shows that equivalised household income decreased with class for each ethnic group), they are of little use for 'controlling out' the impact of socio-economic status when attempting to reveal the extent of a 'pure' ethnic/race effect. This leads to two related problems with approaches that attempt to adjust for socio-economic effects when making comparisons across ethnic groups. The first of these is that if socio-economic status is simply regarded as a confounding factor that needs to be controlled out to reveal the 'true' relationship between ethnicity and health, data will be presented and interpreted once controls have been applied. This will result in the impact of socio-economic factors becoming obscured and their explanatory role lost, just as gender and age effects are not apparent in the majority of the figures shown in Chapter 3. The second is that the presentation of 'standardised' data allows the kind of problems with such data illustrated by Table 5.2 to be ignored, leaving both the author and reader to assume that all that is left is an ethnic/race effect, be that cultural or biological/genetic. Here it is important to remember that not only do such socio-economic indicators inadequately deal with these effects for cross-group comparisons, they also do not account for other forms of disadvantage that might play some role in ethnic variations in health, such as those related to geographical location and the direct effects of racism and discrimination, both described in the introduction to this chapter.

Nevertheless, if these cautions are considered there are some benefits in attempting to control for socio-economic effects. In particular, if controlling for socio-economic effects alters the pattern of ethnic health variations, despite the limitations of the indicators used, we can conclude that at least a part of the variations we have uncovered are a result of such an effect. To do this we need to carefully consider which indicators to use in the process of standardisation for socio-economic status. There are a number of alternatives to those typically used in epidemiological research, including income. However, there are a number of drawbacks associated with income in this survey, most importantly that there was a sufficiently large number of respondents who did not answer the relevant question to make it less useful than it at first appears. Instead, making use of the extensive information this survey collected on the circumstances of its respondents, an index of 'Standard of Living' is used in addition to class and tenure for the process of standardisation.

This index, like the other indicators of socio-economic status used, is household-based, using information on: overcrowding of the accommodation; the presence of basic household amenities; the number of consumer durables the household has; and the number of cars the household has access to. The index has three mutually exclusive points, poor, medium and good, that are inevitably broad, but have been selected both because of their face validity and because they each contain a reasonably large sample size for each ethnic group. Simplifying the index slightly, the 'poor' group consists of those with *any* of the following:

- overcrowded accommodation (one person per room or more);
- lacking sole access to one or more amenity (out of: a bath or shower; a bathroom; an inside toilet; a kitchen; hot water from a tap; and central heating);
- few consumer durables (less than four of: a telephone; television; video; fridge; freezer; washing machine; tumble-drier; dishwasher; microwave; CD-player; and personal computer).

The 'good' group consists of those with *all* of the following:

- less than 0.75 people per room;
- sole access to all of the basic amenities listed above;
- many of the consumer durables listed above (nine or more, or five or more and two cars).

The relationship between this index and ethnic group is shown in Table 5.3. This shows that the white group was the best off, followed closely by the Indian/African Asian group. The Caribbean group was clearly worse off than either of these two, but the Pakistani/Bangladeshi group was by far the worst off.

Table 5.3   Standard of living

column percentages

	Whites	Caribbeans	Indians and African Asians	Pakistanis and Bangladeshis
Standard of living				
Good	43	23	34	9
Medium	49	63	52	41
Poor	8	14	14	50
Weighted base	*2865*	*1567*	*2083*	*1147*
Unweighted base	*2865*	*1205*	*1996*	*1776*

The small percentage of people in the poor band for the white group and the good band for the Pakistani/Bangladeshi group shows why it was necessary for the three bands that make up this index to be relatively broad. However, this raises the possibility that once again different ethnic groups have different locations within a particular band. This is explored in Table 5.4, which looks at the equivalised household income for each band by ethnic group. As expected, within ethnic groups there was a clear relationship between income and the standard of living index. Comparisons across ethnic groups show that the white, Caribbean and Indian/African Asian groups were similar, except for the relatively low income for Indian/African Asians in the medium group. However, for each band the Pakistani/Bangladeshi group had a lower average income. This suggests that the standard of living index still does not adequately control for socio-economic status. Nevertheless, a comparison between the figures presented in Table 5.2 and those in Table 5.4 shows that the ratio between the incomes of the Pakistani/Bangladeshi and white groups for each socio-economic band is smaller in the latter table, suggesting that it should be an improvement over the other indicators of socio-economic status, which are, if anything, even cruder than Registrar General's class.

Table 5.4   Mean equivalised household income and standard of living

	Whites	Caribbeans	Indians and African Asians	Pakistanis and Bangladeshis
Mean income by standard of living (£)*				
Good	225	195	210	155
Medium	145	140	115	80
Poor	105	100	95	65
Weighted base	*2330*	*1274*	*1307*	*824*
Unweighted base	*2410*	*991*	*1283*	*1327*

* based on bands of equivalised household income: the mean point of each band is used to make this calculation, which is rounded to the nearest £5.

The remainder of this chapter shows how standardising for the three indicators of socio-economic status influences the ethnic patterning of health reported in Chapter 3. The data are presented as relative risk scores in comparison to the white group, which is simply the chance of a member of an ethnic minority group to be in the ill-health group compared to a member of the white group, with a value above 1.0 reflecting a greater chance and a value below this reflecting a smaller chance. Ninety-five per cent confidence limits are shown in brackets below each figure. If these limits are both above 1.0 or both below 1.0, the difference between the ethnic minority group and the white group can be considered to be statistically significant. In order to clearly distinguish the 95 per cent confidence limits from 1.0, two decimal points are occasionally used.

As the data have been standardised according to age, gender and the socio-economic indicator in question, once again the Indian and African Asian, and the Pakistani and Bangladeshi groups have been combined. The Chinese group was too small to be included in this process, so has not been considered separately. In addition to this, as there were too few respondents in particular categories above the age of 65 for them to be included, these have also been excluded. This includes the data that are presented in just age and gender standardised form, which means the age and gender standardised relative risks presented here are not identical to those shown in Chapter 3, which include all age groups, although they are similar.

General health

Table 5.5 looks at the effect of various forms of standardisation on the relative risk compared to whites for the respondent to have reported fair or poor health. The most striking finding shown in the table is that standardising for class or tenure makes no difference to the relative risk for either the Pakistani/Bangladeshi or the All Ethnic Minority groups. However, controlling for standard of living reduces the difference between the All Ethnic Minority group and whites to a level that is not statistically significant, and reduces the difference between Pakistani/Bangladeshis and whites to one that is only just statistically significant. For Caribbeans, all three means of standardising for socio-economic status reduces the relative risk to a level that is barely significantly greater than that for whites. For Indian/African Asians, standardising for class and tenure again makes little difference, but controlling for standard of living brings the risk very nearly to statistically significantly lower than that of whites.

Table 5.5   **Relative risk compared with whites of reported fair or poor health standardised for socio-economic factors**

	Caribbeans	Indians and African Asians	Pakistanis and Bangladeshis	All ethnic minorities
Type of standardisation				
Age and gender	1.25	0.99	1.45	1.17
	(1.1 – 1.4)	(0.9 – 1.1)	(1.3 – 1.6)	(1.1 – 1.3)
Class, age and gender	1.15	1.00	1.36	1.14
	(1.03 – 1.3)	(0.9 – 1.1)	(1.2 – 1.5)	(1.1 – 1.2)
Tenure, age and gender	1.17	1.04	1.45	1.18
	(1.04 – 1.3)	(0.9 – 1.2)	(1.3 – 1.6)	(1.1 – 1.3)
Standard of living, age and gender	1.15	0.94	1.24	1.08
	(1.03 – 1.3)	(0.9 – 1.04)	(1.1 – 1.4)	(0.99 – 1.2)

Heart disease

Table 5.6 shows the relative risk compared to whites of reporting a diagnosis of angina or heart disease. The two South Asian groups are of most interest here and, as with the previous table, controlling for class or tenure makes little difference to the data presented, although, if anything it increases the relative risk of these groups. However, controlling for standard of living makes an important difference. The Indian/African Asian group now has a significantly lower risk than whites, while the risk for the Pakistani/Bangladeshi group is also lowered and now no longer significantly greater than the white rate.

Table 5.6   **Relative risk compared with whites of diagnosed heart disease standardised for socio-economic factors**

	Caribbeans	Indians and African Asians	Pakistanis and Bangladeshis	All ethnic minorities
Type of standardisation				
Age and gender	0.95	0.77	1.50	0.97
	(0.6 – 1.4)	(0.5 – 1.1)	(1.1 – 2.0)	(0.7 – 1.3)
Class, age and gender	1.05	0.92	1.49	1.10
	(0.7 – 1.6)	(0.6 – 1.3)	(1.1 – 2.1)	(0.8 – 1.5)
Tenure, age and gender	0.93	0.85	1.57	1.05
	(0.6 – 1.4)	(0.6 – 1.2)	(1.2 – 2.1)	(0.8 – 1.4)
Standard of living, age and gender	1.02	0.67	1.24	0.92
	(0.7 – 1.5)	(0.5 – 0.96)	(0.9 – 1.7)	(0.7 – 1.2)

Table 5.7 includes respondents who reported suffering from severe chest pain in addition to those who reported a diagnosis of heart disease. Once again controlling for class and tenure makes little difference to the relative risks of the two South Asian groups, while controlling for standard of living considerably reduces the risk for both of them. However, for this outcome the risk for Indian/African Asians is just outside being significantly lower than that for whites, and the risk for Pakistani/Bangladeshis is still just about significantly greater.

Table 5.7   Relative risk of diagnosed heart disease or severe chest pain compared with whites standardised for socio-economic factors

	Caribbeans	Indians and African Asians	Pakistanis and Bangladeshis	All ethnic minorities
Type of standardisation				
Age and gender	0.96	0.95	1.88	1.11
	(0.7 – 1.3)	(0.7 – 1.2)	(1.5 – 2.4)	(0.9 – 1.4)
Class, age and gender	0.85	0.93	1.59	1.06
	(0.6 – 1.2)	(0.7 – 1.2)	(1.2 – 2.0)	(0.9 – 1.3)
Tenure, age and gender	0.92	1.05	1.87	1.21
	(0.7 – 1.3)	(0.8 – 1.4)	(1.5 – 2.4)	(0.98 – 1.5)
Standard of living, age and gender	0.89	0.78	1.37	0.96
	(0.7 – 1.2)	(0.6 – 1.01)	(1.1 – 1.7)	(0.8 – 1.2)

Hypertension

Table 5.8 shows the relative risk of having a diagnosis of hypertension compared to whites for each ethnic minority group once the various forms of standardisation had been carried out.

Table 5.8   Relative risk of hypertension compared with whites standardised for socio-economic factors

	Caribbeans	Indians and African Asians	Pakistanis and Bangladeshis	All ethnic minorities
Type of standardisation				
Age and gender	1.49	0.64	0.94	0.94
	(1.2 – 1.8)	(0.5 – 0.8)	(0.8 – 1.1)	(0.8 – 1.1)
Class, age and gender	1.56	0.70	0.88	1.03
	(1.3 – 1.9)	(0.6 – 0.9)	(0.7 – 1.1)	(0.9 – 1.2)
Tenure, age and gender	1.42	0.68	0.95	0.99
	(1.2 – 1.7)	(0.6 – 0.8)	(0.8 – 1.1)	(0.8 – 1.1)
Standard of living, age and gender	1.33	0.60	0.86	0.90
	(1.1 – 1.6)	(0.5 – 0.7)	(0.7 – 1.04)	(0.8 – 1.04)

Interestingly, the pattern for Caribbeans follows that for the South Asian groups in the previous two tables, with controlling for class increasing risk, controlling for tenure making no difference, and controlling for standard of living both reducing their risk and bringing it close to being not significantly different from the white risk. Controlling for standard of living also slightly reduces the risk for the Indian/African Asian and the Pakistani/Bangladeshi groups.

Diabetes

Table 5.9, which focuses on diabetes, shows a similar pattern to previous tables. For both the South Asian groups controlling for class and tenure makes little difference, while for the Caribbean group applying such controls reduces risk, particularly in the case of tenure. For all of the ethnic minority groups, controlling for standard of living slightly reduces the risk of diabetes compared to whites, although differences still remain both statistically significant and large.

Table 5.9   Relative risk of diabetes compared with whites standardised for socio-economic factors

	Caribbeans	Indians and African Asians	Pakistanis and Bangladeshis	All ethnic minorities
Type of standardisation				
Age and gender	2.6	2.6	4.9	3.0
	(1.6 – 4.0)	(1.7 – 3.9)	(3.3 – 7.2)	(2.1 – 4.3)
Class, age and gender	2.8	3.1	5.2	3.5
	(1.8 – 4.3)	(2.0 – 4.6)	(3.4 – 7.8)	(2.4 – 5.0)
Tenure, age and gender	2.3	2.7	4.8	3.1
	(1.4 – 3.6)	(1.8 – 4.1)	(3.3 – 6.9)	(2.2 – 4.4)
Standard of living, age and gender	2.2	2.4	4.1	2.8
	(1.4 – 3.4)	(1.6 – 3.6)	(2.9 – 6.0)	(2.0 – 3.9)

Respiratory disease

Table 5.10 includes respondents who reported that they had either a wheeze or had coughed up phlegm for at least three months of the year. It shows that the effect of controlling for socio-economic group is small for all of the indicators of socio-economic status used and for all of the ethnic minority groups. However, the risk for all of the groups is smallest when standard of living is controlled for. For the Caribbean group, the relative risk compared to whites of reporting respiratory symptoms is not statistically significant if the data are standardised according to class and tenure, but if standard of living is controlled for, the relative risk for Caribbeans becomes, like that for the other ethnic minority groups, significantly lower.

Table 5.10   Relative risk of respiratory symptoms compared with whites standardised for socio-economic factors

	Caribbeans	Indians and African Asians	Pakistanis and Bangladeshis	All ethnic minorities
Type of standardisation				
Age and gender	0.89	0.53	0.65	0.66
	(0.7 – 1.05)	(0.4 – 0.6)	(0.6 – 0.8)	(0.6 – 0.7)
Class, age and gender	0.86	0.53	0.55	0.64
	(0.7 – 1.01)	(0.4 – 0.6)	(0.5 – 0.7)	(0.6 – 0.7)
Tenure, age and gender	0.85	0.58	0.65	0.68
	(0.7 – 1.01)	(0.5 – 0.7)	(0.6 – 0.8)	(0.6 – 0.8)
Standard of living, age and gender	0.83	0.50	0.50	0.61
	(0.7 – 0.98)	(0.4 – 0.6)	(0.4 – 0.6)	(0.5 – 0.7)

Summary

The data presented in Tables 5.5 to 5.10 clearly show that if we wish to examine whether differences in socio-economic status make an important contribution to ethnic variations in health, we must be careful about the indicators of socio-economic status used. Although the index of standard of living is far from perfect in this respect – see Table 5.4, and note that it does not include a lifetime estimate of socio-economic position, which may be of great importance for particular outcomes (Davey Smith *et al.* 1997), nor any aspect of the other forms of social disadvantage, including relative deprivation, faced by ethnic minority people – it is an improvement on the traditional indicators of socio-economic status, class and tenure, that have been used both for the general population and for comparisons across ethnic groups. The difficulties with the use of these traditional indicators for cross ethnic group comparisons are clearly illustrated in Table 5.2.

The data in Table 5.1, taken together with that shown in Table 5.2, suggest that all of the ethnic minority groups considered in this chapter (Caribbeans, Indian/African Asians and Pakistani/Bangladeshis) are disadvantaged compared to whites, although the degree of disadvantage varies across the groups. Consequently, if socio-economic status does contribute to the ethnic variations in health reported in this volume, controlling for socio-economic status should reduce the relative risk of ill-health for all of these ethnic minority groups compared to whites. If the age and gender standardised data is compared to the data that also include controls for standard of living in Tables 5.5 to 5.10 (i.e. if the top and bottom rows of these tables are compared) this pattern is consistently repeated. For only one outcome and one ethnic minority group – Caribbeans and the relative risk compared to whites to report a diagnosis of heart disease – is the risk, once standard of living is controlled, greater than that when only age and gender are considered. In every other case the risk is reduced, although in some instances the reduction is small. In addition, despite the limitations of the standard of living index, in all cases, except diabetes, relative risks that were statistically significantly greater compared to whites are either no longer or only just significantly different once standard of living is controlled for. This suggests that socio-economic status does make an important contribution to ethnic variations in health and, importantly, this applies to the greater risk of heart disease that Pakistani/Bangladeshis reported. It is also worth pointing out that some differences that were not statistically significantly different from the white population when only gender and age are considered, became significantly lower when standard of living was also considered. An important example of this is the risk of diagnosed heart disease for Indian/African Asians.

CONCLUSION AND IMPLICATIONS

The data presented in this chapter show that, as for the general population, socio-economic status is an important predictor of health for ethnic minority groups. Figures 5.1 to 5.12 show that for both general health indicators and those that reflect particular conditions, those in poorer socio-economic groups had poorer health in each ethnic group. In contrast to this, the only comparable study of the health of ethnic minority groups, Marmot *et al.*'s (1984) study of immigrant mortality, came to the conclusion that:

> the relation of social class (as usually defined) to mortality is different among immigrant groups from the England and Wales pattern. (p21)

As suggested earlier, the discrepancy between the conclusions reached here and those reached by Marmot *et al.* (1984) needs careful consideration. Here it is worth highlighting some points that suggest that the data used by the two studies are not directly comparable:

- The definition of ethnicity here is based on country of family origin, while that in Marmot *et al.*'s (1984) study is based on country of birth.

- Data used here are based on self-reports of morbidity, or diagnosis of morbidity, while Marmot *et al.* (1984) use mortality. While the two are related, there are also important differences, as discussed in Chapter 1 and the conclusion of Chapter 3.

- Socio-economic status is defined here according to *current* occupation, tenure, or standard of living, while Marmot *et al.* (1984) use occupation as recorded at time of death. The use of occupation as recorded on death certificates may cause particular problems for immigrant mortality data. This is because the inflating of occupational status on death certificates (where, according to Townsend and Davidson (1982), occupation is recorded as the 'skilled' job held for most of the individual's life rather than the 'unskilled' job held in the last few years of life) will be a particularly significant problem for such data if migration to Britain was associated with significant downward social mobility for members of ethnic minority groups, a process that both Smith (1977), in a previous PSI survey, and Heath and Ridge (1983) have documented. The occupation recorded on the death certificates of migrants, consequently, may well be an inaccurate reflection of experience in Britain prior to death. In addition, given the socio-economic profile of ethnic minority groups in Britain, this inflation of occupational status would only need to happen in relatively few cases for the figures representing the small population in higher classes to be distorted. For example, Table 3.7 in Marmot *et al.* (1984) reports only 212 deaths occurring in the Class I group for those born in the Indian sub-continent in 1970–72 and only 37 for those born in the Caribbean group.

- Finally, differences between the data reported here and by Marmot *et al.* (1984) may reflect genuine differences between the populations studied. Important cohort effects may have operated between the exclusively immigrant ethnic minority population, who had their health assigned by mortality rates, and the ethnic minority population interviewed about 20 years later that included both migrants and those born in Britain and who had their health assessed by self-reported morbidity.

These points suggest not only that the data used in the two studies are not necessarily directly comparable, but also that the data used here are in a number of ways an improvement on the mortality data used by Marmot *et al.* (1984), being nationally representative of the ethnic minority groups used, having more accurate assessments of socio-economic status and ethnicity, and, consequently, being less likely to suffer from artefact effects.

The data presented here also show that traditional indicators of socio-economic status, such as class and tenure, are inappropriate for controlling out socio-economic effects when making comparisons across ethnic groups. Table 5.2 shows that within particular socio-economic bands members of ethnic minority groups were worse of than whites, and that the extent of this varied by ethnic minority group. Tables 5.5 to 5.10 show that for a variety of general and specific indicators of health, controlling for class or tenure makes little or no difference to ethnic variations in health, while controlling for an alternative indicator of socio-economic status, standard of living, improves the health of ethnic minority groups compared to whites in all but one instance for only one of the ethnic minority groups considered.

Again, it is worth pointing out that 'controlling' for socio-economic status cannot be completely done, even if specifically tailored indicators such as standard of living are used. Table 5.4 shows that within bands of standard of living important differences in income between ethnic groups remained. In addition to this, it is also important to recall that taking account of socio-economic status only deals with part of the disadvantage faced by ethnic minority groups. Other important features of the lives of ethnic minority groups may adversely effect their health in comparison to the white population, such as their experiences of racism and discrimination, their perception of the inequality they face in their lives, and their geographical concentration in urban locations. It is likely that differences in the social experiences between ethnic minority and majority groups cannot be reduced to socio-economic status. Despite this, differences between the white and ethnic minority samples were not only reduced once standard of living had been taken into account, but in many instances important differences, such as those for diagnosed heart disease, became no longer statistically significantly different.

The conclusions to be reached, consequently, are that socio-economic status is an important predictor of health within ethnic groups and it also makes an important contribution to the pattern of ethnic variations in health that have been reported both here and elsewhere. This leads back to the concluding comments of Chapter 4, which were concerned with how useful ethnicity is, both as a variable and as a concept, for investigating reasons for differences in health across social groups. This is a particular concern if ethnic health variations are a consequence of the impact of various forms of social disadvantage on health, but the use of ethnicity as a variable in epidemiological research means that socio-economic effects are essentially ignored and explanations are sought in assumed cultural and biological differences. This is an issue which is returned to in Chapter 7.

CHAPTER SIX

Use and Experience of Health Services

INTRODUCTION

Access to and the ease of use of health services is an important potential source of inequality in the health experience of different ethnic groups in Britain. If such inequalities do exist, they may have important influences on both the quality of care received and the outcomes of that care. Consequently, the ethnic variations in health described in preceding chapters may at least be partly attributable to or amplified by differences in health service use. While it is important to note that any differences in health service use may be the result of differences in the *demand* for such services, rather than inequality in access to them, such differences in demand may also be a result of the (in)ability of health services to address the needs and expectations of different ethnic groups. As Smaje (1995a) points out, the demand for, and use of, health services will, in addition to levels of ill-health, be dependent on factors as diverse as: health beliefs and knowledge; attitudes to health services; the geographical distribution of health care resources; the sensitivity of health services to different groups' needs; and variations in the quality of care. All of these factors could vary across ethnic groups and, consequently, produce differences in utilisation rates.

Despite the potential for inequalities in access to the health service across ethnic groups, most of the studies that have attempted to explore possible variations in health service use have found that, on the whole, ethnic minority groups make greater use of the health service than the white majority. For example, the *Black and Minority Ethnic Groups Health and Lifestyles* survey (BMEG) (Rudat 1994), which covered Caribbean, Indian, Pakistani and Bangladeshi ethnic groups, showed that Caribbean men were the only group to have lower rates of registration with a General Practitioner (GP) than the general population, and that even among that group only a very small number (4 per cent) were not registered. In fact, other groups seemed to be more likely to be registered than the general population. The BMEG survey also showed that consultation rates with GPs were higher among ethnic minority groups, particularly Pakistanis and Bangladeshis, than the general population. Similar differences in consultation rates were also uncovered in analysis of the *General Household Survey* data (Balarajan *et al.* 1989) and the third and fourth national *GP Morbidity Surveys* (McCormick and Rosenbaum 1990, Car-Hill *et al.* 1996). These findings have also been supported by smaller scale regional studies, such as that carried out in the West Midlands (Johnson *et al.* 1983). Nevertheless, such studies have a number of drawbacks, some of which can only be partly overcome here. Two of the more serious of these drawbacks are discussed below.

First, differences in the use of health services can only be fully understood in the light of differences in need. Previous chapters have clearly illustrated differences in need both between and within ethnic groups and it may well be that differences in use disappear or even reverse when differences in need are taken into account. Unfortunately, the few studies that have considered differences in health service use by different ethnic groups have not directly accounted for differences in need. However, data from the third national *GP Morbidity Survey* (McCormick and Rosenbaum 1990) suggest that the greater use of primary health care services by ethnic minority patients is largely a result of consultations for illnesses that have a greater prevalence among their various ethnic groups. This implies that the greater use reported is a direct reflection of a greater prevalence of ill-health. Also, Benzeval and Judge (1993) found no significant differences across ethnic groups in the use of hospital services once they had accounted for self-reported ill-health.

Second, assessments of frequency of use give no indidcation of the quality of the services received. The concern here is that the primary health care services used by some ethnic minority groups may not be of the standard used by the majority. The geographical location of ethnic minority populations in predominantly urban areas (Owen 1994) means that they may be more likely to use single-handed, inner-city and non-fundholding general practices with, consequently, fewer resources. It may also be that even within equally resourced practices the quality of the care received may vary across ethnic groups, because of the inability of providers to address the needs of culturally different groups, or because of their reliance on stereotypes about the needs of different ethnic minority groups. A local study in Bristol (Pilgrim *et al.* 1993) attempted to partly address these questions by asking respondents how satisfied they were with the services provided. Results suggested very high levels of satisfaction among all of the groups interviewed, but the authors commented on the difficulties of providing accurate assessments with the instrument they used.

The BMEG survey (Rudat 1994) attempted to assess the quality of GP services in a more direct way across a variety of dimensions. Key findings were:

- Ethnic minority respondents were more likely than the general population to find physical access to their GP difficult, and this was particularly the case for Bangladeshis and Pakistanis.
- The average time spent waiting to see a GP in the surgery was considerably longer for all ethnic minority groups than for the general population.
- Overall, the great majority of South Asians found it easy to understand their GP, although as many as 8 per cent of Bangladeshis said that this was not the case.
- On the whole ethnic minority respondents were just as likely as the general population to feel that their GP had given them a full explanation, although Bangladeshis were *more* likely to believe this.
- Ethnic minority respondents were less likely than the general population to believe that the time their GP spent with them was adequate. This was particularly the case for Bangladeshis, for whom as many as a third of

respondents felt that the time spent with them was inadequate compared with about one in eight of the general population.

- Ethnic minority respondents were less likely than the general population to be happy with the outcome of their consultation. One in eight of the general population were unhappy with the outcome compared to one in five Caribbeans, Indians and Pakistanis and more than one in four Bangladeshis.

So, in the BMEG survey across all but one of these dimensions ethnic minority groups appeared to be disadvantaged compared to whites.

Data presented in this chapter will concentrate on:

- Ethnic differences in the use of health services, both GP and hospital in-patient services, and how these varied by age and gender.
- How the use of these services varied across ethnic groups once respondents' self-assessed health was taken into account.
- The extent to which the language needs of ethnic minority groups were met.
- The preferences of users of these services in terms of the ethnicity and gender for their doctors.
- Variations in the use of other health and social services, such as dentists, alternative practitioners and social workers.

USE OF MEDICAL SERVICES

General Practitioners

All respondents were asked the number of times they had visited their GP in the month leading up to the interview. The first row of Table 6.1 shows that Chinese respondents were less likely than any other group to have visited their GP in the last month. Compared to whites, all of the other ethnic minority groups were more likely to have consulted with their GP, except African Asians who had a similar rate to whites. Less than a quarter of Chinese respondents, compared to about a third of African Asian and white respondents, over two-fifths of Caribbean and Indian respondents, and almost half of Pakistani and Bangladeshi respondents, had consulted their GP about a health problem in the last month.

In terms of the frequency of GP consultations over the past month, variations between ethnic minority groups followed a similar pattern. About one in eleven of the Caribbean, Indian and Bangladeshi respondents, and more than one in ten of the Pakistani respondents had consulted their GP three or more times in the past month. This is compared to about one in 20 white and African Asian respondents and even fewer Chinese respondents.

Table 6.1   Number of visits to the General Practitioner in the past month

column percentages

	White	Caribbean	Indian	African Asian	Pakistani	Bangladeshi	Chinese
Number of times respondent has talked to a GP about his or her health in the past month							
None	66	57	59	68	51	55	77
1 – 2	30	35	33	26	38	36	22
3 – 5	4	7	7	5	10	7	0.4
> 5	0.6	1.8	1.4	0.7	1.8	1.7	0.4
Weighted base	*2856*	*1555*	*1273*	*785*	*853*	*276*	*388*
Unweighted base	*2855*	*1196*	*1251*	*710*	*1171*	*568*	*212*

The first part of Table 6.2 shows how GP consultations varied by gender. Across all ethnic groups women were more likely than men to have visited their GP in the past month. Within gender groups, the ethnic variations in the likelihood of visiting a GP remained as described above.

Table 6.2   Visits to General Practitioner in the past month by age and gender

cell percentages

	White	Caribbean	Indian	African Asian	Pakistani	Bangladeshi	Chinese
Spoken to GP about own health at least once in the last month							
Gender							
Men	30	37	34	27	42	38	21
Women	38	48	47	37	57	52	25
Age							
16 – 24	31	36	28	21	31	25	17
25 – 34	33	36	36	28	42	48	25
35 – 54	31	45	43	33	61	54	23
55 – 74	38	62	61	53	82	69	*
> 74	51	*	*	*	*	*	*
Weighted base	*2856*	*1555*	*1273*	*785*	*853*	*276*	*388*
Unweighted base	*2855*	*1196*	*1251*	*710*	*1171*	*568*	*212*

* small base numbers in the cell make the estimate unreliable

The second half of Table 6.2 shows that age played an important role, both in the likelihood of consulting a GP and in the extent of variations across ethnic groups. All groups except the Chinese had an increased likelihood to have reported a visit to a GP with increasing age, although this pattern was not present in the three younger age groups for whites. For the youngest age group, 16–24, only Caribbeans were more likely than whites to have consulted their GP about their health – and then only slightly more likely. Younger Bangladeshis, African Asians and Chinese were considerably less likely than other ethnic groups to have visited a GP in the past month. For the 25–34 age group the pattern described by the summary statistics presented in Table 6.1 began to emerge. Here all ethnic minority groups were more likely than whites to have consulted their GP except African Asians and Chinese. These differences became greater with increasing age and among those aged 55 to 74 all ethnic minority groups (except the Chinese, for whom no estimate for this age group could be made) were much more likely to have visited their GP than whites, including African Asians.[1] In fact, in this age group Caribbeans and Indians were about one and a half times as likely, Bangladeshis were about one and three-quarters times as likely and Pakistanis were about twice as likely as whites to have visited their GP.

Hospital in-patient services

All respondents were asked whether they had been admitted to a hospital or clinic for one or more nights (shorter stays, such as for day surgery, were not included). Table 6.3 shows responses to this question taking into account both gender and age. Gender differences would be expected to occur as a result of childbearing and the age group 25–34 showed this expected pattern, these women reported a much higher likelihood of being admitted to a hospital than equivalent men. For the other age groups in the table that include childbearing years, gender differences were not so marked or consistent, but were present for Pakistanis, Bangladeshis, younger whites and older Caribbeans.

Table 6.3   Hospital in-patient stays in the past year by age and gender

cell percentages

	White	Caribbean	Indian	African Asian	Pakistani	Bangladeshi	Chinese
Stayed overnight as a hospital in-patient in the last year							
Men							
Age 16 – 24	4	12	4	8	2	2	*
Age 25 – 34	9	2	5	4	2	7	*
Age 35 – 54	9	6	6	6	10	2	*
Age 55 –74	14	11	16	17	20	20	*
Age > 74	24	*	*	*	*	*	*
Total	10	8	8	7	8	6	3
Women							
Age 16 – 24	15	10	8	5	9	20	*
Age 25 – 34	19	18	17	19	17	12	*
Age 35 – 54	8	16	9	6	17	12	*
Age 55 – 74	9	8	10	16	21	9	*
Age > 74	20	*	*	*	*	*	*
Total	13	15	11	11	15	15	9
All respondents	11	12	10	9	11	10	6
Weighted base	*2864*	*1559*	*1286*	*797*	*861*	*284*	*391*
Unweighted base	*2863*	*1199*	*1270*	*726*	*1183*	*589*	*214*

* small base numbers in the cell make the estimate unreliable.

---

1   This is despite this age category having an older average age for whites than for any of the other ethnic groups.

For the men there was a fairly consistent pattern of an increasing likelihood of having a hospital admission with increasing age. The most striking exception to this pattern was the high likelihood of admission for young Caribbean men. This may reflect a high rate of admissions for psychiatric disorders and/or a high accident rate for this group. In fact, responses to the question asking if the respondent had had an accident resulting in hospital treatment in the past year show that for Caribbean men aged 16 to 24 there were 26 such accidents per 100 respondents, compared to 13 for the 25–34 age group, eight for the 35–54 age group, and none for the 55–74 age group. Although other ethnic groups showed a decrease in the rate of accidents for men as they got older, the decrease was not as large for any of them as it was for Caribbean men.

Comparing the ethnic groups for male hospital admissions shows that overall ethnic minority men were less likely than white men to have been admitted. However, as with GP consultations, this difference was related to age. For the oldest age category for which comparisons can be made, 55–74, all of the South Asian groups had a similar or greater rate of admission as whites, and the Caribbean group also seemed to 'catch up' with the white group with increasing age.

For female admissions to hospital it is worth considering those for childbirth separately from others. In this survey, of the female respondents aged 16 to 44 who had reported that they had been admitted to hospital, half were asked if the admission had been for childbirth. For this group, Table 6.4 shows admissions to hospital both for and not for childbirth. For childbirth, white, Indian, African Asian and Caribbean women had similar rates of admission, while Chinese women had lower rates, and Pakistani and Bangladeshi women had higher rates. In contrast, admissions not for childbirth showed a similar pattern to admission rates for men, all ethnic minority groups had a clearly lower rate than whites in the youngest age group and this became less clear with the older age groups.

Table 6.4   Hospital in-patient stays for women in the past year by age and whether for childbirth

cell percentages

	White	Caribbean	Indian	African Asian	Pakistani	Bangladeshi	Chinese
In-patient stays for childbirth							
Age 16 – 24	5	4	6	5*	10	20	*
Age 25 – 34	10	7	12	11	16	11	*
Age 35 – 44	<1	2	<1	<1	8	5*	*
Age 16 – 44	5	5	6	5	11	13	3.5*
In-patient stays not for childbirth							
Age 16 – 24	10	4	3	5*	2	0	*
Age 25 – 34	9	8	9	6	6	0	*
Age 35 – 44	7	20	4	2	18	0*	*
Age 16 – 44	8	9	6	4	8	0	8*
Weighted base	*830*	*297*	*250*	*163*	*150*	*54*	*70*
Unweighted base	*811*	*232*	*242*	*140*	*210*	*126*	*36*

* small base numbers in the cell make the estimate unreliable.

Looking back at Table 6.3 in the light of Table 6.4,[2] suggests that for all ethnic minority groups younger women had a lower rate of hospital admission than whites when childbirth is excluded, but again this appears to change as the respondents get older. Caribbean, Indian and Bangladeshi women appear to have reached a similar rate to that of older white women, while African Asian and Pakistani women had overtaken them. It is worth pointing out again that for both the men and the women in the 55 to 74 age category the average age of white respondents was greater than that for ethnic minority respondents. This suggests that when making *comparisons* for this group we should consider the ethnic minority rates to be under-estimates.

Although respondents were not asked the reason for their hospital admission, they were asked how long they had been admitted for. In an attempt to concentrate on hospital admissions of a more serious nature, Table 6.5 shows the rate of admissions that lasted for more than one week. The first row of the table shows actual levels of hospital admission. To allow for an easy comparison across ethnic groups the second row presents rates that have been standardised to take into account their different age and gender structures.[3]

Table 6.5   Hospital in-patient stays over one week

cell percentages

	White	Caribbean	Indian	African Asian	Pakistani	Bangladeshi	Chinese
Stayed overnight as a hospital in-patient in the last year for more than one week							
Unstandardised	3.5	2.8	1.9	1.4	3.1	1.7	0.3
Age and gender standardised	2.4	2.7	—— 1.7 ——		—— 3.1 ——		1.9
Weighted base	*2864*	*1559*	*1286*	*797*	*861*	*284*	*391*
Unweighted base	*2863*	*1199*	*1270*	*726*	*1183*	*589*	*214*

From the table it can be seen that Indians/African Asians and Chinese respondents had a lower rate of being admitted to hospital for more than one week in the past year than whites. Caribbeans had a similar rate and Pakistanis/Bangladeshis had a higher rate. However, the Pakistani and Bangladeshi result should be treated with some caution. The figures for the unstandardised rates also shown in the table, suggest that Bangladeshis in fact had a much lower rate than Pakistanis. Consequently, the relatively high rate may have applied only to Pakistanis. (In other cases where the Pakistani and Bangladeshi groups have been combined in this volume they have had very similar unstandardised rates.)

2   The two tables cannot be directly compared because the second is based on only half of the ethnic minority sample.

3   See Chapter 3 for an explanation of this, but note that standardisation has been carried out to the age and gender structure of the total ethnic minority population. This effectively reduces the average age of the white group with a consequent reduction in hospital admission rates compared to the unstandardised figures. Another requirement of standardisation is that certain ethnic groups had to be combined, these were Indians with African Asians and Pakistanis with Bangladeshis. Looking at the unstandardised rates for the categories that make up the combined groups, which have similar age and gender structures, allows comparisons of them to be made.

GP consultations and hospital admissions standardised for self-assessed health

As described in the introduction to this chapter, considering rates of GP consultation and of hospital admission without also considering differences in the health status of different ethnic groups can lead to misleading comparisons being made between groups. In this survey respondents were asked to provide general assessments of their health and they were also asked additional questions about particular illnesses. The latter were usually diagnosed by a doctor, reflecting a consultation that had already taken place, so, in terms of understanding differences in consultation rates, whether the respondent had a diagnosis of a particular illness has been ignored. Instead it has been assumed that consultation rates will be influenced by a general sense of well-being, so the focus is on how consultation rates varied across ethnic groups once respondents' perceptions of their overall health had been considered.

All the respondents were asked to rate their health on a five point scale, ranging from excellent to very poor, in comparison to others of the same age. In the following tables this scale has been collapsed into three categories, excellent/good, fair and poor/very poor. Previous tables in this chapter show how differences in response to the questions on consultation with GPs and admission to hospital varied across age and gender groups. Consequently, the tables here have been standardised for both age and gender. As explained in Chapter 3, this means that the Indian group has had to be combined with the African Asian group, and the Pakistani group has had to be combined with the Bangladeshi group.

Table 6.6 shows whether the respondent had consulted a GP about his or her health in the last month, comparing those who considered themselves to be in good, fair and poor health. As expected, the table shows that consultation rates increased for all groups as perceived health got poorer. Chinese respondents at all levels of health status were *less* likely than others to have consulted with their GP, although the small sample size for the Chinese group makes some of these figures unreliable. In contrast, the other ethnic minority groups were all *more* likely than whites to have had one or more consultations, whatever their health status. Although these ethnic minority groups had similar rates to each other, once their health had been taken into account the Pakistani/Bangladeshi group had the highest consultation rates.

Table 6.6　Visits to General Practitioner in the past month by self-assessed general health

cell percentages: age and gender standardised

	White	Caribbean	Indian or African Asian	Pakistani or Bangladeshi	Chinese
Spoken to GP about own health in the last month					
Good/excellent health	24	32	27	35	19
Fair health	48	50	55	66	29*
Poor/very poor health	69	81	83	89	45*
Weighted base	*2856*	*1555*	*2055*	*1124*	*388*
Unweighted base	*2848*	*1194*	*1957*	*1736*	*212*

* small base numbers in the cell make the estimate unreliable.

Table 6.7 uses the same procedure as Table 6.6, but to explore differences in rates of hospital admission in the year prior to interview. Again, for all groups there was an expected rise in the rate of admission with poorer perceived health. As for GP consultation rates, the Chinese group appeared, given the small sample size, to have had lower rates of admission than the other groups. All of the other ethnic groups had remarkably similar rates of hospital admission across all levels of perceived health. This is similar to the findings reported by Benzeval and Judge (1993).

Table 6.7   Hospital in-patient stays in the past year by self-assessed general health

cell percentages: age and gender standardised

	White	Caribbean	Indian or African Asian	Pakistani or Bangladeshi	Chinese
Stayed overnight as a hospital in-patient in the last year					
Good/excellent health	7	7	6	7	6
Fair health	16	13	11	14	7*
Poor health	30	31	31	28	9*
Weighted base	*2863*	*1560*	*2081*	*1141*	*390*
Unweighted base	*2856*	*1197*	*1992*	*1769*	*214*

* small base numbers in the cell make the estimate unreliable.

Summary

The data presented so far suggest that ethnic minority groups, except possibly the Chinese, do not under use either their GPs or hospital in-patient services. Once the perceived quality of the respondent's health was taken into account, ethnic minority respondents were more likely than whites to consult a GP and equally likely to have been admitted to hospital. The process of comparing individuals within the same health category should be regarded with some caution, however. These are broad categories and the extent of ethnic variations in health may mean that within such categories different ethnic groups may have had different average levels of health.

Earlier tables suggested that the differences in consultation rates may vary across age groups, with the higher consultation rates among the ethnic minority groups compared to whites only occurring at older ages. This may partly be a result of the increase in the health differences between ethnic groups with age (see Figure 3.7). In fact, Tables 6.6 and 6.7 show quite clearly how perceived health status influenced consultation rates.

There is an interesting discrepancy between GP consultation rates and hospital admission rates. Differences between ethnic minority groups and whites for the former are larger than for the latter. This is most clearly illustrated when comparing Tables 6.6 and 6.7, but can also be seen when other tables are compared. Two possible explanations seem likely. First, it may be that ethnic minority respondents were more likely to consult their GPs for less serious complaints and, consequently, were less likely to be referred on for hospital treatment. If we accept that there are only minimal ethnic variations in actual health within the broad health categories used in Table 6.6 and that all of the ethnic minority groups behaved similarly in this respect, despite the diversity of their cultures, this would seem to be the most appropriate conclusion. Second, it may be possible that ethnic minority people are less likely to be admitted to hospital than white people when they have a similar level of illness. If this is correct, differences in GP consultation rates should be interpreted as reflecting real differences in levels of illness (which are not adequately controlled for by the broad categories of health status used) that are not translated into differences in hospital admission rates. There are a number of reasons why this might be so – such as not being taken seriously by health care workers, or not being able to communicate symptoms effectively to them – but all would suggest that although ethnic minority people make it into a consultation with their GP, the quality of that consultation is less adequate than that for the white majority. The relative quality of health care received by different ethnic groups is an issue raised in the introduction to this chapter, and one which is explored below using data collected for this survey.

COMMUNICATING WITH A GP AND USE OF IN-PATIENT SUPPORT SERVICES

A basic requirement for effective communication between a doctor and patient is that they share a common language. In order to assess language use, respondents were asked which languages they spoke, and about nine out of ten South Asian and eight out of ten Chinese respondents reported using a language other than English in some circumstances. In addition to this, an assessment of the respondent's English language ability was made by his or her interviewer. This is shown in Table 6.8 for the Asian groups, which clearly illustrates that a significant number of each of the Asian groups had difficulty communicating in English. African Asians had the lowest rate of difficulty, with one in ten respondents judged as speaking English slightly or not at all, compared to one in four Indians and Chinese and two out of five Pakistanis and Bangladeshis. For all groups except the Chinese there were also clear gender differences, women were more likely than men not to speak English. In fact, half of Pakistani women and over half of Bangladeshi women were in this position.

Table 6.8   Interviewer's assessment of English language ability – Asians only

					cell percentages
	Indian	African Asian	Pakistani	Bangladeshi	Chinese
Speaks English only slightly or not at all					
Men	19	8	26	26	24
Women	30	14	50	60	24
Total	25	11	38	41	24
Weighted count	*1283*	*797*	*856*	*285*	*390*
Unweighted count	*1264*	*726*	*1178*	*591*	*213*

The BMEG survey (Rudat 1994) reported that among those whose main language was not English many used one of the South Asian languages to communicate with their GP (that survey did not have any Chinese respondents). However, as many as two out of five of its Indian respondents and a third of its Pakistani and Bangladeshi respondents in this situation had to use English. This suggests that for these groups some problems in communication with a GP may occur.

All ethnic minority respondents to this survey who had spoken to their GP in the last month were asked whether the GP(s) they had consulted had spoken in a language that they could understand. As expected, all of the Caribbean respondents shared a language with their GP. Table 6.9 shows responses to this question for the Asian respondents. From the table it can be seen that there were clear differences both between ethnic groups and between men and women. African Asians were the least likely to have consulted a GP who did not speak a language they could understand, only one in forty were in this situation. Chinese respondents were the most likely to not share a language with their GP, almost one in four were in this situation. However, only 49 Chinese respondents had consulted their GP in the last month and were asked this question, so the extent to which this figure is an accurate reflection of the experience of Chinese people is questionable, although it does mirror the figures on English language ability shown in Table 6.8.

Table 6.9   Whether General Practitioners consulted in the past year spoke a language the respondent understood – Asians only

cell percentages

	Indian	African Asian	Pakistani	Bangladeshi	Chinese
On at least one occasion the GP did not speak a language understood by the respondent					
Men	2.2	1.3	3.7	1.8	*
Women	4.8	3.6	5.7	12.0	*
Total	3.9	2.5	4.8	7.2	28.8
Weighted count	*521*	*248*	*418*	*123*	*85*
Unweighted count	*529*	*245*	*601*	*263*	*49*

* small base numbers in the cell make the estimate unreliable

Looking at the figures by gender shows that for all groups women were more likely than men to consult a GP who did not speak the same language as them. Overall there were few men who had difficulties with the language their GP spoke, the highest figure being 1 in 30 for Pakistani men. For women this was the lowest figure, occurring for African Asian women, and about 1 in 20 Indian and Pakistani women and one in eight Bangladeshi women had difficulties understanding the language their GPs used. As would be expected, this also varied by age. Not shown in the table is that less than 2 per cent of Asians under 25 had difficulties understanding the language used by their GPs compared to almost 7 per cent of those aged 25 or older. Given the conclusions on English language ability arising from Table 6.8, these figures are not surprising. They follow the same gender and, for South Asians, ethnic pattern found in that table. The figures in Table 6.9 are somewhat lower for South Asian, but not for the Chinese, resopondents than those in Table 6.8. This is, presumably, because many South Asians will have a GP of the same or similar ethnicity to themselves, while this may not be the case for the Chinese. In fact, the

BMEG survey (Rudat 1994) suggested that more than four out of five South Asians attend a general practice with a South Asian doctor.

In order to overcome this basic difficulty in communicating with their GPs, respondents used a variety of strategies. The majority, about three-quarters, reported using either family members or friends to translate for them. About one in six said that they managed by using as much English as they knew, sometimes with the help of gestures. A few simply assumed that as their doctor knew about their illness there was no need for further communication. Fewer than one in ten of the respondents who reported language difficulties with their GP had had access to and used an official translator during their consultations. All of these strategies clearly present some difficulties and, of those who did have language problems when communicating with their GP, about a third felt that their GP had not understood them. (There were too few respondents who met the criteria to be asked these questions – only 85 – for responses to be broken down by ethnic group.)

Respondents who had been admitted to hospital in the past year were asked if they had received any assistance from a hospital link worker, an advocate or an interpreter. Responses to this question, shown in Table 6.10, give an indication both of need and of the extent to which it is being met. As can be seen from the table (which, because of the small number of respondents who were admitted to hospital, combines certain groups and omits the Chinese) a third of Pakistani/Bangladeshi respondents had received such services compared to one in seven Indian/African Asians and very few whites and Caribbeans. This pattern did not vary greatly by gender.

Table 6.10   Use of in-patient hospital support services

cell percentages

	White	Caribbean	Indian or African Asian	Pakistani or Bangladeshi
Received assistance from a hospital link worker, advocate or interpreter	4	3	14	30
Weighted count	*324*	*179*	*195*	*123*
Unweighted count	*350*	*150*	*191*	*215*

ETHNIC AND GENDER PREFERENCES FOR DOCTORS

Another way of exploring the extent to which the needs of different ethnic groups vary and are potentially unmet, is to consider their preferences for the ethnicity and gender of the doctor they consult. All of the white respondents and half of the ethnic minority respondents were asked if they preferred to see a doctor of their own ethnic origin. Responses to this question are shown in Table 6.11. Overall, two-fifths of Pakistani and Bangladeshi respondents reported that they preferred to see a doctor of their own ethnic origin, compared to a third of Chinese and Indian respondents, a quarter of white respondents, a fifth of African Asian respondents and just over one in ten Caribbean respondents. There was an interesting variation by gender, white, Indian, Pakistani and Bangladeshi women were more likely than equivalent men to prefer to see a doctor of their own ethnic origin, while there was no difference between Caribbean and African Asian men and women. The much lower rate among Caribbeans than any other ethnic group is also of interest and may reflect the lack of an opportunity to consult with a Caribbean GP. The BMEG survey (Rudat 1994) suggests that less than 1 per cent of both its respondents and the white comparison sample had had access to a Caribbean GP.

Table 6.11 Preferred ethnic origin for doctor by gender

cell percentages

	White	Caribbean	Indian	African Asian	Pakistani	Bangladeshi	Chinese
Ever prefer to see a doctor of own ethnic origin							
Men	21	12	26	21	34	29	*
Women	29	11	33	20	49	54	*
Total	26	12	34	20	41	42	31
Weighted base	*2864*	*775*	*644*	*389*	*419*	*138*	*195*
Unweighted base	*2863*	*607*	*636*	*347*	*582*	*289*	*104*

* small base numbers in the cell make the estimate unreliable.

Not shown in the table is that responses for the Asian groups also varied by language ability, with those who spoke English only slightly or not at all being three times more likely to prefer to see a doctor of their own ethnicity than those who were at least reasonably fluent in English (66 per cent versus 22 per cent). In fact, when respondents who expressed a preference for a doctor with the same ethnicity as themselves were asked why this was so, the majority of South Asian respondents explained their preference in terms of language difficulties. Three-quarters of them said that it enabled them to use their own language and a fifth said that it enabled them to speak directly to the doctor. Other explanations mentioned by South Asian respondents for preferring a doctor of their own ethnicity included 1 in 25 saying it was for religious or cultural reasons and one in eight saying that they felt more comfortable with such a doctor.

Although only a few Caribbean respondents were asked this question (31 in total) it is interesting to note that, in contrast to the result for South Asians, just over half of them said that they preferred a doctor of their own ethnicity because they felt more comfortable with one, and an additional 20 per cent explained their preference as a result of religious or cultural reasons. One in five of the Caribbeans asked this question did not provide an answer. There were also only a few Chinese respondents who were asked this question (25 in total), but the pattern of response for them seemed to broadly follow that for the South Asian respondents.

At first sight it would seem that a preference for a doctor of the same ethnicity as the respondent cannot be explained in terms of language ability for white respondents. However, almost three out of five of the white respondents who expressed such a preference said it was because they had difficulties understanding a non-white doctor. The other reasons white respondents gave for preferring a white doctor more clearly contained elements of prejudice. About one in six of these respondents said that they had less faith in non-white doctors. A similar number said that they preferred to see someone of their own colour, and about one in twelve said that they did not like the approach of non-white doctors. Almost 3 per cent of these respondents used explanations that were explicitly racist. Typical examples of what was said include:

> I'm a racialist to put it bluntly. I just don't like them.

> I'm prejudiced against them, they're in the wrong country. If you were in their country I wouldn't object but they're in my country.

> They stink, I think they smell the Asians.

Table 6.12 shows responses to the question asking respondents if they preferred to see a female or male doctor, which was asked of all of the white respondents and half of the ethnic minority respondents.

Table 6.12   Preferred gender for doctor by gender

cell percentages

	White	Caribbean	Indian	African Asian	Pakistani	Bangladeshi	Chinese
Prefer to see a doctor of own gender							
Men	12	11	16	12	25	10	*
Women	19	29	39	30	75	83	*
Total	15	11	14	10	24	23	8
Weighted base	*2867*	*783*	*646*	*392*	*421*	*138*	*195*
Unweighted base	*2867*	*614*	*638*	*350*	*584*	*289*	*104*

* small base numbers in the cell make the estimate unreliable.

From the table it can be seen that for all ethnic groups women were more likely to say that they preferred to see a doctor of their own gender. (Very few respondents said that they preferred to see a doctor of the opposite gender to them.) However, comparing ethnic groups shows an inconsistent pattern across gender groups. For men, responses were reasonably consistent across all ethnic groups except for Pakistanis. Typically, slightly more than one in ten preferred to consult a male doctor and this rose to almost one in four for Pakistanis. For the women, all ethnic minority respondents except the Chinese were more likely to prefer to see a female doctor than white women, with Pakistani and Bangladeshi women having the highest rates. In fact, almost three out of four Pakistani women and over four out of five Bangladeshi women preferred to see a female doctor. These figures should presumably be interpreted in the light of the cultural and religious traditions among the almost exclusively Muslim Pakistani and Bangladeshi groups, but no follow-up questions were asked in this survey to check on this. Nevertheless such preferences should be noted, as they will undoubtedly influence the quality of a consultation with a doctor. It is also extremely unlikely that the apparent preferences of ethnic minority women, particularly Pakistani and Bangladeshi women, to consult female doctors of the same ethnicity as themselves will be met. For example, the BMEG survey (Rudat, 1994) reports that, while three out of five Pakistani and Bangladeshi female respondents preferred to see a female GP, two-thirds of these women were not always able to do so.

THE USE OF OTHER HEALTH AND SOCIAL SERVICES

All of the white and half of the ethnic minority respondents were asked about their use of a variety of other health and social services in the past year. Responses to these questions are shown in Table 6.13.

Table 6.13   Other health and social services used in the past year

cell percentages

	White	Caribbean	Indian	African Asian	Pakistani	Bangladeshi	Chinese
Per cent who have used the service							
Dentist	62	53	45	46	50	25	47
Physiotherapist	9.0	6.5	5.8	4.1	3.9	0.6	7.9
Psychotherapist	1.1	0.7	0.5	0.8	0.8	0.6	1.3
Alternative practitioner	5.7	2.9	1.7	3.0	1.3	0.6	3.8
Health visitor or district nurse	7.4	8.7	4.2	4.1	4.8	6.9	6.8
Social worker	3.8	5.2	2.2	1.1	1.7	1.7	2.5
Home help	2.1	1.0	0.3	0.1	1.8	0.8	0
Age and gender standardised	0.7	0.9	—— 0.2 ——		—— 1.7 ——		0
Meals on wheels (aged 65+)	3.2	1.8	0	*	3.1*	*	*
Age and gender standardised	2.2	1.7	—— 0 ——		—— 2.0 ——		*
Other	6.9	4.4	1.2	2.9	1.3	2.7	2.3
Weighted base	*2863*	*777*	*646*	*390*	*417*	*138*	*195*
Unweighted base	*2862*	*609*	*638*	*348*	*578*	*289*	*104*

* small base numbers in the cell make the estimate unreliable.

Among the ethnic minority groups there was, on the whole, little variation in the use of these services except for the consistently low use of dentists, physiotherapists and alternative practitioners by Bangladeshis. White respondents were more likely than all of the ethnic minority respondents to have made use of nearly all of these services. The only exception to this was the relatively high use made by Caribbeans of health visitors or district nurses, and social work services. Whether this is the result of institutional beliefs regarding which clients need these particular services, or the result of genuine differences in need is impossible to determine from the data.

Of the services listed, only dental services would be expected to be routinely used. The responses shown in the first row of Table 6.13 are in marked contrast to those shown for GP consultations, which ethnic minority respondents were more likely to have had than white respondents. While more than three-fifths of white respondents had seen a dentist in the past year, only about half of the Caribbean,

Indian, African Asian, Pakistanis and Chinese respondents had. Particularly worrying was that only a quarter of the Bangladeshi respondents had seen a dentist in the last year, a figure also reported in the BMEG survey (Rudat 1994).

The overall greater use by whites of the services listed in Table 6.13 interestingly also applied to alternative practitioners, for which the questioning included the examples of hakims, homeopaths and osteopaths. More than 1 in 20 of the white respondents reported having consulted such a practitioner, compared to around 1 in 30 Caribbeans, African Asians and Chinese, about 1 in 60 Indians and Pakistanis and less than 1 in 100 Bangladeshis.

Not shown in the table is that there was also an interesting variation in the use of these services by gender. For all of the ethnic groups, except Pakistanis and Bangladeshis, women were almost without exception more likely than men to use the services listed. Pakistanis and Bangladeshis followed this general pattern for the use of health visitors or district nurses, whose main work for this relatively young population probably involved providing support for the care of young children, but men were frequently more likely than women to use the other services. This may in part be a reflection of the language needs of Pakistani and, particularly, Bangladeshi women, as shown in Table 6.8.

PRIVATE HEALTH SERVICES

The BMEG survey (Rudat 1994) reports that South Asian groups were less likely than the general population to have private health cover, but that Caribbeans were just as likely. In this survey a limited amount of information was collected on the use of private health care facilities. All of the white and half of the ethnic minority respondents who had spent some time in the past year as a hospital in-patient were asked if their stay had been paid for privately. Nine per cent of white respondents reported that this was the case, compared to about 4 per cent of Indians/African Asians, 2.5 per cent of Caribbeans and less than 2 per cent of Pakistanis/ Bangladeshis. (There were too few Chinese respondents in this situation for a reliable estimate to be made for them.) It seems that three factors may explain these differences. The first is differences in the relative wealth of different ethnic groups, although differences between whites and Indians and African Asians were not that great (Modood *et al.* 1997). Second, given that the majority of private health care insurance is paid through occupational schemes (Laing 1988), the differences in the use of private health care by ethnic groups may reflect differences in the extent of coverage by such schemes as a result of differences in the kinds of occupations they have (Modood *et al.* 1997). Third, different ethnic groups may have different beliefs about the acceptability of private health care, as they do in their orientations to political parties (Modood *et al.* 1997).

This difference in the use of private or Naitonal Health Service (NHS) services was not present for dental services, with 16 per cent of whites, 18 per cent of Indians and African Asians, 20 per cent of Caribbeans and 22 per cent of Chinese using a private dentist. In contrast only 8 per cent of Pakistanis and Bangladeshis used a private dentist.

DISCUSSION

The data presented on both GP visits and hospital in-patient stays suggest that ethnic minority groups were at least as likely as whites to use both primary and secondary medical care. Tables 6.1 and 6.2 show that ethnic minority groups, with the exception of the Chinese, made as much or more use of their GPs as whites. Table 6.2 shows an interesting age variation in this, younger ethnic minority respondents had lower consultation rates and older ethnic minority respondents had higher consultation rates compared to whites. This, in fact, follows the age pattern for ethnic variations in self-assessed health, shown in Figure 3.7. However, even when self-assessed health was taken into account, the greater GP consultation rate compared to whites remained for all ethnic minority groups except the Chinese (Table 6.6). This is consistent with other reports of ethnic variations in the use of health services, as outlined in the introduction (Rudat 1994, McCormick and Rosenbaum 1990, Balarajan *et al.* 1989), and it seems that only two possible explanations can account for this. The first is that the broad groups used to categorise self-assessed health are not internally homogeneous, and within each health category there remain ethnic variations in health that lead to the different consultation rates. The second is that each ethnic minority group is more likely to see GPs as an appropriate source of help for their health problems than the white group and, therefore, are more likely to consult them, even if there are no differences in the relative levels of their health. Whichever explanation is correct, there was no evidence in this survey for the under use of GP services by ethnic minority respondents, except, possibly, by the Chinese.

Tables 6.3, 6.4, 6.5 and 6.7 consider in-patient hospital stays and reach slightly different conclusions to those for GP consultations. The first of these tables shows that ethnic minority respondents were overall less likely to be admitted to hospital, other than for childbirth, than white respondents. When admissions for more than one week were considered (Table 6.5), the same overall pattern emerged. There were changes in these patterns according to age, as there were for variations in GP consultation rates, with ethnic minority groups catching up and, in some cases, overtaking the white rate with increasing age. As suggested above, this may reflect an increase in ethnic variations in health with increasing age. In contrast to GP consultation rates, once self-assessed health was taken into account (Table 6.7) there were no differences in rates of hospital admission across ethnic groups, except perhaps a lower rate among the Chinese. However, this table does not take into account the higher rates of admission that Pakistani and Bangladeshi women had for childbirth (Table 6.4). Given this higher rate and the possibility that the broad health categories used in the table do not adequately control for ethnic variations in health, the discrepancies between Tables 6.6 and 6.7 do raise the possibility that ethnic minority respondents may not receive sufficient hospital-based care, a conclusion also reached by Balarajan *et al.* (1991) in their analysis of the General Household Survey data from 1983 to 1987. A possible reason for this may be that they receive poorer quality primary health care. There is limited evidence to support this proposition. Gillam *et al.* (1989) were able to show that during a consultation with a

GP, ethnic minority patients were less like to receive a follow-up appointment, although this study was based on only one practice.

There are clearly problems with simply looking at utilisation data without taking into account the quality of the services that different groups have access to and receive, even if information on need is taken into account. The data presented in this chapter suggest that primary health care services may not be sufficiently attuned to the needs of certain ethnic minority groups. For example, a significant number of Asian respondents did not understand the language used by their GP and this was particularly the case for Bangladeshi women and Chinese respondents. In fact, as many as one in eight of the female Bangladeshi respondents were in this situation and, although based on small numbers, the figures were even higher for Chinese respondents. Respondents used a variety of strategies to deal with this, although the main one was to use a friend or family member to translate for them. However, despite attempts to improve communication, a large number of these respondents felt that they had not been understood by their GP. This situation is a reflection of three factors: the English language abilities of Asian ethnic groups (see Table 6.8); their opportunities to consult with a GP of a similar ethnicity to themselves; and the scarcity of appropriate translation services – fewer than 10 per cent of respondents who reported language difficulties with their GP had used a translation service. In fact, a number of the ethnic minority respondents did prefer to consult with a GP who was of a similar ethnicity to them, and it is clear both from how this preference increased with decreasing English language ability and the explanations given for such a preference, that for many this was based on a desire to improve the level of communication with their GP.

There is an interesting contrast between the explanations given by ethnic minority respondents and white respondents for preferring a doctor of their own ethnicity. Although many white respondents also explained their preference in terms of not being able to understand ethnic minority doctors, given the language abilities of ethnic minority doctors such an explanation must be questioned and probably contains elements of prejudice. In fact, the other explanations offered for preferring to see a white doctor contained clear elements of prejudice and racism.

Ethnic minority women, with the exception of the Chinese, were more likely to prefer to see a female doctor than white women. This was particularly the case for Pakistani and Bangladeshi women, for whom more than three-quarters had such a preference. However, it seems likely that respondents' preferences for both the ethnicity and gender of their doctors cannot be met even in primary health care and this may have important implications for the quality of the consultations that they have. In addition to this, the data presented in the BMEG report (Rudat 1994), and outlined at the beginning of this chapter, suggest that ethnic minority groups have poorer primary health care across a variety of other dimensions. These include the ease of obtaining access to a GP in addition to the quality of communication with the GP and an overall assessment by the respondent of the quality of consultations.

Ethnic variations in the use of health and social services other than medical services were present in this survey (Table 6.13). Ethnic minority respondents were less likely to make use of all of the services asked about (dentists, physiotherapists, psychotherapists, alternative practitioners, health visitors or district nurses, social workers, home helps and meals on wheels) except for a greater use of health visitors or district nurses, and social workers by Caribbeans. Whether this reflects a greater demand among the Caribbean community for these services, or a perception among providers of a greater need of services for Caribbean children, perhaps as a result of the relatively high rate of single parenthood in this group (Modood *et al.* 1997), or a combination of both of these factors, is impossible to determine from the data. However, given the relative under-utilisation of all of the other services by Caribbeans, and of all services by the other ethnic minority groups, the second explanation should not be ruled out.

Of particular concern among the data on the under-utilisation of health and social services by ethnic minorities compared to whites, are the figures for the use of dental services. While three out of five white respondents had visited a dentist in the past 12 months, this was the case for only half of the Caribbean, Indian, African Asian, Pakistani and Chinese respondents, and for only one in four Bangladeshi respondents – a figure supported by data from the BMEG survey (Rudat 1994). Whether the costs of visiting a dentist are important here is again impossible to tell from the data. However, a significant number of respondents did pay for their dental care privately and, like others (Rudat 1994), the data presented here show that ethnic minority respondents were less likely than whites to have used private health care. Also, consistent with the perspective that cost may be an important barrier to the use of dental care, Pakistanis and Bangladeshis were far less likely to have paid for their dental care privately than all of the other groups.

CHAPTER SEVEN

Conclusion

In the introduction to this volume the context of this survey was fully described. However, some of the issues raised there are worth reiterating prior to an overview of key findings. The first is that this survey was unique in terms of its coverage of ethnic minority populations, the health assessments included in the study, and its coverage of other features of the lives of ethnic minority people in Britain. Most general population surveys do not contain sufficient numbers of ethnic minority people for their samples to be representative of ethnic minority groups, or for the relevant issues to be fully investigated. However, two other national datasets containing morbidity data sufficient to explore ethnic variations in health and health service use are worth considering, the 1991 Census and the Health Education Authority's *Black and Minority Ethnic Groups Health and Lifestyles Survey* (Rudat 1994). Unfortunately both have their limitations. They have been restricted by their limited coverage of ethnic minority populations (Rudat 1994), or their limited assessment of health (the 1991 Census) and the factors beyond ethnicity that may be related to health (Rudat 1994). The most influential work in the epidemiological investigation of ethnic variations in health has, of necessity, relied on immigrant mortality data (Marmot *et al.* 1984, Balarajan and Bulusu 1990, Balarajan 1996). However, these have all of the drawbacks just outlined: they use a one-dimensional indication of health; they have a limited and crude coverage of ethnic minority populations; and they have an inadequate coverage of possible explanatory factors for the observed relationships. All of these limitations should lead to the conclusions drawn from such data being treated with a significant amount of caution.

Consequently, the data that have been reported here can be considered an important benchmark in work on ethnic variations in health, and one that is concerned with providing information on health needs and disadvantage as well as on aetiology. However, two notes of caution need to be sounded in the interpretation of the results presented, both of which are a result of the reliance on a standardised cross-sectional survey instrument. The first is that the assessments of health and health service use are based entirely on self-reports. None of these measures have been clinically validated for cross-cultural reseach. Indeed such self-report could be related to cultural and language differences and, in the case of health service use, the racial discrimination that is a central feature of the lives of ethnic minority people (Modood *et al.* 1997). Consequently, their accuracy could be biased by the ethnicity of the respondent, which could then lead to an inaccurate representation of ethnic variations in health Although we should take seriously the possibility that the data presented are the result of an artefact in reporting style or opportunity for diagnosis, some reassurance about the validity of the measures used can be drawn from the fact that within ethnic groups the expected distribution of health across factors such as age, gender and class was found, and that across ethnic groups different types of health assessment (for example, questions on diagnosis and questions on symptoms) and the assessment of different but related dimensions of health (for example, smoking and respiratory symptoms) showed consistent patterns.

The second note of caution concerns the interpretation of the suggested explanatory relationships. The cross-sectional nature of the survey means that causal direction can only be assumed from these data. So, although they do show clear relationships between suggested explanatory factors and ethnic variations in health, the direction of the relationships shown can not be determined. Some confidence can be drawn from the fact that studies in other populations have repeatedly shown similar relationships (Townsend and Davidson 1982, Blaxter 1987, Townsend *et al.* 1988, Blaxter 1990, Davey Smith *et al.* 1990b, Haynes 1991) and the causal directions assumed in this report have been generally acknowledged as and shown to be appropriate (Davey Smith *et al.* 1990a, Kuh and Wadsworth 1993, Bartley 1994, Benzeval *et al.* 1995, Department of Health 1995).

KEY FINDINGS

The following provides an overview of the findings described in earlier chapters of this volume. On the whole this section is orientated to the interests of epidemiologists and health care planners with an interest in specific illnesses. However, the first section provides a summary of the findings on general health and how this is patterned across ethnic groups, so provides an overview of overall health disadvantage and how this may be related to the position of ethnic minority groups in Britain.

General health

The second chapter shows the large burden of ill-health faced by members of some ethnic minority groups, despite their relatively young age profile compared to whites. Almost 40 per cent of the Pakistani, Bangladeshi and Caribbean groups reported that they either had fair or poor health, a long-standing illness, or were registered disabled, and 20 per cent of the Pakistani and Bangladeshi groups said that their performance of moderately exerting activities, such as climbing one flight of stairs, was in some way limited by their health. In contrast, only just over a quarter of African Asians and Chinese and less than a third of Indians reported that they either had fair or poor health, a long-standing illness, or were registered disabled. Once the age and gender profiles of the different ethnic groups had been taken into account to allow a comparison with whites to be made, the suggestion that there were important differences in the experiences of ethnic minority groups was confirmed. For example, while Pakistani/Bangladeshis and Caribbeans were statistically significantly more likely than whites to report fair or poor health (50 per cent more likely for the former and 30 per cent more likely for the latter), Indian/ African Asians and Chinese had very similar rates to whites. The pattern of findings was consistent across all but one of the assessments of general health used[1] and was very similar to those from the only comparable data source, the 1991 Census (shown in Chapter 3).

Chapters 4 and 5 contain data exploring possible explanations for the relationship between self-assessed general health and ethnic group. Chapter 4 shows that the differences between ethnic minority groups and whites could not be attributed to disadvantage experienced in the country of birth – those that were born in Britain or migrated at an early age were, if anything, more likely than those who migrated aged 11 or older to report that their health was fair or poor. In addition, Chapter 4 shows that if ethnic sub-groups are considered, important differences within particular ethnic minority groups emerge, reinforcing the suggestion in earlier chapters of a lack of uniformity of risk within particular ethnic groups. Chapter 5 uses socio-economic status to explore this variation in risk within ethnic groups in an alternative way. For each of the ethnic groups considered, there was a strong and statistically significant relationship between indicators of socio-economic status and reported fair or poor health. Moreover, once the difficulties with controlling for socio-economic status across ethnic groups had been partially addressed, the relative risk for members of all of the ethnic minority groups compared to whites to report fair or poor health was reduced, although differences between Pakistani/Bangladeshis and whites, and Caribbeans and whites remained statistically significant.

The data on general health from this survey clearly show that levels of ill-health vary markedly across ethnic minority groups, as well as between ethnic minority and majority groups. The implication is that studies that have generalised from ethnic sub-groups to a wider group, such as from Bangladeshis to South Asians (McKeigue *et al.* 1988), will be misleading, as will those that use crude ethnic groupings that are very heterogeneous, such as all ethnic minorities (Benzeval *et al.* 1992, Gould and Jones 1996), or all South Asians (Marmot *et al.* 1984, Balarajan and Bulusu 1990). The data presented in this volume also indicate strongly that a key factor in explaining these ethnic variations in general health is the differing overall socio-economic positions of different ethnic groups. Both within and across ethnic groups socio-economic status showed a strong relationship with health status.

Cardiovascular disease

The data on coronary heart disease presented in this volume also show important differences between ethnic minority groups, and contradict many of the assumptions that have underpinned previous work in this area. Most work on ethnic variations in heart disease has considered South Asians to be a group that is uniformly at greater risk of coronary heart disease (for example, McKeigue *et al.* 1989, McKeigue 1992 and 1993, Gupta *et al.* 1995). However, the data presented in Chapter 2 and Chapter 4

---

1   The only exception to this was the question on long-standing illness, which others (Pilgrim *et al.* 1993, Rudat 1994) and the data shown in Chapter 3, suggest is not a valid indicator for exploring ethnic variations in health. Interestingly, an extension of the question so that it only included long-standing illnesses *that limited work* did, in contrast, show the general pattern just reported.

show important differences in the rates of both diagnosis of and symptoms of coronary heart disease across the groups that comprise South Asians. For example, among those aged 40 or more, almost 25 per cent of Pakistanis and Bangladeshis reported that they had either severe chest pain or diagnosed heart disease, compared to 13 and 12 per cent of Indians and African Asians respectively. In comparison with the white population South Asians as a whole had a higher risk of having either a diagnosis of or symptoms suggestive of heart disease. However, within the South Asian group this greater risk only applied to the Pakistani/ Bangladeshi group, Indian/African Asians had the same risk as whites.

Although these findings do contradict the assumptions underlying much of the work in this area, they are consistent across age and gender groups and across types of question used.[2] In fact, a careful inspection of earlier work that has, despite the difficulties of the task given the quality of data available, attempted to explore differences between South Asian groups in this respect, also suggests that there may be important differences between South Asian groups for coronary heart disease. Consistent with the findings described in both Chapter 2 and Chapter 4 of this volume, Table III of Balarajan *et al.* (1984) suggests that Muslims had a greater proportional mortality ratio for death from myocardial infarction than any other South Asian group. More recent studies of immigrant mortality also suggest that there are important differences between South Asian groups. Again consistent with the findings reported here, Balarajan (1996) shows that those born in Bangladesh followed by those born in Pakistan had the highest rates of mortality from coronary heart disease, although, inconsistent with the data shown here, he shows that those born in India also had higher rates than the general population. Inconsistencies between immigrant mortality data and the fully representative morbidity data used here need to be interpreted in the light of differences between mortality and morbidity health assessments outlined in Chapter 1 and the conclusion to Chapter 3. In particular, it is worth considering evidence that suggests that survival rates following myocardial infarction are higher for better off socio-economic groups (Morrison *et al.* 1997) and for whites compared to South Asians (Shaukat *et al.* 1997, Wilkinson *et al.* 1996).

When possible explanations for the demonstrated ethnic variations in coronary heart disease were explored in Chapters 4 and 5, those that were founded on the belief that South Asians had a shared greater risk, such as the insulin resistance syndrome hypothesis, clearly had to be rejected. (Although, of course this does not mean that insulin resistance does not have a potential role in the aetiology of coronary heart disease, simply that it cannot explain the uncovered ethnic variations, a point that will be returned to later.) Somewhat surprisingly, given the conclusions reached by others working in this field (McKeigue *et al.* 1989), it was found that within ethnic groups there was a strong relationship between socio-economic status and coronary heart disease, that was in many instances statistically significant. Some

---

2   Questions were asked on diagnosis of angina, diagnosis of heart disease, experience of chest pain and
     severity of chest pain. The question on diagnosis of heart disease included 'a heart murmur, a
     damaged heart or a rapid heart', which would cover conditions beyond *coronary* heart disease.
     However, the consistency of response across the questions on diagnosis and those on symptoms
     suggests that the inclusion of the additional items was not too misleading.

support for this finding can be drawn from two studies. The first, in a rural location in western India, also showed a strong relationship between socio-economic status and coronary heart disease (Gupta *et al.* 1994). The second reported that the risk of coronary heart disease in South India was related to low-birthweight and low maternal body weight, leading the authors to conclude that poor maternal nutrition may have been significant (Stein *et al.* 1996). In addition, once socio-economic status had been partially controlled for in this study, the risk of both diagnosed heart disease and symptoms suggestive of heart disease compared to whites dropped for all ethnic minority groups, and the former was no longer statistically significant for the Pakistani/Bangladeshi group. Again, the suggestion is that much of the ethnic variation in heart disease reported here could be attributed to differences in the socio-economic status between different ethnic minority group. Again, it is important to recognise that it was the quality of the data that were available for this analysis that allowed these relationships to be uncovered.

The data on the reporting of a diagnosis of hypertension on the whole follow the pattern described in previous studies (Marmot *et al.* 1984, Balarajan 1991). Chapter 2 shows that Caribbeans had higher rates of diagnosed hypertension than any other ethnic minority group, and Chapter 3 shows that Caribbeans had a greater risk of diagnosed hypertension than whites. However, Chapter 3 also shows that, in contrast to immigrant mortality data, this greater risk applied only to the women in the Caribbean group and did not apply to any of the South Asian groups. In fact, Indian/African Asians appeared to have a lower risk than whites. Given that the questions used relied *solely* on the respondent having had hypertension diagnosed, and that hypertension is an asymptomatic condition so could only be identified if a screening opportunity arose, the accuracy of the data presented is questionable. Nevertheless, Chapter 5 shows once again that within each ethnic group there was an inverse relationship between socio-economic status and the rate of diagnosis of hypertension, which in many cases was statistically significant. In addition, once socio-economic status had been partially controlled for, the relative risk of ethnic minority compared to white respondents to report a diagnosis of hypertension was reduced in every instance.

Diabetes

The ethnic variations for diabetes also followed the pattern found in immigrant mortality data and other studies of diabetes in ethnic minority groups (Marmot *et al.* 1984, Balarajan and Bulusu 1990, McKeigue *et al.* 1991). Chapter 3 shows that all of the ethnic minority groups had a much greater risk of a diagnosis of diabetes than whites and that for all but the Chinese group this difference was statistically significant. Chapters 2 and 3 show that there were also important differences between ethnic minority groups. Among the ethnic minority groups, Chinese respondents reported the lowest rate of diagnosed diabetes, followed by African Asians, Indians and Caribbeans (all with similar rates) and then Pakistanis and Bangladeshis (who also had similar rates). The differences between the South Asian groups are worth highlighting, Pakistani/Bangladeshis had over five times the white rate of diabetes while that for Indian/African Asians was less than three times greater.

In terms of an illness burden, diabetes is clearly a serious problem for ethnic minority groups. Despite the relatively young age profile of these groups, as many as 1 in 13 of the Pakistani and Bangladeshi respondents, 1 in 17 of the Caribbean respondents, 1 in 18 of the Indian respondents, 1 in 25 of the African Asian respondents and 1 in 50 of the Chinese respondents reported that they had had a diagnosis of diabetes. This gives an overall figure of 1 in 18 of all of the ethnic minority respondents to this survey reporting that they had a diagnosis of diabetes.

As for other health outcomes, within ethnic groups there was an inverse relationship between risk of having diagnosed diabetes and socio-economic status. However, uniquely among the outcomes considered here, once socio-economic status had been partially controlled for, the differences between the white group and all of the ethnic minority groups in the rate of diagnosis of diabetes remained large, although the risk of such a diagnosis was reduced.

Respiratory symptoms

The coverage of symptoms suggestive of respiratory illness in this survey focused on questions asking about wheezing or coughing up phlegm. The responses to these questions shown in Chapter 3 illustrated that unlike other health assessments used in this survey, ethnic minority respondents were less likely than whites to report these symptoms, with rates for all of the South Asian and Chinese groups being significantly lower than those for whites, and those for Caribbeans being close to significantly lower.[3] This also is consistent with immigrant mortality data, which show that those born in South Asia and the Caribbean have lower mortality rates from chronic respiratory conditions, a finding that the authors related to the low rates of smoking among ethnic minority groups (Marmot *et al.* 1984).

However, both the data presented by Rudat (1994) and those reported here show that significant numbers of people in some ethnic minority groups do smoke. Not surprisingly, for all ethnic groups smoking was highly related to the rate of reporting these respiratory symptoms, white smokers were 50 per cent and ethnic minority smokers were 80 per cent more likely than their non-smoking counter-parts to report these symptoms (see Table C.12 in Appendix C). In support of the hypothesis that differences in the risk of reporting respiratory symptoms across ethnic groups were the result of differences in rates of smoking, Chapter 3 shows that ethnic minority respondents who smoked had the same risk as their white equivalents. However, non-smoking members of the South Asian groups still had a lower rate of reporting respiratory symptoms than their white counterparts.

Once again, for all ethnic groups the rate of reporting these symptoms was strongly and significantly related to socio-economic status. Also, once socio-economic status had been partially controlled for, the risk for all ethnic minority groups compared to whites to reported these symptoms became even smaller.

---

3 Interestingly, most of the differences reported here related to the question on wheezing rather than that on coughing up phlegm.

Accidents

Respondents were asked about accidents that had occurred to them that resulted in hospital treatment. Chapter 2 shows that for all ethnic groups women were less likely to report having had such accidents than men and that this was particularly true for Pakistani/Bangladeshis. It also shows that among the ethnic minority groups, Caribbeans were much more likely than South Asians to report such accidents, although differences were not so great between Caribbean and Pakistani/Bangladeshi men, particularly for accidents that occurred on the road or pavement. Chapter 3 shows that once this analysis was extended to include a comparison with the white population, all of the ethnic minority groups were much and, except for the Chinese, statistically significantly less likely than whites to have reported such an accident. There is currently very little data with which to compare these findings. Some have suggested that because of the association between accidents and socio-economic disadvantage, those ethnic minority groups that have the greatest socio-economic disadvantage should have a higher risk of accidental injury (Balarajan and Soni Raleigh, 1995). This certainly seems to be a reasonable conclusion to draw, but it is clearly inconsistent with the data presented here, perhaps because this greater risk primarily applies to children who were not covered in this survey.

Overview of health findings

The data just summarised show that there were important variations in the health of ethnic minority compared to majority groups, and that there were also important variations between different ethnic minority groups. When comparing ethnic minority groups, on the whole Pakistanis and Bangladeshis reported the poorest health for both assessments of general health and assessment of coronary heart disease. Caribbeans had the next worst health according to the general health assessments, and had the highest rates of respiratory symptoms and hypertension. The latter was particularly the case for Caribbean women, but this may have reflected the greater opportunity for diagnosis among women compared to men. Among the ethnic minority groups, Indian, African Asian and Chinese respondents reported the best health across all of the dimensions assessed, and when comparisons were made with the white population, it was found that the health of the Indian/African Asian and Chinese groups was very similar, only being worse for diabetes. Both Pakistani/Bangladeshis and Caribbeans reported worse general health and had higher rates of diabetes than whites. In addition, Pakistani/Bangladeshis were more likely than whites to report heart disease and Caribbeans were more likely to report hypertension, although, again, the difference was only present for Caribbean women. In contrast to the other health outcomes included, whites were more likely than all of the ethnic minority groups to report that they had respiratory symptoms, although the differences were not significant when compared to Caribbeans and appeared to be largely due to differences in rates of smoking. They were also more likely to report accidents resulting in hospital treatment.

Within particular ethnic groups there was a strong association between health outcomes and socio-economic position. In addition, once the relatively disadvantaged socio-economic position of ethnic minority groups had been taken into account, their

Figure 7.1   Reduction in relative risk (ln) of ill-health compared with whites after controlling for standard of living

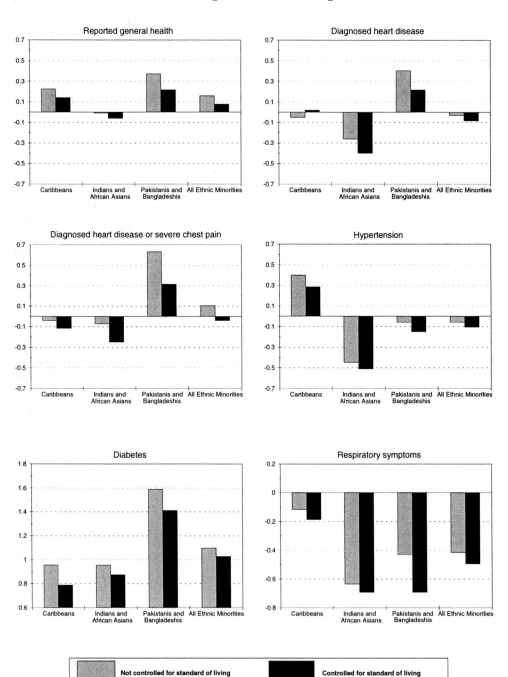

health improved compared to whites across all of the dimensions considered. This is clearly shown in Figure 7.1, which uses the natural logarithm of the relative risk statistic to compare how risk to have ill-health across six key dimensions changes for ethnic minority respondents compared to whites, once socio-economic status is partially controlled for. In the figure a risk equivalent to that for whites is represented by the X-axis (i.e. the value 0), and a figure above this represents a greater risk, while a figure below this a smaller risk. In all but one case, diagnosed heart disease for Caribbeans, the risk for ethnic minority groups compared to whites is reduced once the socio-economic control has been applied. Not shown in the figure is that in many cases the risk changes from being statistically significantly greater than that for whites to not being so, or from not being different to statistically significantly lower than that for whites.

All of this suggests that much of the reported ethnic variations in health can be attributed to socio-economic differences between the groups. However, the specificity of some of the differences – for example Caribbean women reported higher rates of hypertension, while, in contrast, Pakistani/Bangladeshis had higher rates of heart disease – and the data on respiratory symptoms and diabetes, suggests that such a straightforward explanation may not be appropriate. This is discussed later in this chapter.

Health behaviours

In terms of health-related behaviours, the focus in this survey was on smoking and alcohol use, although the chewing of paan was also covered. The data presented in Chapter 2 shows that rates of smoking varied markedly by both ethnicity and gender. Women from the Chinese and all of the South Asian groups had very low rates of smoking, and only about one in five of Indian and African Asian men reported that they currently smoked. In contrast, a third of Pakistani and Chinese men and half of Bangladeshi men reported that they currently smoked. Smoking rates were also high among Caribbeans, but did not show a great gender difference, two out of five Caribbean men and as many as a third of Caribbean women reported that they currently smoked. Among the white respondents there also was not a great gender difference in rates of smoking, about a third of both men and women reported that they smoked. These findings are similar, although the rates are slightly higher, to those reported by Rudat (1994). Worryingly, while as many as two out of five of those white respondents who had ever smoked reported that they had given up, this was only the case for about one out of seven of smokers in the South Asian and Caribbean groups, and among the South Asian groups only 1 in 12 Bangladeshi smokers had given up. This strongly suggests that more could be done in terms of health promotion in this area.

As would be expected, alcohol consumption was closely related to religion. Among the predominantly Muslim Pakistani and Bangladeshi groups, less than 5 per cent of respondents reported that they drank alcohol, although rates were higher for men compared to women. Chapter 4 shows that among the Muslim Indian/African Asians respondents there were also very few respondents who reported that they drank alcohol, although the 10 per cent that did was a greater proportion than for the

Pakistani and Bangladeshi groups. In contrast, two out of five of non-Muslim Indian/African Asians reported that they drank alcohol and, again, rates were much higher for men than for women, three out of five men compared to one out of five women reported that they drank alcohol (see Table D.16 in Appendix D). Among Chinese respondents as many as three out of five reported that they drank alcohol. Four out of five Caribbeans drank alcohol and almost nine out of ten whites drank alcohol. For all of these groups men were slightly more likely to drink alcohol than women.

Both smoking and alcohol consumption appear to be related to age on migration to Britain. For all ethnic minority groups those who were born in Britain or who had migrated at an early age were more likely to have ever smoked and to have drank alcohol than those who migrated aged 11 or older. Many of these differences were statistically significant. Both smoking and alcohol consumption were also related to socio-economic status, although in contradictory ways. For all of the ethnic groups covered, smoking was inversely related to socio-economic status. However, for all but the Caribbean group, alcohol consumption was positively related to socio-economic status. Again many of these differences were statistically significant.

Health care

Respondents were questioned both about their use of primary health care services and about any hospital admissions they had had. The data presented in Chapter 6 show that both South Asian and Caribbean respondents were at least as likely as white respondents to consult with their GP, even after differences in their health had been taken into account. However, Chinese respondents appeared to be less likely to see their GP. In contrast, ethnic minority respondents were, if anything, less likely than whites to be admitted to hospital.

Some attempt was made to look at the quality of care that ethnic minority people might expect from health services. It was found that a significant number of both the South Asian and the Chinese respondents to this survey who had consulted with their GP did not understand the language the GP had used. Despite their attempts to get around this problem, a large number of these respondents felt that their GP still had not understood them. Interestingly, language problems were greater for Chinese compared to South Asian respondents, despite their overall greater fluency in English. This is presumably a result of the fewer opportunities they have to consult with a GP of a similar ethnicity to themselves. A large number of ethnic minority respondents did express a preference to consult with a GP with the same ethnic background as themselves, and this was particularly the case for those who had poor fluency in English. In addition, a large number of ethnic minority women, particularly Pakistanis and Bangladeshis, expressed a preference to see a female doctor. If these findings are considered alongside those from the Health Education Authority survey (Rudat 1994), it does seem that, although members of ethnic minority groups make good use of GP services, they are likely to receive poorer quality care. This poorer care may have led to the discrepancy between the overall greater use of GP services by ethnic minority respondents and their overall lower use of in-patient services.

Ethnic minority respondents also seem less likely than whites to make use of a variety of other health care services. This was particularly the case for dental services, which over the previous year had been used by more than 60 per cent of white respondents compared to about 50 per cent of Caribbean, Indian, African Asian, Pakistani and Chinese respondents and only 25 per cent of Bangladeshi respondents. There was some suggestion that this may have been related to the cost of these services.

EXPLAINING THE RELATIONSHIP BETWEEN ETHNICITY AND HEALTH

In the introduction to this volume the tensions between competing motives and consequent perspectives for carrying out work on ethnic variations in health were described. When adopting a strategy for explaining ethnic variations in health, the clash between these competing perspectives becomes even more obvious. If we are concerned with health disadvantage, then our explanation will undoubtedly be one that can explain overall variations in health. If we are concerned with aetiology, then our explanation will be focused on the variation for a specific disease. In Chapters 4 and 5 and so far in this chapter, a perspective that attempts to evaluate possible explanations for an overall health disadvantage has, on the whole, been adopted, although they have been tested on specific outcomes. This has suggested that ethnic variations in health are overall most likely to relate to differences in socio-economic position. However, the value of such a conclusion is questioned by three pieces of evidence described earlier.

First, as already noted, while socio-economic status may explain ethnic variations in health, it does not necessarily explain the nature they take. Differences between the Caribbean and Pakistani/Bangladeshi groups in comparison to whites illustrate this point well – it seems unlikely that socio-economic factors could in a straight-forward way explain why one group has a greater risk of heart disease, while the other group, or at least the women in it, have a greater risk of hypertension. The most likely explanation for this difference in outcome is that it is the result of an interaction between socio-economic disadvantage and other causal factors that vary across ethnic groups.

Second, the possibility that factors beyond socio-economic status may play an important role is strengthened by the finding of a higher risk of reporting respiratory symptoms for whites compared to all other ethnic groups except Caribbeans. This shows that socio-economic status may not be an over-riding factor in explaining all ethnic variations in health and that in this context at least the culturally related practice of smoking seemed to be far more significant. Nevertheless, *within* ethnic groups socio-economic status did appear important for this outcome and when making comparisons *across* ethnic groups, the advantage that ethnic minority groups had compared to whites became greater once their relatively worse socio-economic position had been partially accounted for.

Indeed, the third piece of evidence, the findings on differences in rates of smoking that are summarised above, illustrates the complexity in the interpretation of these findings. These data confirmed that smoking is culturally related, being more frequently practised in certain ethnic groups. But, smoking behaviour was also highly related to gender in some ethnic groups, and it was also strongly related to socio-economic position for all ethnic groups. What at first sight might appear to be an effect that has straightforward connections with cultural aspects of ethnicity, at closer sight has strong links with other aspects of identity and socio-economic status.

Taken together these three findings raise a central issue for this and other work that has illustrated a relationship between socio-economic status and health. This is a concern with exploring how the relationship between socio-economic status and health is mediated. Implicit in this is the possibility that different health outcomes might be related to different components of socio-economic deprivation, and that the relationship between such an outcome and socio-economic deprivation is contingent on the presence (or absence) of other factors. Certainly the relatively crude materialist perspective that followed the *Black Report* (Townsend and Davidson 1982) has become more sophisticated, both in attempting to specify the role of socio-economic factors in the aetiology of specific disorders and in attempting to unpack the interactions between socio-economic factors with others in the aetiological process (for example, Davey Smith *et al.* 1990b and 1994, Lundberg 1991, Ford *et al.* 1994, Sweeting and West 1995, Vågerö and Illsley 1995).

Figure 7.2 provides an outline of the relationships between factors that were explored as possible explanations for the relationship between ethnicity and health in Chapters 4 and 5 of this volume. It provides a starting point for a discussion that illustrates the complexity of the relevant issues.

Although at first sight the figure might itself seem complex, part of this undoubtedly originates from the multi-dimensional nature of the concepts of ethnicity and race (as described in Chapter 1). For the purposes of the figure, some of these dimensions have been pulled out, and it is postulated that there may be a direct link between both the biological aspects of race and the cultural aspects of ethnicity, and health. A central component of the figure, and the explanation most strongly favoured by the data presented in this volume, is socio-economic status, which the figure proposes may be directly related to the process and consequences of migration, and the process of discrimination on the basis of perceived race. Also within the model is the possibility that differences in health could be the result of differences in the quality of care received, or that the measured relationship between ethnicity and health could be a result of an artefact of the data available, although neither of these possibilities receives support from the data presented here (hence the dotted lines). Other elements that may be important, such as the experience or knowledge of racism being directly related to health (see Benzeval *et al.* 1992 for some evidence of this), have, for the sake of clarity, been left out of the model.

Despite the initial impression of complexity in this causal model, its one-dimensional nature clearly limits it. Some attempt has been made to show that causal effects may be inter-related, so a relationship between class and culture is postulated (and supported by data on smoking), and three inter-related effects that may limit access to and the quality of health services are included. Nevertheless, two important elements of the figure have not been clarified. First, several components of the model, but particularly the central one, remain unexplored. Although the

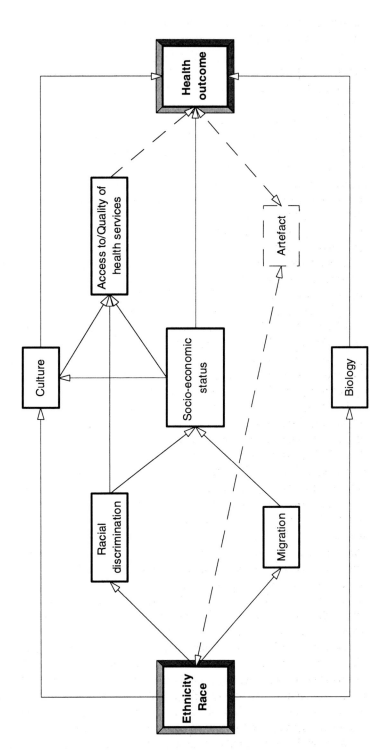

Figure 7.2 Understanding the relationship between ethnicity and health

'Black Box' representing the relationship between ethnicity and health and criticised by Bhopal (1995) (and Arber (1990) in relation to gender), has been unpacked by the figure, within it lies a 'socio-economic' black box that, as described earlier, also needs to be unpacked. In addition, the model does not allow for any interactive effects in the causal pathway. As the differences between Caribbeans and Pakistani/Bangladeshis in comparison to whites show, this may be particularly important when we want to understand particular health outcomes. It may well be that a non-specific material disadvantage interacts with other particular forms of disadvantage, or particular cultural and biological attributes, to produce specific types of health disadvantage.

In terms of an overall understanding of health differences, then, it seems that we can conclude that ethnic variations in health are largely a consequence of relative socio-economic position, and operate through differences in material circumstances. But if we want to understand variations in particular health outcomes, it seems that the specificity of the variations between different ethnic minority groups and whites can only be explained by an interaction between material circumstances and attributes that vary across ethnic minority groups in similar socio-economic positions. The data presented in this volume give an example of how complex this may be. For respiratory symptoms, the greater rate of smoking among whites compared to other ethnic groups appears to have put them at greater risk despite their overall better socio-economic position. Indeed, once this better socio-economic position had been accounted for, they were even more likely to report respiratory symptoms. However, this reveals an important socio-economic effect that acts in addition to the smoking related risk, within all of the ethnic groups socio-economic position was strongly related to the reporting of respiratory symptoms. But, perhaps even more importantly, the data also show that within each ethnic group socio-economic position was related to smoking, suggesting that these factors can only be fully understood as highly inter-related effects.

TAKING RESEARCH ON ETHNICITY AND HEALTH FORWARD

Two central messages can be taken from the data presented in this volume. The first is that the quality of health care received by patients is related to their ethnic background. In addition to a possible need for more culturally sensitive services, there is also an important need, in health care settings, for both staff with appropriate language abilities and adequate translation facilities. The data show that communication, which is the central feature of a consultation with a doctor, is a significant problem for a large number of ethnic minority patients. In addition, the low use made by Chinese respondents of health services may have been, at least partly, related to the language problems they faced when attempting to access them. According to Rudat (1994) about 80 per cent of South Asians have access to a South Asian GP, many of whom will presumably speak relevant South Asian languages. This may be a consequence of the relatively high concentration in particular localities of members of South Asian groups (Owen 1994) and, given that the South Asians covered by the BMEG survey did not include those that did not live in such areas, Rudat's figures may have been an over-estimate of access to South Asian doctors. The data presented by Rudat (1994) also suggest that very few people have access to a Chinese GP. This means that the number of staff with such language abilities and appropriate translation services should not only be increased in areas with a large South Asian population they should also be introduced into areas with moderate and small South Asian populations and more generally for the Chinese population, which tends to be more dispersed than other ethnic minority groups. This of course needs careful thought about how to encourage the recruitment of people with such skills into the health service.

The relatively low referral rate of ethnic minority people to secondary health care, implied by the data here and elsewhere (Balarajan *et al.* 1991), warrants further detailed investigation. In addition to the communication difficulties that occur, this could be a consequence of ethnic minority people being more likely to use poorer resourced primary health care facilities. As others have commented in more general terms (Harris *et al.* 1996), to address this some thought also needs to be given to the funding of the relatively poorly resourced general practices in inner-city areas that will be used by many members of ethnic minority groups. For example, one study contrasting inner London with other areas found that 46 per cent of inner London GP premises were below standard compared with just 7 per cent of those in England as a whole (Jarman and Bosanquet 1992).

Nevertheless, the suggestion that ethnic minority people receive poorer quality care than whites requires further substantiation. Although the structural problems relating to communication and resources should be addressed, it is essential that more detailed comparative studies of the care received by patients from different ethnic groups are undertaken to assess the full extent and nature of any possible problems.

The second message is that much of the ethnic variations in health uncovered appears to be the result of differences in socio-economic position. This finding illustrates the great importance of collecting data on socio-economic position when exploring the relationship between ethnicity and health. Two common approaches, to ignore socio-economic position altogether, or to use ethnicity as a surrogate indicator of socio-economic status (as in the index of deprivation used by Jarman 1983) are clearly unacceptable. Certainly it is the case that the current failure to collect information on socio-economic status alongside the collection of data relating to the ethnicity of patients admitted to hospital, needs to be rectified (McKenzie and Crowcroft 1994), as others have also commented. Unfortunately, the analysis presented in Chapter 5 shows that taking account of socio-economic factors when exploring ethnic variations in health is not a straightforward process. It seems likely that few, if any, studies in this area will have the luxury of the depth of relevant information provided by this survey. Consequently, when making comparisons across ethnic groups, researchers should be aware of the limitations of data that only contain crude overall indicators of socio-economic status, such as occupational class or housing tenure and car ownership. While these indicators might prove effective for exploring socio-economic variations within ethnic groups, an important task in its own right, they are clearly inadequate if investigators want to 'control out' socio-economic effects in order to focus on ethnic ones. Indeed, the claim that after attempts to control out socio-economic factors the residual effect that remains must be attributable to something inherent in ethnicity – such as culture or biology – ignores both the difficulties in controlling out and the need to make direct measurements of effects rather than assuming that they operate. Both cultural and biological differences need to be measured and their contribution to differences in outcome assessed.

In fact, beyond the practical problems shown in Chapter 5, there are other issues that need to be considered before attempting to control for socio-economic status and before interpreting results that purport to do this. The most obvious is that an important dimension of interpretation and explanation becomes lost from view in such a process. This then gives the impression that different types of explanation operate for ethnic minority groups compared to the general population. While for the latter factors relating to socio-economic status are shown to be crucial, for the former they are not visible, so differences are assumed to be related to some aspect of ethnicity or race, even though, as shown here, socio-economic factors are important determinants of health for all groups. In addition, ethnicity may also be important for explaining the health disadvantage of whites – as the evidence on smoking and respiratory symptoms illustrates – adding further support to the proposition that we should be careful not to apply different types of explanation to different ethnic groups without strong empirical support. This also highlights an equally fundamental problem with the use of data that has had socio-economic status controlled for. In this chapter it has been argued that both the inter-relationships between different types of explanation for health variations, and the interactive effects between them, need to be examined. The process of controlling out a key explanatory factor assumes that the former are of no interest and the latter do not occur, both assumptions are clearly unsatisfactory.

One possible implication of what has been concluded so far is that ethnicity per se is of minimal interest in understanding health variations. If socio-economic factors are the over-riding explanation for health variations, including ethnic variations in health, the suggestion is that rather than exploring the relationship between ethnicity and health, we should focus on the relationship between socio-economic status and health (Navarro 1990, Sheldon and Parker 1992). From this perspective, insofar as ethnicity is important it would only be in terms of exploring the production of particular class fractions and consequent disadvantage through the process of racialisation (Miles 1989). However, a reconsideration of the three purposes for undertaking research on ethnicity and health, discussed in the introduction, shows that this may be mistaken. Despite the importance of socio-economic status in explaining ethnic variations in health, a consideration of the position of ethnic minority groups will still benefit from an understanding of their relative health. Indeed, if we are to improve on the delivery of health care to any group in our society, it seems crucial to consider its health needs. In addition, as the discussion on the specificity of outcomes suggests, epidemiological investigations may continue to help in the understanding of the aetiology of specific diseases, particularly if more attention is paid to investigating 'Black Boxes'.

Finally, in terms of meeting Health of the Nation targets for ethnic minority groups, Balarajan's (1996) presentation of the most up to date immigrant mortality data suggests that we still have a long way to go. The data presented in this volume show that a number of broadly defined health promotion activities can be improved. First, the smaller proportion of ethnic minority people who have given up smoking compared to their white counterparts suggests that we have been relatively unsuccessful in getting health promotion messages through. However, other work has suggested that messages do get through and are understood, despite difficulties with delivery, but do not in themselves provide sufficient motivation for behaviour change (Beishon and Nazroo 1997). Some thought needs to be given to how such motivation for change can be increased and obstacles preventing change overcome. In addition, the relatively disadvantaged socio-economic position of ethnic minority groups compared to whites needs to be addressed. While this is clearly beyond the immediate remit of the Department of Health (Department of Health 1995), the consequences of such socio-economic disadvantage for both individuals and health care services need to be carefully considered across government departments, and cross-departmental solutions sought.

References

Ahmad, W. (1995) 'Review article: "race" and health', *Sociology of Health and Illness,* vol. 17, no. 3, pp. 418–429

Ahmad, W.I.U. (1993a) *'Race' and Health in Contemporary Britain.* Buckingham: Open University Press

Ahmad, W.I.U. (1993b) 'Making black people sick: 'race', ideology and health research'. In W.I.U. Ahmad (ed.) *'Race' and Health in Contemporary Britain.* Buckingham: Open University Press

Ahmad, W.I.U., Kernohan, E.E.M. & Baker, M.R. (1989) 'Influence of ethnicity and unemployment on the perceived health of a sample of general practice attenders', *Community Medicine,* vol. 11, no. 2, pp. 148–156

Alwash, R. & McCarthy, M. (1988) 'Accidents in the home among children under 5: ethnic differences or social disadvantage', *British Medical Journal,* vol. 296, pp. 1450–3

Arber, S. (1990) 'Opening the "Black Box": Understanding inequalities in women's health'. In P. Abbott & G. Payne (eds) *New Directions in the Sociology of Health.* Brighton: Falmer Press

Aspinall, P. (1995) 'Department of Health's requirement for mandatory collection of data on ethnic group of inpatients', *British Medical Journal,* vol. 311, pp. 1006–9

Balarajan, R. (1991) 'Ethnic differences in mortality from ischaemic heart disease and cerebrovascular disease in England and Wales', *British Medical Journal,* vol. 302, pp. 560–564

Balarajan, R. (1996) 'Ethnicity and variations in the nation's health', *Health Trends,* vol. 27, no. 4, pp. 114–119

Balarajan, R. & Bulusu, L. (1990) 'Mortality among immigrants in England and Wales, 1979–83'. In M. Britton (ed.) *Mortality and Geography: A Review in the mid-1980s, England and Wales.* London: Office of Population Censuses and Surveys

Balarajan, R. & Soni Raleigh, V. (1993) *The Health of the Nation: Ethnicity and Health.* London: Department of Health

Balarajan, R. & Soni Raleigh, V. (1995) *Ethnicity and Health in England.* London: HMSO

Balarajan, R., Bulusu, L., Adelstein, A.M. & Shukla, V. (1984) 'Patterns of mortality among migrants to England and Wales from the Indian subcontinent', *British Medical Journal,* vol. 289, pp. 1185–87

Balarajan, R., Soni Raleigh, S. & Yuen, P. (1991) 'Hospital care among ethnic minorities in Britain', *Health Trends,* vol. 23, no. 3, pp. 90–93

Balarajan, R., Yuen, P. and Raleigh, V. (1989) 'Ethnic differences in general practitioner consultations', *British Medical Journal,* vol. 289, pp. 958–960

Barker, D. (1991) 'The foetal and infant origins of inequalities in health in Britain', *Journal of Public Health Medicine*, vol. 13, pp. 64–68

Bartley, M. (1994) 'Unemployment and ill health: understanding the relationship', *Journal of Epidemiology and Community Health*, vol. 48, pp. 333–337

Bartley, M., Montgomer, S., Cook, D. & Wadsworth, M. (1996) 'Health and work insecurity in young men'. In D. Blane, E. Brunner & R. Wilkinson (eds) *Health and Social Organisation*. London: Routledge.

Bebbington, P. & Nayani, T. (1995) 'The psychosis screening questionnaire', *International Journal of Methods in Psychiatric Research*, vol. 5, pp. 11–19

Beishon, S. & Nazroo, J.Y. (1997) *Coronary Heart Disease: Contrasting the health beliefs and behaviours of South Asian communities in the UK*. London: Health Education Authority

Benzeval, M. & Judge, K. (1993) *The development of population-based need indicators from self-reported health care utilisation data*. London: King's Fund Institute

Benzeval, M., Judge, K. & Solomon, M. (1992) *The Health Status of Londoners*. London: King's Fund Institute

Benzeval, M., Judge, K. & Whitehead, M. (1995) *Tackling Inequalities in Health: an agenda for action*. London: King's Fund Institute

Ben-Shlomo, Y., White, I.R. & Marmot, M. (1996) 'Does the variation in the socioeconomic characteristics of an area affect mortality?' *British Medical Journal*, vol. 312, pp. 1013–4

Bhopal, R.S. (1995) *Ethnicity, race, health and research: racist black box, junk or enlightened epidemiology*, presented at Society for Social Medicine Scientific Meeting, Royal Holloway University of London

Bhopal, R.S. (1996) 'Setting priorities for health care for ethnic minority groups'. In S. Rawaf & V. Bhal (eds) *Assessing the Health Needs of People from Black and Ethnic Minorities*. London: Department of Health

Blalock, H.M. (1985) *Social Statistics*. Singapore: McGraw-Hill

Blane, D., Bartley, M., Davey Smith, G., Filakti, H., Bethune, A. & Harding, S. (1994) 'Social patterning of medical mortality in youth and early adulthood', *Social Science and Medicine*, vol. 39, no. 3, pp. 361–366

Blane, D., Power, C. & Bartley, M. (1996) 'Illness behaviour and the measurement of class differentials in morbidity', *Journal of the Royal Statistical Society*, Series A, vol. 159, Part 1, pp.77–92

Blaxter, M. (1987) 'Evidence of inequality in health from a national survey', *The Lancet*, July 4, pp. 30–33

Blaxter, M. (1990) *Health and Lifestyles*. London: Tavistock/Routledge

Bloor, M.J., Robertson, C. & Samphier, M.L. (1989) 'Occupational status variations in disagreements on the diagnosis of cause of death', *Human Pathology*, vol. 30, pp. 144–148

Bradby, H. (1995) 'Ethnicity: not a black and white issue. A research note', *Sociology of Health and Illness*, vol. 17, no. 3, pp. 405–417

Brown, C. (1984) *Black and White Britain: The Third PSI Survey*. London: Heinemann

Brown, C. & Ritchie, J. (1981) *Focussed Enumeration: the Development of a Method for Sampling Ethnic Minority Groups*. London: Policy Studies Institute/SCPR

Carr-Hill, R.A., Rice, N. & Roland, M. (1996) 'Socioeconomic determinants of rates of consultation in general practice based on fourth national morbidity survey of general practices', *British Medical Journal*, vol. 312, pp. 1008–13

Chaturvedi, N. & McKeigue, P. (1994) 'Methods for epidemiological surveys of ethnic minority groups', *Journal of Epidemiology and Community Health*, vol. 48, pp. 107–111

Clarke, M., Clayton, D.G., Mason, E.S. & MacVicar, J. (1988) 'Asian mothers' risk factors for perinatal death – the same or different? A 10 year review of Leicestershire perinatal deaths', *British Medical Journal*, vol. 297, pp. 384–387

Cruickshank, J.K., Cooper, J.E., Burnett, M., MacDuff, J. & Drubra, U. (1991) 'Ethnic differences in fasting plasma C-peptide and insulin in relation to glucose tolerance and blood pressure', *The Lancet*, vol. 338, pp. 842–847

Cruickshank, J., Beevers, D., Osbourne, R., Haynes, J., Corlett, J. & Selby, S. (1980) 'Heart attack, stroke, diabetes, and hypertension in West Indians, Asians and whites in Birmingham, England', *British Medical Journal*, vol. 281, p. 1108

Daniel, W.W (1968) *Racial Discrimination in England*. London: Penguin

Davey Smith, G., Bartley. M. & Blane, D. (1990a) The Black report on socioeconomic inequalities in health 10 years on', *British Medical Journal*, vol. 301, pp. 373–377

Davey Smith, G., Blane, D. & Bartley, M. (1994) 'Explanations for socio-economic differentials in mortality: evidence from Britain and elsewhere', *European Journal of Public Health*, vol. 4, pp.131–144

Davey Smith, G., Hart, C., Blane, D., Gillis, C. & Hawthorne, V. (1997) 'Lifetime socio-economic position and mortality: prospective observational study', *British Medical Journal*, vol. 314, pp. 547–552

Davey Smith, G., Shipley, M.J. & Rose, G. (1990b) 'Magnitude and causes of socioeconomic differentials in mortality: further evidence from the Whitehall study', *Journal of Epidemiology and Community Health*, vol. 44, p. 265

Department of Health (1995) *Variations in Health. What Dan the Department of Health and the NHS Do?* London: Department of Health

Donovan, J. (1984) 'Ethnicity and health: a research review', *Social Science and Medicine*, vol. 19, no. 7, pp. 663–670

Dunnell, K. (1993) *Sources and Nature of Ethnic Health Data*. London: North East and North West Thames RHA

Fenton, S., Hughes, A. & Hine, C. (1995) 'Self-assessed health, economic status and ethnic origin', *New Community*, vol. 21, no. 1, pp. 55–68

Ford, G., Ecob, R., Hunt, K., Macintyre, S. & West, P. (1994) 'Patterns of class inequality in health through the lifespan: Class gradients at 15, 35 and 55 years in the West of Scotland', *Social Science and Medicine*, vol. 39, no. 8, pp. 1037–50

Fox, K. & Shapiro, L. (1988) 'Heart disease in Asians in Britain', *British Medical Journal*, vol. 297, pp. 311–312

Gillam, S.J., Jarman, B., White, P. & Law, R. (1989) 'Ethnic differences in consultation rates in urban general practice', *British Medical Journal*, vol. 299, pp. 953-957

Gordon, T (1982) 'Further mortality experience among Japanese Americans', *Public Health Reports*, vol. 97, pp. 973–984

Gould, M.I. & Jones, K. (1996) 'Analyzing perceived limiting long-term illness using UK census microdata', *Social Science and Medicine*, vol. 42, no. 6, pp. 857-869

Gupta, R., Gupta, V.P. & Ahluwalia, N.S. (1994) 'Educational status, coronary heart disease, and coronary risk factor prevalence in a rural population of India', *British Medical Journal*, vol. 309, pp. 1332–6

Gupta, S., de Belder, A. & O'Hughes, L. (1995) 'Avoiding premature coronary deaths in Asians in Britain: Spend now on prevention or pay later for treatment', *British Medical Journal*, vol. 311, pp. 1035–36

Hall, S. (1992) 'The question of cultural identity'. In S. Hall, D. Held and T. McGrew (eds) *Modernity and its Futures*. Cambridge: Polity

Halpern, D. (1993) 'Minorities and Mental Health', *Social Science and Medicine*, vol. 36, no. 5, pp. 597–607

Harris, T., Silver, T., Rank, E. & Hilton, S. (1996) 'Vocational training for general practice in inner London. Is there a dearth? And if so what's to be done?' *British Medical Journal*, vol. 312, pp. 97–101

Haynes, R. (1991) 'Inequalities in health and health service use: evidence from the General Household Survey', *Social Science and Medicine*, vol. 33, no. 4, pp. 361–368

Heath, A. & Ridge, J. (1983) 'Social mobility of ethnic minorities', *Journal of Biosocial Science, supplement*, vol. 8, pp. 169–184

Howlett, B., Ahmad, W. & Murray, R. (1992) 'An exploration of white, Asian and Afro-Caribbean peoples' concepts of health and illness causation', *New Community*, vol. 18, no. 2, pp. 7–13

Humphrey, K. & Carr-Hill, R. (1991) 'Area variations in health outcomes: artefact or ecology', *International Journal of Epidemiology*, vol. 20, no. 1, pp. 251–258

Jarman, B. (1983) 'Identification of underprivileged areas', *British Medical Journal*, vol. 286, pp. 1705–8

Jarman, B. & Bosanquet, N. (1992) 'Primary health care in London – changes since the Acheson report', *British Medical Journal*, vol. 305, pp. 1130–1133

Johnson, M., Cross, M. & Cardew, S. (1983) 'Inner-city residents, ethnic minorities and primary health care', *Postgraduate Medical Journal*, vol. 59, pp. 664–667

Joint Committee of the Royal Colleges of Physicians and Pathologists (1982) 'Medical aspects of death certification', *Journal of the Royal College of Physicians*, vol. 16, pp. 205–218

Jones, T. (1993) *Britain's Ethnic Minorities*. London: Policy Studies Institute

Kelly, S. M. & Miles-Doan, R. (1997) 'Social inequality and injuries: Do morbidity patterns differ from mortality', *Social Science and Medicine*, vol. 44, no. 1, pp. 63–70

Khan, V. (1979) *Minority Families in Britain: Support and Stress*. London: Macmillan

Knight, T.M., Smith, Z., Whittles, A., Sahotaa, P., Lockton, J.A., Hogg, G., Bedford, A. & Toop, M. (1992) 'Insulin resistance, diabetes, and risk markers for ischaemic heart disease in Asian men and non-Asian men in Bradford', *British Heart Journal*, vol. 67, pp. 343–350

Krieger, N. (1994) 'Epidemiology and the web of causation: has anyone seen the spider?' *Social Science and Medicine*, vol. 39, no. 7, pp. 887–903

Kuh, D.J.L. & Wadsworth, M.E.J. (1993) 'Physical health status at 36 years in a British national birth cohort', *Social Science and Medicine*, vol. 37, no. 7, pp. 905–916

Laing, W. (1988) *Laing's Review of Private Health Care 1988/9*. London: Laing and Buisson

Lewis, G., Pelosi, A.J., Araya, R. & Dunn, G. (1992) 'Measuring psychiatric disorder in the community: a standard assessment for use by lay interviewers', *Psychological Medicine*, vol. 22, pp. 465–486

Lundberg, O. (1991) 'Causal explanations for class inequality in health – an empirical analysis', *Social Science and Medicine*, vol. 32, no. 4, pp. 385–393

MRC (1982) *American Thoracic Society News*, vol. 8, pp. 12–16

Macintyre, S., Maciver, S. & Soomans, A. (1993) 'Area, class and health: should we be focusing on places or people?' *Journal of Social Policy*, vol. 22, no. 2, pp. 213–234

Markowe, H. (1993) 'The work of the Central Health Monitoring Unit in the Department of Health (England)', *Journal of Epidemiolgy and Community Health*, vol. 47, pp. 6–9

Marmot, M.G., Adelstein, A.M., Bulusu, L. & OPCS (1984) *Immigrant Mortality in England and Wales 1970–78: Causes of Death by Country of Birth*. London: HMSO

Mather, H.M. & Keen, H. (1985) 'The Southall diabetes survey: prevalence of known diabetes in Asians and Europeans', *British Medical Journal*, vol. 291, pp. 1081–84

Mather, H.M., Verma, N.P.S., Mehta, S.P., Madhu, S. & Keen, H. (1987) 'The prevalence of known diabetes in Indians in New Delhi and London', *Journal of Medical Association of Thailand*, vol. 70, pp. 54–58

McCormick, A. & Rosenbaum, M. (1990) *Morbidity statistics from General Practice, Third National Study: Socioeconomic analysis*. London: HMSO

McKeigue, P. (1992) 'Coronary heart disease in Indians, Pakistanis and Bangladeshis: aetiology and possibilities for prevention', *British Heart Journal*, vol. 67, pp. 341–342

McKeigue, P. (1993) *Coronary heart disease and diabetes in South Asians*. London: North East and North West Thames RHA

McKeigue, P. & Marmot, M. (1988) 'Mortality from coronary heart disease in Asian communities in London', *British Medical Journal*, vol. 297, p. 903

McKeigue, P., Marmot, M. Syndercombe Court, Y., Cottier, D., Rahman, S. & Riermersma, R. (1988) 'Diabetes, hyperinsulinaemia, and coronary risk factors in Bangladeshis in East London', *British Heart Journal*, vol. 60, pp. 390–396

McKeigue, P., Miller, G. & Marmot, M. (1989) 'Coronary heart disease in South Asians overseas: a review', *Journal of Clinical Epidemiology*, vol. 42, no. 7, pp. 597–609

McKeigue, P., Shah, B. & Marmot, M. (1991) 'Relation of central obesity and insulin resistance with high diabetes prevalence and cardiovascular risk in South Asians', *The Lancet*, vol. 337, pp. 382–386

McKenzie, K.J. & Crowcroft, N. (1994) 'Race, ethnicity, culture, and science', *British Medical Journal*, vol. 309, pp. 286–287

Miles, R. (1989) *Racism*. London: Routledge

Modood, T., Berthoud, R., Lakey, J., Nazroo, J., Smith, P., Virdee, S. & Beishon, S. (1997) *Ethnic Minorities in Britain: Diversity and Disadvantage*. London: Policy Studies Institute

Modood, T, Beishon, S. & Virdee, S. (1994) *Changing Ethnic Identities*. London: Policy Studies Institute

Morrison, C., Woodward, M., Leslie, W. & Tunstall-Pedoe, H. (1997) 'Effect of socioeconomic group on incidence of, management of, and survival after myocardial infarction and coronary death: analysis of community coronary event register', *British Medical Journal*, vol. 314, pp. 541–546

Mossey, J. & Shapiro, E. (1982) 'Self-rated health: a predictor of mortality among the elderly', *American Journal of Public Health*, vol. 72, pp. 800–808

Nazroo, J.Y. (1997) *Mental Health and Ethnicity: Findings from a National Community Survey*. London: Policy Studies Institute (forthcoming)

Navarro, V. (1990) 'Race or class versus race and class: mortality differentials in the United States', *The Lancet*, Nov 17, pp. 1238–40

Odugbesan, O., Rowe, B., Fletcher, J., Walford, S & Barnett, A.H. (1989) 'Diabetes in the UK West Indian community: the Wolverhampton study', *Diabetic Medicine*, vol. 9, pp. 641–645

Office of Population Censuses and Surveys (1991) *General Household Survey 1989.* London: HMSO

Office of Population Censuses and Surveys (1994) Undercoverage in Great Britain (Census User Guide no. 58). London: HMSO

Owen, D. (1994) 'Spatial variations in ethnic minority groups populations in Great Britain', *Population Trends,* vol. 78, pp. 23–33

Pilgrim, S., Fenton, S., Hughes, T., Hine, C., & Tibbs, N. (1993) *The Bristol Black and Ethnic Minorities Health Survey Report.* Bristol: University of Bristol

Robinson, V. (1989) 'Race, space and place: the geographical study of UK ethnic relations 1957–1987', *New Community,* vol. 14, no. 1, pp. 186–197

Roman, E., Beral, V., Inskip, H., McDowall, M. & Adelstein, A. (1984) 'A comparison of standardized and proportional mortality ratios', *Statistics in Medicine,* vol. 3, pp. 7–14

Rose, G.A. & Blackburn, H. (1986) *Cardiovascular Survey Methods.* Geneva: World Health Organisation

Rudat, K. (1994) *Black and Minority Ethnic Groups in England: Health and Lifestyles.* London: Health Education Authority

Senior, P.A. & Bhopal, R. (1994) 'Ethnicity as a variable in epidemiological research', *British Medical Journal,* vol. 309, pp. 327–330

Shaukat, N. & Cruickshank, J. (1993) 'Coronary artery disease: impact upon black and ethnic minority people'. In A. Hopkins and V. Bahl (eds) *Access to Health Care for People from Black and Ethnic Minorities.* London: Royal College of Physicians

Shaukat, N., Lear, J., Fletcher, S., de Bono, D.P. & Woods, K.L. (1997) 'First myocardial infarction in patients of Indian subcontinent and European origin: comparison of risk factors, management, and long term outcome', *British Medical Journal,* vol. 314, pp. 639–642

Sheldon, T.A. & Parker, H. (1992) 'Race and ethnicity in health research', *Journal of Public Health Medicine,* vol. 14, no. 2, pp. 104–110

Simmons, D., Williams, D.R.R. & Powell, M.J. (1989) 'Prevalence of diabetes in a predominantly Asian community: preliminary findings of the Coventry diabetes study', *British Medical Journal,* vol. 298, pp. 18–21

Sloggett, A. & Joshi, H. (1994) 'Higher mortality in deprived areas: community or personal disadvantage', *British Medical Journal,* vol. 309, pp. 1470–74

Smaje, C. (1995a) *Health, 'Race' and Ethnicity: Making Sense of the Evidence.* London: King's Fund Institute

Smaje, C. (1995b) 'Ethnic Residential Concentration and Health: evidence for a positive effect?', *Policy and Politics,* vol. 23, no. 3, pp. 251–69

Smith, D. (1977) *Racial Disadvantage in Britain.* Harmondsworth: Penguin

Smith, P. (1996) 'Methodological aspects of research amongst ethnic minorities', *Survey Methods Centre Newsletter,* vol. 16, no. 1, pp. 20–24

Smith, P. & Prior, G. (1997) *The Fourth National Survey of Ethnic Minorities: Technical Report.* London: Social and Community Planning Research

Stein, C.E., Fall, C.H., Kumaran, K., Osmond, C., Cox, V. & Barker, D.J. (1996) 'Fetal growth and coronary heart disease in south India', *The Lancet,* vol. 348, pp. 1269–1273

Sweeting, H. & West, P. (1995) 'Family life and health in adolescence: A role for culture in the health inequalities *debate?', Social Science and Medicine,* vol. 40, no. 2, pp. 163–175

Syme, S., Marmot, M., Kagan, H. & Rhoads, G. (1975) 'Epidemiologic studies of CHD and stroke in Japanese men living in Japan, Hawaii and California', *American Journal of Epidemiology,* vol. 102, pp. 477–480

Thomas, R. & Purdon, S. (1994) 'Using the results of the 1991 Census question on limiting long-term illness', *Survey Methods Centre Newsletter,* vol. 14, no. 2, pp. 7–13

Townsend, P. & Davidson, N. (1982) *Inequalities in Health (the Black Report).* Middlesex: Penguin

Townsend, P., Phillimore, P. & Beattie, A. (1988) *Health and Deprivation: Inequality and the North.* London: Routledge

Vågerö, D. & Illsley, R. (1995) 'Explaining health inequalities: beyond Black and Barker', *European Sociological Review,* vol. 11, no. 3, pp. 219–239

Ware J.E. & Sherbourne, C.D. (1992) 'The MOS 36–Item Short-Form Health Survey (SF–36) 1: Conceptual framework and item selection', *Medical Care,* vol. 30, no. 6, pp. 473–483

White, A., Nicolaas, G., Foster, K., Browne, F. & Carey, S. (1993) *Health Survey for England 1991.* London: HMSO

Wild, S. & McKeigue, P. (1997) 'Cross sectional analysis of mortality by country of birth in England and Wales, 1972–92', *British Medical Journal,* vol. 314, pp. 705–710

Wilkinson (1994) *Unfair Shares.* Illford: Barnardo's

Wilkinson, P., Sayer, J., Koorithottumkal, L., Grundy, C., Marchant, B., Kopelman, P. & Timmis, A.D. (1996) 'Comparison of case fatality in south Asian and white patients after acute myocardial infarction: observational study', *British Medical Journal,* vol. 312, pp. 1330–1333

Williams, R. (1993) 'Health and length of residence among South Asians in Glasgow: a study controlling for age', *Journal of Public Health Medicine,* vol. 15, no. 1, pp. 52–60

Williams, R., Bhopal, R. & Hunt, K. (1993) 'Health of a Punjabi ethnic minority in Glasgow: a comparison with the general population', *Journal of Epidemiology and Community Health,* vol. 47, pp. 96–102

Appendix A: Health Questionnaire

HEALTH

H1 | I would now like to ask you about your health and the use you make of health services.

Please think back over the last 12 months about how your health has been. Compared to people of your own age, would you say that your health has on the whole been...READ OUT...

...excellent,	1
good,	2
fair,	3
poor,	4
or very poor?	5
Can't say	8

2918

H2a) | Do you have any long-standing illness, disability or infirmity? By long-standing I mean anything that has troubled you over a period of time that is likely to affect you over a period of time?

Yes	1	ASK b)
No	2	GO TO H3

2919

IF YES

H2b) What is the matter with you?   2920-39

TRY TO OBTAIN A MEDICAL
DIAGNOSIS OR ESTABLISH
MAIN SYMPTOMS

c) INTERVIEWER CODE

    Complaint on Reference Card RA   1   2940

    All others   2

IF ILLNESS/DISABILITY/INFIRMITY

d) Does this problem limit the kind of paid work
   that you can do (or could do if wanted to)?

    Yes   1   2941

    No   2

.H3 Can I check, are you registered as a
    disabled person, either with Social
    Services or with a green card?

    Yes   1   2942

    No   2

    Unsure   8

28   E2/H

H4 | Are you currently taking or using any
medicines, pills, ointments or injections
of any kind?

INCLUDES "ALTERNATIVE"
HEALTH REMEDIES   Yes | 1 | ASK H5   2943

                                                  No | 2 | GO TO H6

IF YES AT H4
H5a) | Please could you tell me what they are.   2944-71

PROBE FOR FULL DETAILS OF <u>MEDICINES</u>, <u>PILLS</u>,
<u>OINTMENTS</u>, AND <u>INJECTIONS/IMPLANTS</u>

ASK TO SEE BOTTLES IF
IF POSSIBLE

MEDICINES: ---------------------------------

PILLS: ---------------------------------

OINTMENTS: ---------------------------------

INJECTIONS/IMPLANTS: ---------------------------------

                    ----

b) | INTERVIEWER CODE
                        Medication on Reference Card RB   1   2972
                                           All others   2

CARD 30

H6 | Do you now have or have you ever had any of the following conditions?

READ OUT AND RING ONE CODE FOR EACH

	Yes	No	
High blood pressure, sometimes called hypertension (apart from during pregnancy)?	1	2	3014
A stroke?	1	2	3015
Diabetes?	1	2	3016
Angina?	1	2	3017
A heart attack - including a heart murmur, a damaged heart or a rapid heart?	1	2	3018

H7a) | **CHECK H6 AND RECORD:**

Has or had diabetes	1	ASK b)	3019
Others	2	GO TO H8	

IF HAS OR HAD DIABETES

b) | Do you attend a diabetes treatment clinic?

Yes	1	3020
No	2	

H8a) | **INTERVIEWER CHECK A1a) AND RECORD:**

Respondent aged 40 or over	1	CHECK b)	3021
Respondent aged under 40	2	GO TO H10	

b) | **INTERVIEWER CHECK H6 AND RECORD:**

Respondent reported no heart problems (CODE 2 FOR ANGINA AND HEART ATTACK)	1	ASK H9	3022
Respondent reported heart problems	2	GO TO H10	

H9a) | Have you ever had any pain or discomfort in your chest?

Yes	1	ASK b)	3023
No	2	GO TO H10	

30   E2/H

IF YES
H9b) Have you ever had a severe pain across the front
of your chest lasting for more than half an hour?

Yes | 1 | ASK c)   3024
No | 2 | GO TO H10

IF YES
c) Did you see a doctor because of this pain?

Yes | 1 | ASK d)   3025
No | 2 | GO TO H10

IF YES
d) What did the doctor say?

Angina   1   3026

Heart attack   2

Did not say   3

Other (SPECIFY) --   4

ALL

H10 The following questions are about activities you might do during a typical day.

a) Does your health limit you when you take part in ...

READ OUT AND CODE ONE FOR EACH IN GRID AT a)
IF "YES" AT (a), ASK b)

b) How much does your health limit you in - (ACTIVITY) - a lot or a little?

RING ONE CODE FOR EACH IN GRID UNDER (b)

	(a)			(b)		
	Yes	No	Wouldn't ever do	Limited a lot	Limited a little	
... vigorous activities, such as running, lifting heavy objects or participating in strenuous sports?	1	2	3	1	2	3027-28
... moderate activities such as moving a table, pushing a vacuum cleaner, bowling or playing golf?	1	2	3	1	2	3029-30
...lifting or carrying groceries?	1	2	3	1	2	3031-32
...climbing several flights of stairs?	1	2	3	1	2	3033-34
...climbing one flight of stairs?	1	2	3	1	2	3035-36

		(a)		(b)	
			Wouldn't ever do	Limited a lot	Limited a little
	Yes	No			
...bending, kneeling or stooping?	1	2	3	1	2	3037-38
...walking <u>more than a mile</u>?	1	2	3	1	2	3039-40
...walking <u>half a mile</u>?	1	2	3	1	2	3041-42
...walking 100 yards?	1	2	3	1	2	3043-44
...bathing or dressing yourself?	1	2	3	1	2	3045-46

(3047-50)

H11a) Have you had attacks of wheezing or whistling in your chest at any time in the last 12 months?

Yes 1   3051

No 2

b) Have you ever had attacks of shortness of breath with wheezing?

Yes | 1 | ASK c)   3052

No | 2 | GO TO H12

33   E2/H

IF YES

H11c) Is your breathing absolutely normal between attacks?

                                        Yes   1   3053

                                        No   2

d) Have you at any time in the last twelve months been woken at night by an attack of shortness of breath?

                                        Yes   1   3054

                                        No   2

H12a) Do you <u>usually</u> bring up any phlegm from your chest first thing in the morning in the winter?

                                        Yes | 1 | GO TO c) | 3055

                                        No | 2 | ASK b) |

IF NO

b) Do you usually bring up any phlegm from your chest during the day or night in the winter?

                                        Yes | 1 | ASK c) | 3056

                                        No | 2 | GO TO H13 |

IF YES

c) Do you bring up phlegm like this on most days for as much as three months each year?

                                        Yes   1   3057

                                        No   2

34   E2/H

H13a) | Would you say that for your height you are...

READ OUT...

...about the right weight,   1   3058

too heavy,   2

or too light?   3

Can't say   8

b) | Have you ever seriously tried to lose weight?

Yes   1   3059

No   2

H14a) | Have you ever smoked a cigarette (IF **ASIAN**: or Bidi),
a cigar or a pipe?

| Yes | 1 | ASK b) | 3060 |
| No | 2 | GO TO H15 |

IF YES
b) | Do you smoke cigarettes (IF **ASIAN**: or Bidis) at all
nowadays?

| Yes | 1 | GO TO e) | 3061 |
| No | 2 | ASK c) |

IF NO
c) | Have you ever smoked cigarettes (or Bidis)?

| Yes | 1 | ASK d) | 3062 |
| No | 2 | GO TO H15 |

35   E2/H

IF YES

H14d) Did you smoke cigarettes (or Bidis) regularly or
occasionally? By regularly, I mean at least one
cigarette (or Bidi) a day.

Regularly	1	
Occasionally	2	GO TO H15
Never really smoked, just tried it once or twice	3	

3063

CURRENT SMOKERS

e) About how many cigarettes (or Bidis) a day do you usually
smoke on <u>weekdays</u>?

WRITE IN NUMBER: ☐☐   3064-65

OR CODE: Can't say   98

f) And about how many cigarettes (or Bidis) a day do you usually
smoke at <u>weekends</u>?

WRITE IN NUMBER: ☐☐   3066-67

OR CODE: Can't say   98

H15a) Have you ever had paan (betel)?

Yes	1	ASK b)
No	2	GO TO H16

3068

IF YES

b) Do you have paan (betel) nowadays?
IF YES: Do you have it regularly or just
occasionally?

Yes, regularly	1
Yes, occasionally	2
No	3

3069

H16 | How often, if ever, do you drink alcohol?

Once a week or more often	1		3114
		ASK H17	
Less often than once a week	2		
Never drink alcohol	3	GO TO H18	

IF DRINK ALCOHOL

H17 | Thinking about the last three months only, have you at any time

... READ OUT AND CODE YES OR NO FOR EACH ...	<u>Yes</u>	<u>No</u>	Can't say	
... found that your hands were shaking in the morning after drinking the previous night?	1	2	8	3115
... had a drink first thing in the morning to steady your nerves or get rid of a hangover?	1	2	8	3116

37   E2/H

H18 | The next few questions are about how you feel in
yourself - your general well-being.

a) | Have you noticed that you've been getting tired
in the past month?

Yes	1	GO TO c)	3117
No	2	ASK b)	

IF NO
b) | During the past month, have you felt you've
been lacking in energy?

Yes	1	ASK c)	3118
No	2	GO TO H19	

IF TIRED OR LACKING IN ENERGY
c) | Do you know why you have been feeling
(tired/lacking in energy)?

Yes	1	ASK d)	3119
No	2	GO TO H19	

IF YES
d) | SHOW CARD HA. What is the main reason? Please choose
from this card?

CODE ALL THAT APPLY

Problems with sleep	1	3120-26
Medication	2	
Physical illness	3	
Working too hard (inc. housework, looking after baby)	4	
Stress, worry or some other psychological reason	5	
Physical exercise	6	
Other (SPECIFY)_____	7	

38   E2/H

ALL

H19a) In the past month, have you been having problems with
      trying to get to sleep or with getting back to sleep if
      you were woken?

                                                    Yes   1   3127
                                                    No   2

b) Has sleeping more than you usually do been a problem
   for you in the last month?

                                                    Yes   1   3128
                                                    No   2

c) INTERVIEWER CHECK a) AND b) AND RECORD:
                     Respondent has sleep problems
                        ('Yes' AT a) AND/OR b)) | 1   ASK H20 | 3129
             Respondent does <u>not</u> have sleep problems | 2   GO TO H21 |

IF SLEEP PROBLEMS

H20a) Do you know why you are having problems with your
      sleep?

                                                    Yes | 1   ASK b) | 3130
                                                    No | 2   GO TO H21 |

IF YES

b) SHOW CARD HB. What is the main reason for these problems?
   Please choose from this card?

   CODE <u>ALL</u> THAT APPLY   Noise   01   3131-48
                        Shift work/too busy to sleep   02
                               Illness/discomfort   03
                                     Worry/thinking   04
                        Needing to go to the toilet   05
          Wake to do something (e.g. look after baby)   06
                                           Tired   07
                                      Medication   08
            Other (SPECIFY) _____ 09

                                                                                     (3149)

ALL

H21a) Almost everyone becomes sad, miserable or depressed
at times.
Have you had a spell of feeling sad, miserable or
depressed in the past month?

	Yes	1	ASK b)	3150
	No	2	GO TO c)	

IF YES

b) Have you had such a spell in the
past <u>week</u>?

	Yes	1		3151
	No	2		

c) During the past <u>month</u>, have you been able to
enjoy or take an interest in things as much as
you usually do?

	Yes	1	GO TO e)	3152
No/No enjoyment or interest		2	ASK d)	

IF NO

d) Have you felt unable to enjoy or take an interest
in things during the past <u>week</u>?

	Yes, unable to take an interest in things	1	3153
	No	2	

e) **INTERVIEWER CHECK:**

	'Yes' AT (b) OR AT (d)	1	ASK H22	3154
	Others	2	GO TO H26	

IN QUESTIONS H22 TO H24, READ 'depressed'
IF RESPONDENT SAID 'Yes' TO b); READ "UNABLE TO TAKE AN INTEREST IN
THINGS" FOR THE REMAINDER

40

IF DEPRESSED/UNABLE TO TAKE INTEREST

H22a) Since last... (DAY OF WEEK)... on how many days have you .felt depressed (unable to take an interest in things)?

4 days or more	1
2 to 3 days	2
1 day	3
Can't say	8

3155

b) Have you felt depressed (unable to enjoy or take an interest in things) for more than 3 hours in total on any day in the past week?

Yes	1
No	2

3156

41   E2/H

H23a) | SHOW CARD HC. What sort of things made you feel
       | depressed (unable to enjoy or take
       | an interest in things) in the past week? Can you
       | choose from this card?

RING AS MANY CODES AS APPLY IN COLUMN (a)

	(a)	(b) Main Thing
Members of the family	01	01
Relationship with spouse/partner	02	02
Relationships with friends	03	03
Housing	04	04
Money/bills	05	05
Own physical health (inc. pregnancy)	06	06
Own mental health	07	07
Work or lack of work (inc. student)	08	08
Legal difficulties	09	09
Political issues/the news	10	10
Harassment	11	11
Other (SPECIFY) _____	12	12
Can't say	98	98

(a)

3157-76

(b)

3177-78

IF 2+ ANSWERS AT a), ASK b)
b) | What was the main thing that made you feel like
   | this?

RING ONE CODE ONLY ABOVE IN COLUMN (b)

c) | In the past week when you felt depressed (unable
   | to enjoy or take an interest in things),
   | did you ever become happier when something
   | nice happened, or when you were in company?

CARD 32

Yes	1	3214
No	2	

(3215)

E2/H

H23d) | How long have you been feeling depressed
(unable to take an interest
in things) as you have described?

less than 2 weeks	1
2 weeks but less than 6 months	2
6 months but less than 1 year	3
1 year but less than 2 years	4
2 years or more	5

3216

H24a) | In the past week were these feelings worse in
the morning or in the evening, or did this make no
difference?

Worse in the morning	1
Worse in the evening	2
No difference/Other	3

3217

b) | When you have felt sad, miserable or depressed (unable
to take an interest in things) in the past week, have
you been so restless that you couldn't sit still?

Yes	1
No	2

3218

c) | And have you been doing things more slowly, for
example, walking more slowly?

Yes	1
No	2

3219

H24d) | Have you been less talkative than normal?

| | Yes | 1 | 3220 |
| | No | 2 | |

e) | Again, thinking about the past seven days, have you on at least one occasion felt guilty or blamed yourself when things went wrong when it <u>hasn't</u> been your fault?

| | Yes | 1 | 3221 |
| | No | 2 | |

f) | During the past week, have you been feeling you are not as good as other people?

| | Yes | 1 | 3222 |
| | No | 2 | |

g) | Have you felt hopeless at all during the past week, for instance about your future?

| | Yes | 1 | 3223 |
| | No | 2 | |

h) | INTERVIEWER CHECK e), f) AND g) AND RECORD:

| 'Yes' e), f) OR g) | 1 | ASK H25 | 3224 |
| Others | 2 | GO TO H26 | |

44   E2/II

IF CODE 1 AT H24h)

H25a) In the past week, have you felt that life isn't
worth living?

Yes	1	ASK b)	3225
Yes, but not in the past week	2	GO TO H26	
No	3		

IF YES
b) In the past week, have you thought of committing
suicide?

Yes	1	ASK b)	3226
Yes, but not in the past week	2	GO TO H26	
No	3		

IF YES
c) Have you talked to your doctor about these
thoughts (of committing suicide)?

Yes	1	GO TO H26	3227
No	2	READ d)	

IF NO
d) (You have said that you thought about
committing suicide). Since this is a very
serious matter, it is most important that
you talk to your doctor about these thoughts.

45   E2/H

ALL

H26   (Thank you for answering those questions on how
      you have been feeling). I would now like to ask
      you a few questions about worries you might have.

a)   Have you been feeling anxious or nervous in the
      past month?

                                          Yes   1   3228

                                          No   2

b)   In the past month, did you ever find your muscles
      felt tense or that you couldn't relax?

                                          Yes   1   3229

                                          No   2

H26c) Some people have phobias; they get nervous or uncomfortable about particular things or situations when there is no real danger.

In the past month, have you felt anxious, nervous or tense about any particular things or situations when there was no real danger?

IF NECESSARY: For example, you may get nervous when speaking or eating in front of strangers, when you are far from home or in crowded rooms, or you may have a fear of heights. You may become nervous at the sight of things like blood or spiders.

Yes	1	ASK H27	3230
No	2	GO TO H28	

IF YES

H27 | SHOW CARD HD. Can you look at this card and tell me
which of the situations or things listed made you
the most anxious in the past month?

CODE ALL THAT APPLY

Crowds or public places, including travelling alone or being far from home	1	3231-36
Enclosed spaces	2	
Social situations, including eating or speaking in public, being watched or stared at	3	
The sight of blood or injury	4	
Any specific single cause including insects, spiders and heights	5	
Other things	6	

H28a) | INTERVIEWER CHECK H26a), b) AND c) AND CODE FIRST TO APPLY

'Yes' AT a) OR b)	1	ASK b)	3237
'Yes' AT c)	2	GO TO c)	
Others	3	GO TO H29	

48   E2/H

IF CODE 1 AT a)

H28b) Which, if any, of the following symptoms did
       you have when you felt anxious?

READ OUT AND CODE YES OR NO FOR EACH   <u>Yes</u>   <u>No</u>

                      Heart racing or pounding   1   2   3238

                      Hands sweating or shaking   1   2   3239

                               Feeling dizzy   1   2   3240

       -
                    Difficulty getting your breath   1   2   3241

                       Butterflies in stomach   1   2   3242

                                 Dry mouth   1   2   3243

       -
       Nausea or feeling as though you wanted to vomit 1   2   3244

       IF CODE 1 OR 2 AT a)

   c) Thinking about the last month, did your anxiety
       or tension ever get so bad that you got into a
       panic, for instance, make you feel that you might
       collapse or lose control unless you did something
       about it?

                                            Yes   1   3245

                                            No   2

49   E2/H

ALL

H29 Over the past year, have there been times when you
     felt very happy indeed without a break for days on
     end?

Yes	1	ASK H30	3246
Unsure	2		
		GO TO H31	
No	3		

IF YES

H30a) Was there an obvious reason for this?

Yes	1	3247
Unsure	2	
No	3	

b) Did your relatives or friends think it was
    strange or complain about it?

Yes	1	3248
Unsure	2	
No	3	

ALL

H31a) Over the past year, have you ever felt that
       your thoughts were directly interfered with
       or controlled by some outside force or person?

Yes	1	ASK b)	3249
Unsure	2		
		GO TO H32	
No	3		

50   E2/H

H31b) **IF YES**
Did this come about in a way that many people
would find hard to believe, for instance, through
telepathy?

Yes	1	3250
Unsure	2	
No	3	

H32a) Over the past year, have there been times when
you felt that people were against you?

Yes	1	ASK b)	3251
Unsure	2	GO TO H33	
No	3		

b) **IF YES**
Have there been times when you felt that people
were deliberately acting to harm you or your
interests?

Yes	1	3252
Unsure	2	
No	3	

c) Have there been times you felt that a group of
people were plotting to cause you serious harm
or injury?

Yes	1	3253
Unsure	2	
No	3	

51   E2/11

H33 | Over the past year, have there been times when you felt that something <u>strange</u> was going on?

Yes	1	ASK H34	3254
Unsure	2		
		GO TO H35	
No	3		

IF YES
H34 | Did you feel it was so strange that other people would find it very hard to believe?

Yes	1	3255
Unsure	2	
No	3	

ALL
H35a) | Over the past year, have there been times when you heard or saw things that other people couldn't?

Yes	1	ASK b)	3256
Unsure	2		
		GO TO H36	
No	3		

IF YES
b) | Did you at any time hear voices saying quite a few words or sentences when there was no one around that might account for it?

Yes	1	3257
Unsure	2	
No	3	

52   E2/H

H36 | INTERVIEWER RECORD ANY COMMENTS MADE SPONTANEOUSLY
WHICH WOULD HELP INTERPRETATION OF ANSWERS H29-H35

ALL

H37 | Over the past month, approximately how many
times have you talked to, or visited a GP or
family doctor about your own health? Please
do not include any visits to a hospital, or
visits you made while abroad.

One or two	1	
Three to five	2	
Six to ten	3	ASK H38
More than ten	4	
None	5	GO TO H39
Can't say	8	

3258

IF VISITED IN PAST MONTH

H38a) | Did the doctor speak a language you could
clearly understand?

Yes	1	GO TO H39
No	2	ASK b)
Some did, some didn't	3	

3259

53   E2/H

IF NO/SOME DID AND SOME DIDN'T

H38b) How did you manage to communicate to the
doctor(s) who did not speak a language you
could understand?   3260-7:

PROBE FULLY. RECORD VERBATIM

CARD 33

c) Do you think the doctor understood you?

                                        Yes   1   3314
                                        No   2

54

E2/H

H39a) In the past twelve months have you spoken to a GP or family doctor on your own behalf, either in person or by telephone, about being anxious or depressed or a mental, nervous or emotional problem?

Yes	1	ASK b)
No	2	GO TO H40

3315

IF YES

b) What did the doctor say was the matter with you?

3316-31

TRY AND OBTAIN A MEDICAL DIAGNOSIS OR ESTABLISH SYMPTOMS

c) INTERVIEWER CODE

Complaint on Reference Card RA	1	
All others	2	

3332

ALL

H40a) In the last 12 months, that is since ...(MONTH) 1992/1993 have you had any kind of accident as a result of which you saw a doctor or went to hospital?

Yes	1	ASK b)
No	2	GO TO H41

3333

IF YES

b) Have you had more than one accident, in the last year? IF YES: How many?

One only 1   3334

Two 2

Three 3

Four or more 4

ASK c) AND d) FOR EACH ACCIDENT IN PAST 12 MONTHS STARTING WITH MOST RECENT

c) In which year and month did ... (accident) happen?

ENTER YEAR AND MONTH IN COLUMN (c) IN GRID

d) Where did this accident happen? PROMPT AS NECESSARY AND RING ONE CODE IN COLUMN (d) ON GRID

	(c) When happened		(d) Where accident happened							
Accident	Year	Month	Sports facilities	Workplace	Home/ garden	School/ College	Motor/ vehicle	Road/ pavement	Other (SPECIFY)	
Most recent			1	2	3	4	5	6	7_____	3335-39
2nd most recent			1	2	3	4	5	6	7_____	334:-44
3rd most recent			1	2	3	4	5	6	7_____	33-5-49
4th most recent			1	2	3	4	5	6	7_____	325:-54
5th most recent			1	2	3	4	5	6	7_____	3355-59

56   E2/H

H41a) In the last 12 months, that is since ... (MONTH) ...
1992/1993, you been in hospital or in a clinic as an in-patient
overnight or longer?

INCLUDE CHILDBIRTH

Yes	1	ASK b)
No	2	GO TO H44

3360

IF YES
b) Since ... (MONTH) ... 1992/1993, in all, how many days
have you spent in hospital or in a clinic as an
in-patient?

WRITE IN NO. OF DAYS: [|]   3361-62

OR CODE: Can't remember/Can't say   98

c) Did you receive any assistance from a hospital
linkworker, advocate or interpreter?

Yes   1   3363

No   2

d) Was (were) your hospital stay(s) free under the
NHS or paid for privately?

All free under the NHS   1   3364

All paid for privately   2

Some NHS/some private   3

Can't say   8

57   E2/1

H42 | INTERVIEWER CHECK A1a) AND RECORD:

Respondent is female and under 45 | 1 | ASK H43 | 336

Others | 2 | GO TO H44

IF CODE 1 AT H42
H43 | Were any of these hospital stays for
child-birth?

Yes, all   1   336

Yes, some   2

No   3

ALL
H44a) | When attending your GP or hospital, would you
prefer to be seen by a doctor of - (ETHNIC ORIGIN) -
origin?

Yes | 1 | ASK b) | 33

No | 2

Depends | 3 | GO TO H46

Can't say | 8

IF YES
b) | Why is that?   3368-

PROBE FULLY AND RECORD VERBATIM

H45 NOT USED

58

E2/H

H46 | When visiting a GP or hospital, do
you prefer to be seen by a...

CARD 34
(3414-25)

READ OUT...

...female doctor,   1   3426

a male doctor,   2

or doesn't it matter to you?   3

(Can't say)   8

59   E2/H

ALL

H47a) Finally, here is a list of some health and welfare
services. Please tell me for each service, whether it is
something you have made use of in the last 12 months, that
is since - (MONTH) - in last year?

READ OUT AND RING ONE CODE FOR EACH IN GRID AT (a)

b) **ASK (b) FOR EACH SERVICE USED**
Thinking of - (SERVICE) - , was this provided by
the NHS or Social Services, or was it provided
by a private or voluntary agency?

RING ONE CODE FOR EACH IN GRID IN (b)

	(a) Used			(b) Provider				
	Yes	No	Unsure	NHS	Social services	Private/ vol agency	Unknown	
Dentist	1	2	8	1	2	3	8	3427-28
Physiotherapist	1	2	8	1	2	3	8	3429-30
Psychotherapist	1	2	8	1	2	3	8	3431-32
Social Worker or Welfare Officer	1	2	8	1	2	3	8	3433-34
Alternative medical practitioner (e.g. Hakim, homeopath, osteopath)	1	2	8	1	2	3	8	3435-36

60   E2/11

	(a) Used			(b) Provider			
	Yes	No	Unsure	NHS	Social services	Private/ vol agency	Unknown
Health Visitor or District Nurse	1	2	8	1	2	3	8	3437-38
Home Help	1	2	8	1	2	3	8	3439-40
(IF AGED 65+) Meals on wheels	1	2	8	1	2	3	8	3441-42
Some other health or Welfare service	1	2	8	1	2	3	8	3443-44

Appendix B: Additional Tables for Chapter 3

Table B.1   Report of health compared to others of same age

cell percentages: age and gender standardised

	White	All ethnic minorities	Caribbean	All South Asians	Indian or African Asian	Pakistani or Bangladeshi	Chinese
Those reporting fair or poor health	27	32	34	32	27	39	26
Weighted base	2864	5180	1565	3226	2085	1142	389
Unweighted base	2860	5182	1201	3767	1996	1771	214

Table B.2   Reported long-standing illness

cell percentages: age and gender standardised

	White	All ethnic minorities	Caribbean	All South Asians	Indian or African Asian	Pakistani or Bangladeshi	Chinese
Those reporting a long-standing illness	27	21	27	18	17	21	15
Weighted base	2865	5184	1566	3229	2085	1144	389
Unweighted base	28650	5190	1203	3773	1999	1774	214

Table B.3   Reported long-standing illness limiting work

cell percentages: age and gender standardised

	White	All ethnic minorities	Caribbean	All South Asians	Indian or African Asian	Pakistani or Bangladeshi	Chinese
Those reporting long-standing illness limiting work	11	12	13	12	11	13	7
Weighted base	2853	5160	1559	3212	2081	1131	389
Unweighted base	2839	5156	1194	3748	1992	1756	214

Table B.4   Moderately exerting activities* limited by health

cell percentages: age and gender standardised

	White	All ethnic minorities	Caribbean	All South Asians	Indian or African Asian	Pakistani or Bangladeshi	Chinese
Men	8	12	6	15	12	20	8
Women	13	19	21	19	14	27	12
Total	11	15	14	17	13	24	10
Weighted base	2866	2584	795	1590	1035	554	199
Unweighted base	2866	2573	613	1856	985	871	104

* includes any of: moderate activities; climbing one flight of stairs; walking half a mile; or carrying groceries.

Table B.5   Score of three or more on index of general health*

cell percentages: age and gender standardised

	White	All ethnic minorities	Caribbean	All South Asians	Indian or African Asian	Pakistani or Bangladeshi	Chinese
Men	10	12	11	13	11	18	8
Women	11	14	17	13	12	15	6
Total	11	13	14	13	11	17	7
Weighted base	*2850*	*5092*	*1552*	*3151*	*2051*	*1100*	*389*
Unweighted base	*2839*	*5090*	*1191*	*3685*	*1959*	*1726*	*214*

* score calculated as sum of: Fair reported health = 1;   Poor or very poor health = 2;   Long-standing illness = 1
Long-standing illness limiting work = 2;   Registered disabled = 2

Table B.6   Psycho-social health

cell percentages: age and gender standardised

	White	All ethnic minorities	Caribbean	All South Asians	Indian or African Asian	Pakistani or Bangladeshi	Chinese
Those reporting tiredness, lacking in energy or sleep problems	54	39	49	34	34	35	42
Weighted base	*2867*	*2587*	*795*	*1593*	*1038*	*555*	*199*
Unweighted base	*2867*	*2579*	*614*	*1861*	*988*	*873*	*104*

Table B.7   Diagnosed heart disease

cell percentages: age and gender standardised

	White	All ethnic minorities	Caribbean	All South Asians	Indian or African Asian	Pakistani or Bangladeshi	Chinese
Those reporting diagnosed angina or heart attack	4.2	4.0	3.7	4.2	3.3	6.0	3.0
Weighted base	*2864*	*5183*	*1564*	*3230*	*2087*	*1143*	*389*
Unweighted base	*2864*	*5187*	*1202*	*3771*	*1998*	*1773*	*214*

Table B.8   Severe chest pain or diagnosed heart disease by age for respondents aged 40 or over

cell percentages: age and gender standardised

	White	All ethnic minorities	Caribbean	All South Asians	Indian or African Asian	Pakistani or Bangladeshi	Chinese
Aged 40 to 44	5	6	6	6	2	16	*
Aged 45 to 59	14	15	12	17	13	24	*
Aged 60 or over	20	24	22	26	22	35	*
Total	14	15	13	17	13	25	8
Weighted base	*1046*	*1875*	*552*	*1181*	*772*	*409*	*142*
Unweighted base	*1592*	*1989*	*494*	*1412*	*822*	*590*	*83*

Table B.9   Hypertension

cell percentages: age and gender standardised

	White	All ethnic minorities	Caribbean	All South Asians	Indian or African Asian	Pakistani or Bangladeshi	Chinese
Men	11	10	13	9	10	8	4
Women	12	12	21	8	6	13	6
Total	12	11	17	9	8	11	5
Weighted base	*2863*	*5172*	*1558*	*3225*	*2083*	*1142*	*389*
Unweighted base	*2862*	*5173*	*1195*	*3764*	*1994*	*1770*	*214*

Table B.10   Perceived obesity

cell percentages: age and gender standardised

	White	All ethnic minorities	Caribbean	All South Asians	Indian or African Asian	Pakistani or Bangladeshi	Chinese
Those reporting themselves overweight	41	25	34	22	22	22	13
Weighted base	*2849*	*2507*	*777*	*1536*	*1008*	*529*	*194*
Unweighted base	*2839*	*2486*	*602*	*1782*	*955*	*827*	*102*

Table B.11   Diabetes

cell percentages: age and gender standardised

	White	All ethnic minorities	Caribbean	All South Asians	Indian or African Asian	Pakistani or Bangladeshi	Chinese
Those with diabetes	1.7	5.7	5.3	6.2	4.7	8.9	3.0
Weighted base	*2867*	*5196*	*1568*	*3238*	*2093*	*1146*	*389*
Unweighted base	*2867*	*5196*	*1205*	*3777*	*2001*	*1776*	*214*

Table B.12 Prevalence of respiratory symptoms

cell percentages: age and gender standardised

	White	All ethnic minorities	Caribbean	All South Asians	Indian or African Asian	Pakistani or Bangladeshi	Chinese
Woken by shortness of breath	5	4	5	4	3	6	3
Coughing up phlegm							
Smokers	9	13	12	16	16	16	*
Non-smokers	3	5	4	6	6	7	*
Total	7	7	7	8	7	9	6
Wheezing or coughing up phlegm							
Men	25	18	21	17	15	20	*
Women	28	17	25	15	14	16	*
Smokers	31	27	27	30	32	28	*
Non-smokers	20	15	21	13	12	15	*
Total	27	18	23	16	15	18	12
Weighted base	*2867*	*2587*	*795*	*1593*	*1038*	*555*	*199*
Unweighted base	*2867*	*2579*	*614*	*1861*	*988*	*873*	*104*

* cell numbers too small for a reliable estimate.

Table B.13 Accidents resulting in hospital treatment over the past 12 months

rate per 100: age and gender standardised

	White	All ethnic minorities	Caribbean	All South Asians	Indian or African Asian	Pakistani or Bangladeshi	Chinese
Accidents resulting in hospital treatment	13	6	9	4	4	5	8
Weighted base	*2867*	*2587*	*795*	*1593*	*1038*	*555*	*199*
Unweighted base	*2867*	*2579*	*614*	*1861*	*988*	*873*	*104*

Appendix C: Additional Tables for Chapter 4

Table C.1   Reported health compared to others of the same age by age on migration to Britain

cell percentages: age and gender standardised

Age on migration to Britain	Caribbean[1]		Indian or African Asian[2]		Pakistani or Bangladeshi[3]	
	British born or <11	11 or older	British born or <11	11 older	British born or <11	11 or older
Those reporting fair or poor health	27	17	22	18	21	20
Weighted base	*368*	*118*	*335*	*428*	*252*	*198*
Unweighted base	*316*	*111*	*322*	*480*	*316*	*376*

[1] only those aged 30 to 44;   [2] only those aged 25 to 39;   [3] only those aged 20 to 34

Table C.2   Reported long-standing illness by age on migration to Britain

cell percentages: age and gender standardised

Age on migration to Britain	Caribbean[1]		Indian or African Asian[2]		Pakistani or Bangladeshi[3]	
	British born or <11	11 or older	British born or <11	11 older	British born or <11	11 or older
Those reporting a long-standing illness	21	10	10	8	9	7
Weighted base	*368*	*118*	*335*	*428*	*252*	*199*
Unweighted base	*316*	*111*	*323*	*480*	*316*	*378*

[1] only those aged 30 to 44;   [2] only those aged 25 to 39;   [3] only those aged 20 to 34

Table C.3   Hypertension by age on migration to Britain

cell percentages: age and gender standardised

Age on migration to Britain	Caribbean[1]		Indian or African Asian[2]		Pakistani or Bangladeshi[3]	
	British born or <11	11 or older	British born or <11	11 older	British born or <11	11 or older
Those reporting hypertension	8.2	9.0	3.6	1.3	2.5	4.7
Weighted base	*364*	*118*	*333*	*427*	*252*	*196*
Unweighted base	*314*	*111*	*321*	*479*	*316*	*377*

[1] only those aged 30 to 44;   [2] only those aged 25 to 39;   [3] only those aged 20 to 34

Table C.4   Respiratory symptoms by age on migration to Britain

cell percentages: age and gender standardised

Age on migration to Britain	Caribbean[1]		Indian or African Asian[2]		Pakistani or Bangladeshi[3]	
	British born or <11	11 or older	British born or <11	11 older	British born or <11	11 or older
Those reporting wheezing or coughing up phlegm	21	11	14	8	8	8
Weighted base	*174*	*68*	*155*	*230*	*123*	*99*
Unweighted base	*160*	*61*	*152*	*241*	*163*	*186*

[1] only those aged 30 to 44;   [2] only those aged 25 to 39;   [3] only those aged 20 to 34

Table C.5   Smoking by age on migration to Britain

cell percentages: age and gender standardised

Age on migration to Britain	Caribbean[1]		Indian or African Asian[2]		Pakistani or Bangladeshi[3]	
	British born or <11	11 or older	British born or <11	11 older	British born or <11	11 or older
Those who have ever smoked	43	33	19	11	24	19
Weighted base	*174*	*68*	*155*	*230*	*123*	*99*
Unweighted base	*160*	*61*	*152*	*241*	*163*	*186*

[1] only those aged 30 to 44;   [2] only those aged 25 to 39;   [3] only those aged 20 to 34

Table C.6   Alcohol use by age on migration to Britain

cell percentages: age and gender standardised

Age on migration to Britain	Caribbean[1]		Indian or African Asian[2]		Pakistani or Bangladeshi[3]	
	British born or <11	11 or older	British born or <11	11 older	British born or <11	11 or older
Those who never drink alcohol	17	34	49	62	94	99
Weighted base	*174*	*68*	*155*	*230*	*123*	*99*
Unweighted base	*160*	*61*	*152*	*241*	*163*	*186*

[1] only those aged 30 to 44;   [2] only those aged 25 to 39;   [3] only those aged 20 to 34

Table C.7   Reported health compared to others of the same age by religious group (Indians and African Asians only)

cell percentages

	Hindu	Sikh	Muslim	Christian	All Indians and Arican Asians
Those reporting fair or poor health	27	28	32	26	28
Weighted base	*883*	*799*	*193*	*86*	*2083*
Unweighted base	*819*	*704*	*284*	*85*	*1996*

**Table C.8 Reported long-standing illness by religious group
(Indians and African Asians only)**

					cell percentages
	Hindu	Sikh	Muslim	Christian	All Indians and Arican Asians
Those reporting a long-standing illness	17	16	20	18	17
Weighted base	*883*	*799*	*194*	*86*	*2084*
Unweighted base	*819*	*706*	*285*	*85*	*1999*

Table C.9 Diagnosed heart disease by religious group (Indians and African Asians only)

					cell percentages
	Hindu	Sikh	Muslim	Christian	All Indians and Arican Asians
Those reporting diagnosed heart disease	1.7	3.9	5.8	7.7	3.3
Weighted base	*883*	*801*	*194*	*86*	*2086*
Unweighted base	*819*	*706*	*285*	*85*	*1998*

**Table C.10 Severe chest pain or diagnosed heart disease among those aged 40 or older
by religious group (Indians and African Asians only)**

				cell percentages
	Hindu	Sikh	Muslim	All Indians and Arican Asians
Those reporting symptoms or diagnosis suggestive of heart disease	7.7	14.1	18.5	12.2
Weighted base	*346*	*301*	*85*	*813*
Unweighted base	*345*	*285*	*111*	*822*

Table C.11 Hypertension by religious group (Indians and African Asians only)

					cell percentages
	Hindu	Sikh	Muslim	Christian	All Indians and Arican Asians
Those reporting hypertension	6.4	8.6	9.4	13.0	8.0
Weighted base	*883*	*797*	*193*	*86*	*2082*
Unweighted base	*819*	*702*	*284*	*85*	*1994*

Table C.12   Diabetes by religious group (Indians and African Asians only)

cell percentages

	Hindu	Sikh	Muslim	Christian	All Indians and Arican Asians
Those reporting diabetes	5.1	4.6	4.3	6.6	4.9
Weighted base	*883*	*802*	*194*	*86*	*2088*
Unweighted base	*819*	*707*	*285*	*85*	*2000*

Table C.13   Respiratory symptoms by religious group (Indians and African Asians only)

cell percentages

	Hindu	Sikh	Muslim	All Indians and Arican Asians
Those reporting wheezing or coughing up phlegm	14	14	18	7
Weighted base	*437*	*393*	*96*	*1037*
Unweighted base	*407*	*344*	*139*	*988*

Table C.14   Smoking by religious group (Indians and African Asians only)

cell percentages

	Hindu	Sikh	Muslim	All Indians and Arican Asians
Those who have ever smoked	13	6	20	14
Weighted base	*437*	*393*	*96*	*1037*
Unweighted base	*407*	*344*	*139*	*988*

Table C.15   Use of paan by religious group (Indians and African Asians only)

cell percentages

	Hindu	Sikh	Muslim	All Indians and Arican Asians
Ever used paan	50	11	49	34
Weighted base	*437*	*390*	*95*	*1032*
Unweighted base	*407*	*343*	*138*	*985*

Table C.16   Alcohol use by religious group (Indians and African Asians only)

cell percentages

	Hindu	Sikh	Muslim	All Indians and Arican Asians
Those who never drink alcohol				
Men	38	31	85	38
Women	81	82	96	79
Total	59	60	91	59
Weighted base	*437*	*393*	*95*	*1034*
Unweighted base	*407*	*344*	*138*	*986*

Appendix D: Additional Tables for Chapter 5

Table D.1   Reported fair or poor health by class

	White	All ethnic minorities	Caribbean	Indian or African Asian	Pakistani or Bangladeshi
			percentages: age, gender and class standardised		
Class					
Non-manual	21	24	25	20	30
Manual	23	30	29	27	35
No full-time worker in household	37	38	38	34	44
Total	27	30	31	27	36
Weighted base	*2227*	*4334*	*1438*	*1873*	*1023*
Unweighted base	*2110*	*4434*	*1060*	*1782*	*1592*

Table D.2   Reported fair or poor health by tenure

	White	All ethnic minorities	Caribbean	Indian or African Asian	Pakistani or Bangladeshi
			percentages: age, gender and class standardised		
Tenure					
Owner-occupier	23	28	27	24	35
Tenant	34	39	40	34	45
Total	26	31	30	27	38
Weighted base	*2322*	*4536*	*1465*	*1962*	*1109*
Unweighted base	*2173*	*4617*	*1077*	*1848*	*1692*

Table D.3   Angina or heart attack by class

	White	All ethnic minorities	Caribbean	Indian or African Asian	Pakistani or Bangladeshi
			percentages: age, gender and class standardised		
Class					
Non-manual	3.0	2.4	3.3	1.4	2.8
Manual	2.7	3.7	2.7	3.1	6.1
No full-time worker in household	3.9	4.5	4.0	4.3	5.4
Total	3.2	3.5	3.4	2.9	4.8
Weighted base	*2227*	*4333*	*1437*	*1874*	*1022*
Unweighted base	*2110*	*4436*	*1060*	*1783*	*1593*

Table D.4 Angina or heart attack by tenure

percentages: age, gender and class standardised

	White	All ethnic minorities	Caribbean	Indian or African Asian	Pakistani or Bangladeshi
Tenure					
Owner-occupier	3.0	3.2	2.7	2.5	5.2
Tenant	4.1	4.0	3.8	3.5	5.2
Total	3.3	3.5	3.1	2.8	5.2
Weighted base	*2322*	*4538*	*1466*	*1963*	*1110*
Unweighted base	*2173*	*4620*	*1077*	*1849*	*1694*

Table D.5 Severe chest pain or diagnosed heart disease by class for respondents aged 40 or over

percentages: age, gender and class standardised

	White	All ethnic minorities	Caribbean	Indian or African Asian	Pakistani or Bangladeshi
Class					
Non-manual	8	8	9	7	10
Manual	11	15	11	11	27
No full-time worker in household	19	17	12	17	24
Total	13	13	11	12	20
Weighted base	*749*	*1440*	*468*	*637*	*334*
Unweighted base	*919*	*1498*	*369*	*654*	*475*

Table D.6 Severe chest pain or diagnosed heart disease by tenure for respondents aged 40 or over

percentages: age, gender and class standardised

	White	All ethnic minorities	Caribbean	Indian or African Asian	Pakistani or Bangladeshi
Tenure					
Owner-occupier	11	14	11	11	23
Tenant	16	17	11	18	21
Total	12	15	11	13	23
Weighted base	*778*	*1498*	*472*	*665*	*361*
Unweighted base	*939*	*1568*	*374*	*680*	*514*

Table D.7   Hypertension by class

percentages: age, gender and class standardised

	White	All ethnic minorities	Caribbean	Indian or African Asian	Pakistani or Bangladeshi
Class					
Non-manual	8	8	15	5	6
Manual	12	11	15	9	10
No full-time worker in household	11	12	18	8	11
Total	10	10	16	7	9
Weighted base	*2228*	*4326*	*1434*	*1871*	*1021*
Unweighted base	*2111*	*4426*	*1055*	*1780*	*1591*

Table D.8   Hypertension by tenure

percentages: age, gender and class standardised

	White	All ethnic minorities	Caribbean	Indian or African Asian	Pakistani or Bangladeshi
Tenure					
Owner-occupier	9	9	14	6	9
Tenant	13	12	17	9	12
Total	10	10	15	7	10
Weighted base	*2321*	*4531*	*1461*	*1961*	*1110*
Unweighted base	*2173*	*4610*	*1072*	*1846*	*1692*

Table D.9   Diabetes by class

percentages: age, gender and class standardised

	White	All ethnic minorities	Caribbean	Indian or African Asian	Pakistani or Bangladeshi
Class					
Non-manual	1.1	4.1	4.1	2.8	6.4
Manual	1.1	4.5	3.2	3.5	8.3
No full-time worker in household	2.1	6.3	4.5	7.1	7.6
Total	1.4	5.0	3.9	4.4	7.4
Weighted base	*2228*	*4336*	*1438*	*1876*	*1023*
Unweighted base	*2111*	*4437*	*1059*	*1785*	*1593*

Table D.10 Diabetes by tenure

percentages: age, gender and class standardised

	White	All ethnic minorities	Caribbean	Indian or African Asian	Pakistani or Bangladeshi
Tenure					
Owner-occupier	1.1	4.3	2.5	3.7	7.6
Tenant	2.7	6.2	6.0	5.9	6.9
Total	1.6	4.8	3.5	4.3	7.4
Weighted base	*2322*	*4540*	*1464*	*1964*	*1111*
Unweighted base	*2174*	*4621*	*1076*	*1851*	*1694*

Table D.11 Respiratory symptoms (coughing up phlegm or a wheeze) by class

percentages: age, gender and class standardised

	White	All ethnic minorities	Caribbean	Indian or African Asian	Pakistani or Bangladeshi
Class					
Non-manual	23	14	16	13	13
Manual	23	17	28	13	12
No full-time worker in household	35	21	26	17	20
Total	27	17	23	14	15
Weighted base	*2230*	*2135*	*721*	*927*	*487*
Unweighted base	*2113*	*2186*	*534*	*872*	*780*

Table D.12 Respiratory symptoms (coughing up phlegm or a wheeze) by tenure

percentages: age, gender and class standardised

	White	All ethnic minorities	Caribbean	Indian or African Asian	Pakistani or Bangladeshi
Tenure					
Owner-occupier	24	16	21	12	16
Tenant	32	24	27	24	21
Total	26	18	22	15	17
Weighted base	*2324*	*2247*	*728*	*979*	*539*
Unweighted base	*2176*	*2292*	*546*	*910*	*836*

Table D.13 Regular current smoking by class

percentages: age, gender and class standardised

	White	All ethnic minorities	Caribbean	Indian or African Asian	Pakistani or Bangladeshi
Class					
Non-manual	21	16	24	9	16
Manual	33	18	30	8	18
No full-time worker in household	46	25	39	19	18
Total	33	20	31	12	17
Weighted base	*2230*	*2135*	*721*	*927*	*487*
Unweighted base	*2113*	*2186*	*534*	*872*	*780*

Table D.14 Regular current smoking by tenure

percentages: age, gender and class standardised

	White	All ethnic minorities	Caribbean	Indian or African Asian	Pakistani or Bangladeshi
Tenure					
Owner-occupier	24	14	21	8	14
Tenant	45	27	41	18	24
Total	30	17	27	11	17
Weighted base	*2324*	*2247*	*728*	*979*	*539*
Unweighted base	*2176*	*2292*	*546*	*910*	*836*

Table D.15 Ever drinks alcohol by class

percentages: age, gender and class standardised

	White	All ethnic minorities	Caribbean	Indian or African Asian	Pakistani or Bangladeshi
Class					
Non-manual	95	49	81	45	7
Manual	91	46	83	39	5
No full-time worker in household	84	46	84	41	2
Total	90	47	83	42	5
Weighted base	*2229*	*2128*	*720*	*925*	*483*
Unweighted base	*2112*	*2181*	*533*	*870*	*778*

Table D.16 Ever drinks alcohol by tenure

percentages: age, gender and class standardised

	White	All ethnic minorities	Caribbean	Indian or African Asian	Pakistani or Bangladeshi
Tenure					
Owner-occupier	94	45	80	42	4
Tenant	83	44	86	33	4
Total	91	45	82	39	4
Weighted base	*2324*	*2240*	*726*	*977*	*537*
Unweighted base	*2175*	*2287*	*545*	*908*	*834*

Tables and Figures

CHAPTER 4

CHAPTER 5

CHAPTER 6

CHAPTER 7

Index

The Fourth National Survey of Ethnic Minorities

• **Lead title** •

ETHNIC MINORITIES IN BRITAIN
Diversity and Disadvantage

Tariq Modood, Richard Berthoud, Jane Lakey, James Nazroo, Patten Smith, Satnam Virdee and Sharon Beishon

The most comprehensive study available of the economic and social circumstances of Britain's ethnic minorities, in a series which has established itself as a key reference and required reading for all academics and policy makers involved in these issues.

This is the fourth in a series of major studies by the Policy Studies Institute which have charted the experiences of ethnic minorities in Britain since the 1960s. It reports on changes in such key fields as family structure, education, employment and housing. And it introduces new topics which have not been examined thoroughly in the past: poverty, health, racial harassment and cultural identity.

Ethnic Minorities in Britain is required reading for anyone concerned about multi-cultural Britain.

Contents: Foreword by Professor Bhikhu Parekh • Introduction • People, Families and Households • Qualifications and English Language • Employment • Income and Standards of Living • Neighbourhoods and Housing • Health and Health Services • Racial Harassment • Culture and Identity • Conclusion

£17.50, paperback, ISBN 0 85374 670 2
June 1997, 234x153mm, 440 pages

PSI publications are available from Grantham Book Services Ltd
Isaac Newton Way, Alma Park Industrial Estate, Grantham, Lincs NG31 9SG
Orders: (Tel) 01476 541080 (Fax) 01476 541061

The Fourth National Survey of Ethnic Minorities

• **Forthcoming** •

ETHNICITY AND MENTAL HEALTH

James Nazroo

For the first time in such an extensive study of ethnic minorities, the Fourth National Survey has included a section on mental health, which has been validated in follow-up research. There is no comparable information available on the mental health of ethnic minority groups in Britain. Indeed previously available data has been restricted by a reliance on information on hospital admissions, limited coverage of ethnic minority populations, and no coverage of socio-economic factors which might be related to mental health.

This survey will provide the first ever report on rates of both psychotic and neurotic illness among a nationally representative community sample of ethnic minority and white respondents. The report will focus on how rates of illness vary across and within ethnic groups, how this variation is influenced by socio-economic factors, and how the findings challenge existing assumptions about the mental health of ethnic minority groups.

£14.95 paperback ISBN 0 85374 718 0
September 1997 234x153mm 192 pages

PSI publications are available from Grantham Book Services Ltd
Isaac Newton Way, Alma Park Industrial Estate, Grantham, Lincs NG31 9SG
Orders: (Tel) 01476 541080 (Fax) 01476 541061

The Fourth National Survey of Ethnic Minorities

CHANGING ETHNIC IDENTITIES

Tariq Modood, Sharon Beishon and Satnam Virdee

The British population includes over 3 million people with origins outside Europe. New cultures are taking root in and adapting to Britain, and as part of the new trend in 'identity politics', British race relations are increasingly being shaped by new forms of minority ethnic and religious assertiveness.

What are these new forms of identities? To what extent are they rooted in cultural difference? Or are they mainly a reaction to racism? Do different minority groups emphasise different aspects of their heritage, and how do they reconcile a commitment to those heritages with being British?

This book represents the first comparative study based on original fieldwork covering two generations of Caribbeans and the main South Asian groups on what their ethnic background means to them.It examines the basis of ethnic identity in family life, community languages, religion, marriage choices and in experiences of racial exclusion and forms of political solidarity. It highlights the changes that have taken place and are taking place between the migrant and British-born generation, and challenges those who think in terms of the simplistic oppositions of British–Alien or Black–White.

The authors conclude that we need a new view of Britishness and the varieties and forms that it can encompass, a Britishness which allows minorities to make a claim upon it, and to be accepted without having to conform to a narrow cultural norm.

£15.00 paperback ISBN 0 85374 646 X
1995 229x145mm 144 pages

*PSI publications are available from Grantham Book Services Ltd
Isaac Newton Way, Alma Park Industrial Estate, Grantham, Lincs NG31 9SG
Orders: (Tel) 01476 541080 (Fax) 01476 541061*

The Fourth National Survey of Ethnic Minorities

RACIAL VIOLENCE AND HARASSMENT

Satnam Virdee

Serious attacks on African Caribbean and South Asian people have made racial violence and harassment an issue of widespread public concern.

Any useful discussion of how racial violence and harassment should be tackled needs to be based on a thorough understanding of the nature and scale of the problem. The official figures on the extent of racial violence and harassment in Britain are based on police statistics and the British Crime Survey. This book offers a critical evaluation and assessment of these sources to see if the problem has, as some claim, increased. The report reviews a number of small-scale studies in local areas where racial violence and harassment is known to be a problem. Detailed questioning about the experience of racial violence and harassment -- particularly 'low-level' harassment -- among a sample of African Caribbean and South Asian respondents then reveals:

- where such incidents take place;
- who the perpetrators are;
- what, if anything, the people subject to such violence and harassment try to do about it; and
- the extent to which people's lives are affected, beyond the actual harassment that takes place.

The report concludes with a discussion of the key issues involved in addressing the problem more effectively.

£9.95 paperback ISBN 0 85374 647 8
1995 229x145mm 96 pages

PSI publications are available from Grantham Book Services Ltd
Isaac Newton Way, Alma Park Industrial Estate, Grantham, Lincs NG31 9SG
Orders: (Tel) 01476 541080 (Fax) 01476 541061

The Fourth National Survey of Ethnic Minorities

ASIAN SELF-EMPLOYMENT

The interaction of culture and economics in England

Hilary Metcalf, Tariq Modood and Satnam Virdee

Self-employment has grown disproportionately among South Asians. Today one third of Asian men in paid employment are self-employed, compared to one fifth of white men. In some parts of the UK, Asian businesses are expanding more rapidly than those of any other group. Yet these positive trends mask a more complex and less optimistic picture than is commonly painted. There are sharp differences in levels of business success between various groups in the Asian community, and indications suggest that the remarkable growth seen over recent decades is losing its momentum, as the first generation British Asians encourage their children to move into professional and salaried careers.

This unique study offers, for the first time, a detailed comparison of different Asian communities, and challenges the common assumption that all Asian groups can be regarded as the same. Among its findings it identifies:

- ways in which culture and religion could impact on entry into self-employment;
- how negative factors such as racism at work and 'dead-end jobs' have led to increased levels of self-employment;
- barriers to success in business, and how specific problems are more prevalent among specific Asian groups;
- the need to target assistance; and
- evidence that Asian self-employment may not continue at its currently high rates.

£14.95 paperback ISBN 0 85374 698 2
November 1996 216x135mm 128 pages

PSI publications are available from Grantham Book Services Ltd
Isaac Newton Way, Alma Park Industrial Estate, Grantham, Lincs NG31 9SG
Orders: (Tel) 01476 541080 (Fax) 01476 541061

• **Student text** •

BRITAIN'S ETHNIC MINORITIES

Trevor Jones

Research in the 1960–1980s showed that Britain's ethnic minority population had substantially lower living standards than white people. Since then, of course, Britain has experienced major social and economic restructuring. *Britain's Ethnic Minorities* is an examination of how such changes have been reflected in the social and economic circumstances of ethnic minority groups.

Drawing on the Labour Force Survey and other comparative data, the book includes an extensive analysis of the labour market position of the main ethnic minority groups. It covers population size and geographical location; age and family structure; labour force participation; industrial distribution; job levels; trade union membership; unemployment; job search; and patterns of tenure. A key theme is the growing diversity within and between different ethnic minority groups, as some make greater progress than others into education and the labour market.

This book provides a comprehensive introduction to the socio-economic position of Britain's ethnic minorities. It will be of considerable interest to teachers and students of sociology, social policy and politics.

£9.95 paperback ISBN 0 85374 684 2
1996 229x145mm 192 pages

*PSI publications are available from Grantham Book Services Ltd
Isaac Newton Way, Alma Park Industrial Estate, Grantham, Lincs NG31 9SG
Orders: (Tel) 01476 541080 (Fax) 01476 541061*

• **Just published** •

CREDIT USE AND ETHNIC MINORITIES

Alicia Herbert and Elaine Kempson

Britain's ethnic minorities who live on low incomes are likely to have a high level of need for credit – a need which is often unmet by high-street banks and building societies.

This is the first available assessment of the ways in which members of these communities find and use credit. The authors have made detailed case studies of Bangladeshi, Pakistani and Afro-Caribbean communities to present a unique guide to patterns of credit use among ethnic minorities and the ways in which these patterns vary from the wider picture among low-income households. Using extensive desk research, consultations with community leaders and over 50 in-depth interviews, they give a clear account of:

- attitudes to credit, the need for credit, and the range of sources available and used;
- the extent to which people have access to the high-street credit market, and the barriers that prevent further access;
- levels of use of local credit markets, such as moneylenders and pawnbrokers, and the associated costs;
- the nature and extent of unlicensed credit markets within specific ethnic minority communities, and the need for legislation to protect vulnerable groups from these markets;
- the types of 'informal' responses which ethnic minority groups have devised, how they work, the extent and purpose of their use, and the costs and opportunities associated with them; and
- how such community initiatives might be encouraged so as to widen the choice of credit sources.

This is essential reading for those working in the credit markets, as well as for those involved in issues of race and ethnicity.

£9.95 paperback ISBN 0 85374 695 8
1996 216x135mm 128 pages

*PSI publications are available from Grantham Book Services Ltd
Isaac Newton Way, Alma Park Industrial Estate, Grantham, Lincs NG31 9SG
Orders: (Tel) 01476 541080   (Fax) 01476 541061*

NURSING IN A MULTI-ETHNIC NHS

Sharon Beishon, Satnam Virdee and Ann Hagell

Approximately 8 per cent of National Health Service nursing and midwifery staff are from ethnic minority groups. This major study of the careers of nurses and midwives found large gaps between equal opportunity policies on the one hand, and actual practices in the workplace on the other.

Drawing conclusions from both a qualitative study of six nurse employers and 150 interviews, and a nationally representative postal survey of over 14,000 staff, the book shows that many ethnic minority and white nurses felt that the allocation of training and promotion opportunities was unfair, that racial harassment of ethnic minority nursing staff by patients and colleagues was widespread, that management was not doing enough to tackle the problem of racial harassment and that they were forced to accept it as 'part of the job'. Moreover, some groups of ethnic minority nurses, in particular black nurses, had not advanced a far up the grading structure as their white colleagues.

This study reveals significant gaps between written policies and nurses' experiences which need to be addressed, and discusses the policy implications behind these findings.

£24.95 paperback ISBN 0 85374 662 1
1995 229x145mm 320 pages

*PSI publications are available from Grantham Book Services Ltd
Isaac Newton Way, Alma Park Industrial Estate, Grantham, Lincs NG31 9SG
Orders: (Tel) 01476 541080 (Fax) 01476 541061*

• New •

CHURCH, STATE AND RELIGIOUS MINORITIES

Edited by Tariq Modood

The relationship between religion and state has not been a major issue for over a century. Yet the development of a new multicultural and multi-state situation in Britain is once again opening up some old constitutional debates, in particular about 'establishment', the privileged position of the Church of England in the British state. The Prince of Wales' highly publicised remark about not wanting to be 'Defender of the Faith' but a 'Defender of Faith' has now dramatically brought the question of the implications of recent multi-faith developments for establishment, the monarchy and British national identity to the centre of public attention.

This collection of essays, covering a range of faiths and secular views, explores these issues and the public role of religion in a plural society. The introduction provides an overview of the debate. Part One explores the issue in relation to concepts such as citizenship, equality, secularism and national identity. In Part Two, 'establishment' is defended and rejected by Christians and secular critics, while Part Three gives the perspectives of leading members of different minority faiths.

These thought-provoking chapters from prominent members of Jewish, Sikh, Buddhist, Muslim and Hindu communities, as well as Christian churches and varieties of secular opinion, make this the first book to explore the church–state relationship in Britain through focusing on the concerns of minority faiths.

£10.95 paperback ISBN 0 85374 724 5
May 1997 216X135mm 120 pages

*PSI publications are available from Grantham Book Services Ltd
Isaac Newton Way, Alma Park Industrial Estate, Grantham, Lincs NG31 9SG
Orders: (Tel) 01476 541080   (Fax) 01476 541061*

ETHNIC MINORITIES AND HIGHER EDUCATION

Why are there differential rates of entry?

Tariq Modood and Michael Shiner

Since 1990, when ethnic origin data collection began, it has been apparent that there are significant differences in rates of entry into higher education between ethnic groups.

This report, using official figures from UCCA and PCAS 1992, is the first to submit the data to a rigorous multivariate analysis to identify what accounts for the differences. It uncovers several significant ethnic differences on rates of admission,one of the most worrying of which is the significant 'under-admission' of Pakistanis and Black Caribbeans to the 'old' universities.

£5.95 paperback ISBN 0 85374 633 8
1994 229x145mm 64 pages

PSI publications are available from Grantham Book Services Ltd
Isaac Newton Way, Alma Park Industrial Estate, Grantham, Lincs NG31 9SG
Orders: (Tel) 01476 541080   (Fax) 01476 541061

RACIAL JUSTICE AT WORK

Enforcement of the Race Relations Act 1976 in Employment

Christopher McCrudden, David J Smith and Colin Brown

Twenty years after it was first made unlawful, racial discrimination in employment continues at a substantial level. The Race Relations Act 1976 extended the scope of earlier legislation and attempted to strengthen the mechanisms of enforcement. Yet many problems and difficulties have arisen in practice. It is time to review the successes and failures of the use of law in this field, and to point the way to more effective policy.

This book sets out the results of a detailed and wide-ranging review of the enforcement of the 1976 Act – and shows that none of the main elements of the 1976 strategy has worked as intended. In particular, methods of encouraging employers to adopt positive action policies have been inadequate, and individual complainants have remained heavily reliant on expert advice and assistance which is not always available. These conclusions emerge from a detailed study covering the industrial tribunals, the policy and practice of CRE, CRE's use of strategic and formal investigations, conciliation and the role of ACAS, and the employer's perspective on different methods of enforcement.

Racial Justice at Work will inform not only policy makers, academics and those campaigning for ethnic equality in the UK or working in the field of employment law, but individual employers seeking to eradicate racial discrimination, and employees looking to know more about their rights, and the problems they may encounter in the workplace.

£29.95 hardback ISBN 0 85374 470 X
1991 229x145mm, 320 pages

*PSI publications are available from Grantham Book Services Ltd
Isaac Newton Way, Alma Park Industrial Estate, Grantham, Lincs NG31 9SG
Orders: (Tel) 01476 541080   (Fax) 01476 541061*